Praise for
NEVER IN FINER COMPANY

"An exceptionally vivid tale of men at war. Unsparing and dramatic, *Never in Finer Company* illuminates the sacrifice, courage, and leadership of American doughboys in combat, as well as the toll wrung from them after the shooting stopped. Edward G. Lengel has written a rich and compelling story."
—Rick Atkinson, Pulitzer Prize–winning and *New York Times* bestselling author of *The Liberation Trilogy*

"The Great War remade our world and continues to cast its shadow more than one hundred years later. Edward G. Lengel, one of the great chroniclers of that conflict, has revealed a hidden war within that war and masterfully tells one of WWI's paramount stories. By carefully building the backstory of the main characters of the Lost Battalion, Sergeant York, and the intrepid war correspondent who initially captured this story, Lengel's powerful prose transports the reader back in time in a gripping, searing narrative of the men who transcended the bounds of human endurance and courage."
—Patrick K. O'Donnell, bestselling author of *The Unknowns*

"Edward G. Lengel body-slams us into the muddy trenches of the Argonne Forest alongside the besieged doughboys of the Lost Battalion to confront the very nature of courage, cowardice, and heroism. Through the eyes of four men whose lives intersected in those awful woods, *Never in Finer Company* reveals how World War I not only changed them fundamentally but how it transformed America as well."
—John F. Ross, author of *Enduring Courage*

"The story of the 'Lost Battalion' is one of the great legends of the so-called Great War, and this new volume, written by a foremost historian of World War I, presents this tale in a new way by stripping away the legend to expose the more intriguing tale underneath...A tale of bravery, courage, and sacrifice, tempered with the knowledge that these men carried their burdens of loss, terror, and guilt far beyond the Meuse-Argonne forest."
—*New York Journal of Books*

"[An] expert recounting of a devastating incident involving American soldiers...Lengel vividly shows how the Germans unexpectedly pinned down and cut off the 77th in an isolated pocket of the [Argonne] forest, trapping the soldiers for seven days without ammunition, food, water, or medicine...A must-read for anyone interested in WWI and the experiences of soldiers in battle."
—*Publishers Weekly*

"The timely account of the bloody ordeal endured by New York City's 77th Division of the U.S. Army in northern France's Argonne Forest in October 1918."
—*New York Times*

"*Never in Finer Company* does a great job telling the story of some of America's greatest moments. The addition of this book in time for the World War I centennial will hopefully trigger greater interest by the American public in one of the most important epochs in our history."
—*ARMY Magazine*

"[A] masterful account of the battle and the Lost Battalion's heroic stand."
—*American Heritage*

"Lengel writes in a straightforward, entertaining style...The average reader will get a clear glimpse into nearly forgotten World War I history...[A] riveting account."
—*Internet Review of Books*

"In this excellent account, we look at the Lost Battalion from four viewpoints, men whose lives were forever changed because of what they experienced."
—*WTBF Radio*

NEVER IN FINER COMPANY

The Men of the Great War's Lost Battalion

EDWARD G. LENGEL

New York

Copyright © 2018 by Edward G. Lengel

Hachette Book Group supports the right to free expression and the value of copyright. The purpose of copyright is to encourage writers and artists to produce the creative works that enrich our culture.

The scanning, uploading, and distribution of this book without permission is a theft of the author's intellectual property. If you would like permission to use material from the book (other than for review purposes), please contact permissions@hbgusa.com. Thank you for your support of the author's rights.

Hachette Books
Hachette Book Group
1290 Avenue of the Americas
New York, NY 10104
HachetteBooks.com
Twitter.com/HachetteBooks
Instagram.com/HachetteBooks

Printed in the United States of America
First Paperback Edition: November 2021

Published by Hachette Books, an imprint of Perseus Books, LLC,
a subsidiary of Hachette Book Group, Inc.

The Hachette Speakers Bureau provides a wide range of authors for speaking events. To find out more, go to www.hachettespeakersbureau.com or call (866) 376-6591.

The publisher is not responsible for websites (or their content) that are not owned by the publisher.

Editorial production by Christine Marra, *Marra*thon Production Services.
www.marrathoneditorial.org

Book design by Jane Raese
Set in 10.5-point Utopia

Library of Congress Cataloging-in-Publication Data has been applied for.

ISBN 978-0-306-82568-2 (hardcover); ISBN 978-0-306-92140-7 (paperback);
ISBN 978-0-306-82569-9 (ebook)

LSC-C

PRINTING 1, 2021

TO CAITLIN
for rescuing me when I was lost

CONTENTS

	List of Maps	ix
PROLOGUE	Four Men	1
ONE	Playing the Game	7
TWO	War's Story	37
THREE	The Country Awakens	53
FOUR	The Adventure Begins	69
FIVE	First Blood	95
SIX	Through the Forest Gate	115
SEVEN	Into the Pocket	135
EIGHT	Surrounded	147
NINE	Friendly Fire	167
TEN	The Test	195
ELEVEN	The Quality of Courage	213
TWELVE	The Crisis	225
THIRTEEN	Heroes	245

CONTENTS

FOURTEEN	Unknown Soldiers	267
FIFTEEN	Homecomings	307
	Acknowledgments	321
	Notes	323
	Bibliography	339
	Index	343
	About the Author	358

MAPS

Western Meuse-Argonne 118

The Lost Battalion 145

(PROLOGUE)

FOUR MEN

The soldier came down through the woods to the battlefield. It was morning. Almost a day had passed since the fighting stopped, and the wounded forest was quiet. Nearby lay a canteen, and some distance away from that a helmet. Both were riddled with bullet holes. The ground was saturated with bullets, and spongy under the soldier's feet. Tattered bushes drooped dejected in every direction. In one place bullets had slashed a lane through them wide enough for a man to pass.

Two stretcher-bearers followed the soldier and stopped as he paused and turned his head to peer into the bracken. He was tall, red-haired, with a trimmed mustache and light, almost blond eyebrows over haunted blue eyes. Yesterday, he had performed deeds that would inspire millions of people long past the day he passed from the world. But he did not think of himself as a hero, and he had no thought for the future. Dozens of men had died on this ground. Some were friends and others strangers, including enemies whom he had slain. Many of these had died close enough for him to see the expressions on their faces as they went, all unprepared, to meet their maker.

One thought consumed the soldier's mind: somewhere, there must be a survivor.

The graves collection team had been efficient. No bodies were visible. Still, the three men tramped back and forth across the small ravine, crunching underfoot the scattered detritus of war. They could not help noticing the darker sticky patches where blood stained the fallen autumn leaves.

The soldier cried out, calling the names of men he remembered. Dymowski. Weiler. Waring. Wins. Swanson. And his best friend, Savage. With each name, he saw a face in his mind's eye. They were all dead, but he would have settled for a response from anyone. Friend. Stranger. American. German. Any answering call that could coax a remnant of life from a shattered ground where he could see only death. Behind him the stretcher-bearers called too; but the forest had no reply.

After a time, the silence became terrible and the three men turned, dejected, to retrace their path uphill into the forest. The soldier had grown up in the hills and understood the woodland rhythm, but there was no peace for him among these trees. He had never wanted to visit this foreign land, and now it had claimed his comrades. He thought of each of them as he walked, especially Savage. Never again would they share a blanket, read the Bible, or discuss their faith. The others too, men from backgrounds he had never thought to understand, had become a part of him: Greeks, Italians, Poles, Jews.

In a strange way that the soldier could not begin to comprehend, the Germans too had entered into his soul and he knew that they would never leave. Yesterday, he had almost single-handedly broken an entire German battalion. Many of them he and his comrades had taken prisoners. But the soldier had also killed dozens of men mechanically, even ruthlessly, and a part of him had thrilled at the sound of their dying shrieks. His conscious mind could hardly deal with this knowledge of what lay inside himself, but he knew it was there. And he asked God for healing, and guidance. Walking on, he prayed for the enemy, dead and living, as brothers.

Survivors packed the dressing stations and hospitals, and the soldier visited everyone he could in the days that followed. One of his friends had taken five bullets in the body and one in the arm, and miraculously survived. Another had fallen beneath a hail of enemy fire that shattered his helmet and shredded his uniform, but taken no more than a bullet in the arm. He encountered them not as a triumphant gladiator but as a friend, and imparted such comfort as he could. Always and again a thought surfaced to lash his mind: why them, and not me? During the battle, he had seen two comrades fall dead to his left and right, and two more behind him, and yet he had never been touched. Alvin C. York would grapple with this thought—threatening despair, and firing inspiration—for the remainder of his life.[1]

York was only one of thousands of men to trace brooding footpaths through the Argonne Forest on that morning of October 9, 1918. Just a couple of miles away, several dozen wretched doughboys sat slump shouldered on wooden benches in a hut, their faces bathed in the flickering glare of a movie screen. Their tall, bespectacled commanding officer sat with them, hoping that Charlie Chaplin could help them briefly forget the sodden, filthy pocket of woodland that had been their unwilling home for the past six days. Like York, they had made certain to leave no dead or wounded behind. Not until the last ambulance and stretcher departed had they consented to stand up, brush mud from their uniforms, assemble in something like formation, and walk away. Now they were safe, but the Little Tramp's antics didn't help much to fill the emptiness inside them. Some forced a chuckle, but nobody laughed.

The press had already branded the bespectacled officer and his second in command, a burly, wizened-looking man now being tended in a field hospital, as heroes among heroes. One of them was a lawyer, another a stockbroker. Neither had ever poked his head inside a forest before coming to France, except for the occasional leisurely stroll. They were city men born and bred, with feet accustomed to walking macadamed streets and hands suited to wielding pen and paper instead of rifles. Inside, though, Charles Whittlesey and George McMurtry had become more like Alvin C. York—a man they had yet to meet—than anyone they knew back home. Not one thought of himself as a hero. Each struggled with the same surging feelings of guilt, and grasped at the first fleeting glimpses of hope and renewal.

A fourth man had met Whittlesey and McMurtry the previous day and spoken with them about their experiences. Then he had stood and watched as they trudged painfully out of the woods at the head of their band of doughboys past a whirring motion picture camera. Now he sat behind a portable typewriter and wrote about them. He was of medium height, and wore a neatly tailored but now mud-caked uniform. His face was oddly angular, almost ugly. But the first thing you noticed was the intensity of his eyes. The spectacles that he wore and the constant cloud of cigarette smoke that wreathed his face did not mask them. They bored deeply into each subject of their gaze—without cruelty, but with an unflappable determination to understand.

Damon Runyon was a veteran, but no one would ever call him a hero. Born to the country and an adept of the city, his job was to observe and tell stories. Now he was a war correspondent for the *New York American*. In company with his fellow journalists, he would study the American soldier, present him to the public, and confer on him a kind of immortality. Yet Damon Runyon was different. His unique desire to understand the common man gave voice to the doughboys and helped them to redefine what it meant to be an American. And just like them he had thoughts to process: dreams, fancies, and torments that he would spend years laboring to transform into inspiration.

York, Whittlesey, McMurtry, and Runyon would never have known each other had it not been for the First World War. Each had trod a unique path to the October days that engulfed them in the same stricken forest in eastern France known as the Argonne. They all fought in the same bitter contest, and were all transformed. But their stories did not end there. Afterward, they would live, speak to the public, and sometimes meet in places like New York City, Washington, DC, and tiny Pall Mall, Tennessee, experiencing along with other veterans the long journey home, but without any hope of healing privacy. Each man was haunted in his own way. None, however, ever ceased to struggle for meaning, or to turn his personal demon into a servant of good. And none of them ever stopped giving, and sacrificing. In the process they touched thousands, and changed America.

(CHAPTER ONE)

PLAYING THE GAME

New York City never sleeps, but fate—or evil—sometimes catches it unawares. Two hours after midnight on July 30, 1916, a massive fireball shook Manhattan and engulfed New York Harbor with light. The city's twin beacons of hope—the Statue of Liberty and nearby Ellis Island—disappeared in a storm of shrapnel that chipped stone and shattered windows. The blast knocked sleepers out of their beds in Manhattan and Brooklyn. Carousers on Broadway gaped at skyscrapers looming ominously from aerial haloes. Windows flew open. Neighbors shouted. Men and women assembled on street corners and quizzed bewildered policemen.

Twenty minutes later the echoes of an even more powerful explosion tore through the city. Glass exploded in Times Square. Brooklyn Bridge shuddered. Horses reared in terror, and motorists swerved crazily behind shattered windshields. Crowds filled the streets, unhindered by police. Some people declared it was an earthquake; others thought the city was being bombarded by some mysterious enemy. Minutes passed before New Yorkers decided that something had happened along the waterfront near Battery Park, or perhaps in the harbor, and began streaming in that direction.

Gawkers lining Manhattan's south shore witnessed a conflagration. Looking west across the harbor past Ellis Island and the Statue of Liberty on Bedloe's Island, now barely visible in the glare, they could see the industrial docks of Jersey City. A promontory known as Black Tom, thick with warehouses, marked the docks' lower end. The entire place was in flames, shaken by intermittent explosions that sent debris hurtling hundreds of feet into the air. A newspaper reporter likened it to a "terrible yellow blossom." Watchers slowly realized that the Black Tom warehouses, and many of the barges moored nearby, were packed with munitions—shells of all sizes intended to fuel the war then consuming western Europe.

Like soldiers rushing into battle, heedless of their safety, firemen assaulted the blaze. Finding the water mains wrecked, they drew water from the harbor and turned it on the warehouses. As they worked a three-masted schooner and five explosives-laden barges burned away from their moorings and drifted into the harbor directly toward Ellis Island. The buildings there were filled with hundreds of immigrants who had fled war and poverty in search of hope in America. If the barges, already spitting munitions, made landfall they might incinerate the lot.

A courageous few saved the many. From Manhattan and New Jersey, a flotilla of fireboats, tugboats, and cutters surged valiantly to intercept the barges. Somehow, they managed not only to snare and tow the vessels out to open water and subdue their flames, but to do so without injury. No one had seen anything like it. In the fashion of emergency responders everywhere, however, these heroes did not stop to leave their names. In time they would fade into obscurity.

Not so the Statue of Liberty. Smoke and flames concealed her for hours, and New Yorkers wondered if the explosions had obliterated their beloved beacon. Dawn at first revealed nothing. Acrid smoke still wreathed the harbor. Soon, however, "the surly black smoke that sought to smother the goddess sullenly admitted its defeat and the torch and then the whole figure of Liberty emerged." The torch still glowed—Lady Liberty's own flame had kept ablaze all night.[1]

The Black Tom explosion killed several people—accounts vary—and injured hundreds. Two policemen died in the second blast, along with a small child in Manhattan, hurled from his bed by the blast's shock. The promontory where the explosion had occurred was a smoking ruin. On the morning after the blast, rescue workers picked over thirteen warehouses, eighty-seven railway cars, and six piers that had been obliterated. They walked around a gigantic wreckage-strewn crater that gushed full of harbor water. And they stared up at the Statue of Liberty, pockmarked by shrapnel but still standing proud, and the tattered buildings on Ellis Island. Orders went out for the immigrants to be evacuated.

After a brief panic that saw police searching for nonexistent bombs planted in their headquarters, law enforcement officials announced that the explosion was not deliberate but an accident caused by negligence. Arrest warrants were issued for the chiefs of the Lehigh Valley Railroad, the National Dock and Storage Company, and the Johnson Lighterage and Towing Company that shared responsibility for the operations at Black Tom. Not until several years later would evidence emerge that agents of the German government, then still at peace with the United States, had set off the explosion in an act of sabotage. No one then called it terrorism.[2]

Whatever its cause, the Black Tom disaster jolted New York City and the United States. The global war that began in 1914 and claimed millions of lives had seemed a distant affair. The US government's supply of funding and munitions to Europe, particularly to the western allies of France and Great Britain, caused no widespread concern outside the German American community. After Black Tom, however, which one reporter likened to an "American Verdun" akin to the horrendous battle then raging in France, no one could deny that the war might impact the United States and cost American lives.[3]

The millions of citizens who scanned their newspapers that summer for updates on Black Tom, however, included many who hesitated to consider New York City part of what they called America. Every schoolchild knew how the city had once been an epicenter of the American Revolution. George Washington had fought a great battle on Long Island in 1776, and said farewell to his officers at Fraunces Tavern in Lower Manhattan. From 1785 to 1790 it had been the capital of the United States. Since then, however, the city had changed profoundly, becoming something unique, unrecognizable, even threatening to traditional notions of American life.

New York City in the summer of 1916 bore similarity to a Picasso painting. It was a misfit, hodgepodge kind of place, its pieces not quite fitting together; a city of contrasts. On the surface, and to foreign observers, it represented all that was muscular and energetic about the United States. In America, however, some pundits denounced the metropolis as an abomination, a twisted mutation of the old white Anglo-Saxon Protestant America, a pool of vice, corruption, and greed. Only after a thorough scrubbing, they said, could New York City recover the golden age it had lost many years before.

Manhattan ignored the naysayers. Its golden age was just beginning. Long a major railway junction, the city embraced the automobile after the turn of the century. New modes of mechanical transportation dominated its teeming smoky streets, fueling construction projects such as the Queensboro and Manhattan Bridges and Penn Station, which opened in 1910. The subway opened in 1904, ushering businessmen, workers, and revelers into Manhattan. Times Square, named after the central offices of the *New York Times*, became the acknowledged city center and erupted into light as the city electrified. Broadway between 23rd and 34th Streets, emblazoned with glowing advertisements, became known as the Great White Way. Overhead, the city skyline took shape. The Singer Building opened in 1908, the Metropolitan Life Insurance Company Tower in 1909, and the Woolworth Building—then the world's tallest building—in 1913.

Popular entertainment bedazzled Americans in 1916 just as it would a century later, but New York—not Hollywood, then regarded as little more than a sunbaked backwater populated by eccentrics and crazies—was where they looked for it. Broadway had not fully matured to its golden age, but theaters sprang up everywhere to cater to the well-heeled, late-night crowds hungry for plays, vaudeville, and silent movies. Most joy seekers went to Times Square, the Tenderloin District at Sixth Avenue and 30th Street, or to Luna Park on Coney Island. Others headed to Madison Square Garden (MSG), built in 1890, where they took in bicycle races, wrestling, and boxing matches. On March 25, 1916, MSG crowds watched Jess Willard successfully defend his world heavyweight title against challenger Frank Moran in ten rounds.

New Yorkers adored baseball. They had three teams to choose from. The American League Yankees and National League Giants both played at the Polo Grounds (Yankee Stadium wouldn't be built until 1923), uptown at the city's edge near Coogan's Bluff. The Brooklyn Base Ball Club was known alternately as the Robins or the Dodgers. Hated and hating rival of the Giants, it played at Ebbets Field in Flatbush, just opened in 1913. Of the three teams, the Robins were by far the best in 1916—they reached the World Series that year, but lost to the Boston Red Sox in five games, in a showdown between the batting of the Robins' Casey Stengel and the pitching of the Sox' Babe Ruth. Even with so much baseball on tap, the three teams regularly played to capacity crowds. New York fans were demanding and smart—and insisted on quality sports writing.[4]

No city in the world was more dependent on newspapers. Commuters clutched them on subway trains, families read them at dining room tables, and fans carried them to ball games. In an era when people had the patience to read thousands of words at a sitting, New York City papers were a rich source of entertainment and information. City reporters were keen observers and top-notch writers who chronicled every element of city life. Newsmen watched, participated in, and infiltrated events and gatherings. They described what they saw but also registered moods on the street. Competition was fierce. Papers owned by Joseph Pulitzer and William Randolph Hearst vied for lucrative advertising revenue by scooping top stories in politics, world news, and sports. Even the high-class papers scandal-mongered to hold off the emerging tabloids.

Even amid so much reportage, middle- and upper-class New Yorkers remained largely ignorant of the poverty that gripped much of the city. For some two-thirds of New York City's approximately five million inhabitants, daily life featured poor housing, miserable sanitation, and toil. On the Lower East Side and other parts of the city, poor folks crowded into crumbling tenements that once had been affluent single-family homes. Thousands of new tenement buildings were erected in the later nineteenth century to house the massive inflow of impoverished immigrants. Although some legislation was enacted toward improving conditions, by 1916 not much had changed.

The hordes of immigrants who crowded places like the Lower East Side—scrabbling for low-paying jobs, forming gangs, or just loafing in the streets—threatened to subvert the city's allegedly pure past. The flood had begun in the mid–nineteenth century with Irish and Germans. The Irish faced resentment for their Catholic religion, their nonconformist culture, and their racial heritage. Then came a new wave of immigrants beginning in the 1880s. This one seemed like a barbarian invasion. Often dark skinned, wearing strange clothes and speaking unintelligible languages, and practicing unfamiliar religious rituals, they came from places like Russia (including Poland, Lithuania, and Ukraine), Austria-Hungary, Spain, Italy, Greece, China, and the Middle East, with sprinklings of Mexicans, Africans, and others. And most of them entered the United States through New York.

Immigrants who passed the check and quarantine at Ellis Island were routinely cheated at the docks of their small family savings, and sometimes harassed or beaten. Many moved inland, but most sought refuge in the city among communities of folks who shared their language and culture. There they lived, overcrowded and suspicious of the world around them, competing with adjacent immigrant communities for the same scant resources. Men, women, and children worked in the most menial of industries. Women struggled to raise large families. Hordes of orphaned children left behind by impoverished or dead parents fought to survive on the streets. Violence figured prominently in their daily lives.

Despite half-hearted attempts at civic education, most first- and second-generation immigrants spoke little English and understood nothing about the American government. The American president seemed just as distant as their own czars, kings, and potentates. They viewed municipal authorities as gangsters—bullies and thugs who stole from the poor to line their own pockets in return for dubious "protection." No wonder many immigrants distrusted vested authority and kept to themselves or turned to fringe political movements.

Most immigrants, however, had crossed the ocean because the United States had beckoned them with promises of freedom and opportunity. As they sailed into New York Harbor, they had looked up at the Statue of Liberty with longing and pride. Though unwilling to discard their cultures, they yearned to adopt their new country, and for it to accept them. They just didn't know how. The strange potpourri of cultures and outlooks that characterized New York City in 1916 was no melting pot but a bubbling mélange of opposites that stubbornly refused to meld. Only after thousands of former immigrants returned from the war wearing American uniforms would this begin to change in any tangible way.

As the excitement over Black Tom faded in the autumn of 1916, the presidential election campaign found Americans still clinging to a neutralist dreamland. President Woodrow Wilson, a Democrat, campaigned for and won reelection on the platform "he kept us out of war." In Democratic-controlled New York City, the president garnered vital support from newspaper mogul William Randolph Hearst. This flamboyant purveyor of "yellow journalism" and former political candidate was closely connected to the party centers of power, and ardently advocated neutrality. That did little to erode readership of his newspapers in a city that preferred doing business to making war.

American neutrality began evaporating even before Wilson took the inaugural oath for his second term. On January 31, 1917, Germany announced that it was about to resume unrestricted submarine warfare. Henceforth sub commanders could fire torpedoes without warning at any ships, including neutrals, headed for Allied ports. Americans responded with outrage. A chagrined Wilson broke off relations with Berlin, and Congress passed an arms appropriations bill in case of war. The coup de grâce came on March 1, three days before Wilson's inauguration, when the government announced its discovery of the notorious Zimmermann telegram. In it, the German minister to Mexico tried to get that country to declare war on the United States in return for the promise of California, Arizona, and New Mexico. Readers disgustedly slapped down newspapers on dining room tables across the country.

With Americans in an uproar, neither Hearst nor anyone else could continue toeing a neutral line. New York's city hall joined the rest of the country in demanding unity and "one hundred percent Americanism." Openly sectional and ethnic identity politics suddenly became anathema in the world's most diverse city.

John Purroy Mitchel, the thirty-six-year-old "boy mayor of New York," tried to cement the city's common American identity by issuing a petition that became as ubiquitous as ticker tape. Armies of street hawkers scurried across Manhattan, shoving copies under the noses of elusive passersby. City agents placed the petition everywhere imaginable. Check into a hotel and it was there. Send a telegram and it was there. Walk into a deli and it was there. Grab a beer in the corner bar and it was there. Get hauled into a police station and it was there. One million New Yorkers signed it, pledging:

> As an American, faithful to the American ideals of justice, liberty and humanity, and confident that the government has exerted its most earnest efforts to keep us at peace with the world, I hereby declare my absolute and unconditional loyalty to the Government of the United States and pledge my support to you [President Wilson] in protecting American rights against unlawful violence upon land and sea, in guarding the Nation against hostile attacks, and in upholding international right.

New York's primary German American newspaper, the *Fatherland*, released its final issue on Valentine's Day, declaring "America First," and changed its name to the *New World*. Hearst abandoned neutralism and his editorial columns opened fire on the German kaiser. City newspapers filled columns with patriotic ditties. Songwriters worked overtime in Tin Pan Alley. Twenty-eight-year-old Irving Berlin told New Yorkers to sing "Now is the time, To fall in line / You swore that you would so be true to your vow / Let's all be Americans now."[5]

On April 2, a contingent of Regular Army troops, grim faced and deeply tanned from service on the Mexican border, landed at Governor's Island within sight of the rebuilding docks at Black Tom. Before dawn on April 6 the soldiers boarded a small flotilla of tugs and cutters that carried them across the harbor to

Hoboken. In a coordinated operation at sunrise, the men climbed on board twenty-seven docked German vessels and seized them in the name of the US government. Afterward, the soldiers escorted over one thousand German sailors away at gunpoint. The sailors were dispatched to shrapnel-scarred Ellis Island, where they spent the rest of the war. City authorities made certain that they had no access to beer.[6] President Woodrow Wilson signed the declaration of war against Germany in the White House at 1:18 P.M. The mood in New York City was tense. Mayor Mitchel's ebullient proclamation of Americanism produced no genuine unity. Ugly feelings, rooted in suspicions and division, bubbled to the surface instead. Sentries watched for shadowy enemy agents. On Long Island, a marine opened fire on two twelve-year-old boys joyriding in an automobile, killing one of them. Two "skulkers" were shot in New Jersey.

The city's first act of mobilization for war came on the afternoon of April 7, when several hundred naval militiamen marched down Fifth Avenue to board trains at Penn Station. Crowds gathered to walk alongside the militiamen. At the Union League Club on East 37th Street they passed Mayor Mitchel with some officials on a reviewing stand. The crowds cheered lustily. At one point, bystanders attacked a young man who forgot to remove his hat in tribute to the militiamen. At Penn Station, police arrested another young man. Rumors spread that he had threatened to blow up the station. The man, who was merely a miscreant detained on an old warrant, barely escaped lynching before the police hurried him away.[7]

Star-spangled displays sprouted along Fifth Avenue and throughout most of the city that spring, but underneath the mood of fear remained strong. Wary of growing ethnic paranoia, many German businesses switched to Anglo-Saxon names.

Shopkeepers who hesitated were liable to find their windows smashed and the premises looted. In the tenements, immigrants felt the country's insistence that they "prove" their Americanism by uncovering the traitors among them.

Not just Germans were under suspicion. Millions of recent immigrants hailed from German-allied Austria-Hungary, an empire that sprawled across much of the Balkans and eastern Europe. Anyone with an eastern-European- (or Jewish-) sounding name was a potential enemy. One day a man named Morris Lifschitz wandered into the subcellar of the Western Union Telegraph Company with a pair of pliers. He was arrested under suspicion of planning sabotage. His name condemned him in the public's eyes. With New York City in mind, the state governor took steps to shift all "alien workers" away from essential war industries.[8]

New York City's vociferous demonstrations of patriotism lacked inner conviction. Even with a war on, business stood paramount. Morning and evening rush hours remained hectic as always. Commuters still buried themselves in the business and sports sections of their newspapers. And within a week of the declaration of war, the stream of young men entering armed service recruitment offices dwindled to a trickle. Patriotic journalists and activists denounced "slackers" to no purpose.

"Wake Up America Day" was scheduled for April 19 in an effort to boost recruiting. Posters appeared all over the city, and baseball clubs promoted the event in their ballparks. On the big day—the anniversary of the 1775 battles of Lexington and Concord—a parade of sixty thousand patriots, mostly women and children, marched down Fifth Avenue. Airplanes dropped patriotic leaflets as the marchers walked beneath huge flags and banners. But something was off. Men stayed at work instead of joining the parade, and the crowd seemed listless.

Among the juvenile marchers, reporters noticed that the boys seemed distracted and apathetic. Girls, by contrast, swarmed in happy droves bedecked in red, white, and blue ribbons. They sang cheerfully and behaved like natural-born soldiers, for "their carriage was more erect and their attention to orders far more punctilious." President Wilson, however, could not beat the Germans with an army of eight-year-old girls. Two days after the march took place, newspapers decisively declared it a "failure" as recruiting continued to slump.[9]

Americans in general were reluctant to volunteer for overseas service. By the end of April only seventy-three thousand men had enlisted—a pathetically small number for a nation of 103 million people. The principle of voluntary service had died even before it was born. Congress accordingly passed the Selective Service Act on April 28, and it was enacted three weeks later. Men ages twenty-one to thirty immediately became eligible for the draft, and everyone up to middle age had to register by June 5. Secretary of War Newton D. Baker drew the first name in the lottery on July 20 for an army that eventually totaled nearly five million men.

Potentially hundreds of thousands of new soldiers would come from greater New York City, but not everyone viewed the prospect hopefully. At a time when the Confederacy was often regarded as the apogee of American military achievement, Alabama farm boys seemed like ideal soldier material. Yankees and westerners could do themselves proud too, provided they descended from good American stock. But what of the rabble from Lower East Side tenements who barely spoke English? Or blacks? Patriots warned General John J. Pershing, commanding the American

Expeditionary Forces (AEF), to beware of un-American influences in his ranks from places like New York City.[10]

The War Department did not at first hesitate to accept men of any background provided they were healthy. Filling the ranks was its first priority. Only after the draft was fully under way did military officials begin to ponder the diversity of American manpower. Black soldiers could be and were cordoned off into segregated units. Immigrants posed a more complex challenge. Their interests and motivations were suspect. How could they be taught to work and fight in unison?

Much depended on the officers chosen to lead them. These would have to be exceptional individuals, shining examples of American values, and leaders in their communities. Identifying them was difficult. The prewar regular army was too small for the purpose, and had no organized reserve officer corps to draw upon. It did, however, have thousands of graduates of the so-called Plattsburg movement: patriotic young men of good family with no real military experience but a deep sense of civic responsibility. These were the men who would lead the 77th Division into the field, and in some cases sacrifice everything.

The idea for the Plattsburg movement began before the war. Recognizing the army's lack of reserve officers, Army Chief of Staff Leonard Wood established camps in four states where educated young men could pay twenty-seven dollars and fifty cents for several weeks of summer training with professional army officers. When the European war began, business executives and political leaders in New York lobbied successfully for the creation of a new camp at Plattsburg (later Plattsburgh) Barracks, on Lake Champlain near the Canadian border. It was called the Businessman's Camp to emphasize the kind of leaders Mayor Mitchel and other promoters had in mind. Journalistic wits quickly dubbed it the "Tired Businessmen's Camp." Mitchel and *New York Times* manager Julius Ochs Adler were among the camp's first recruits, along with former president Roosevelt's sons Theodore Jr. and Quentin.

The first Plattsburg camp opened on August 10, 1915. Twelve hundred attendees, including blue bloods, sports stars, financiers, policemen, and politicians, arrived by car and train from all over the state. The atmosphere was festive. Recruits swam in the lake, chatted and backslapped, explored the town, and girded themselves for wholesome exercise. In the first few days the men set up cots, chopped wood, unloaded trucks, and proudly showed off their blisters. They received brand new Springfield rifles for target practice. Most of the men had never handled weapons before, so instructors spent as much time dodging for cover as they did issuing directions.

A week after the camp opened, the *New York Sun* published the mocking headline "Rookies Seek Bed Early," and reported that sore-shouldered men filled the injured list. Bruised, battered, and weary, dozens of campgoers quit, pleading the press of business. But those who stuck grew in pride and confidence. Instructors instilled in them the importance of virtue, responsibility, and leading by example. At the beginning of September, the men participated in full-scale field war games. They enjoyed these like children at a rowdy affair of capture the flag.

On September 6, 1915, the Montreal Express train arrived at New York City's Grand Central Terminal with three hundred "bronzed and happy-looking" young men in khaki. Mayor Mitchel came first off of the train, showed off his new muscles to waiting reporters, and then fled to Long Beach for a well-earned rest.

Others spoke of their adventures as Wood looked genially on. In truth, they hadn't learned much. But they had made a statement about preparedness, civic duty, and the kind of men who would lead American troops if and when the country entered the war.

Several thousand men enlisted by spring 1916 for the next edition, which included several camps from June through September. Once again campgoers endured a strenuous routine of exercise and military discipline, their enthusiasm undampened even when heavy rains turned the June camp into a "surging sea of uncensored mud." The blue bloods returned, and reporters noted approvingly that "scions of old families do neat jobs in trench digging." Most of the men, however, came from New York City's professional classes.

On July 12, a series of special trains arrived at Plattsburg carrying thirty-two hundred businessmen for the year's third camp. Under a blazing sun they got right to work, picking up rocks, hefting baggage, and digging ditches. The men went through a course of drill wearing thick regulation uniforms. For dinner, the recruits consumed a spartan repast that they pronounced "better than anything they might have got on Broadway." Among the men munching creamed potatoes and cold meat at table that evening was Condé Nast, owner of *Vogue* and *Vanity Fair*; famed attorney Elihu Root Jr.; intercollegiate swimming champion Eben Cross; and a gangly, bespectacled thirty-two-year-old New York lawyer named Charles White Whittlesey.[11]

At first glance, Whittlesey seemed like the ideal bunkmate. He was not a blue blood but still came from a good family, and partnered in a successful city legal practice. He was fit, earnest, and patriotic; steady, sympathetic, and well educated. He imbibed the Plattburg program, especially its values, with enthusiasm. Deep down, though, Whittlesey remained for all of his life an outsider.

Charles Whittlesey had been born in 1884 in Florence, Wisconsin, a small town in the far northeastern corner of the state on the Michigan border. He was the second of six children in a prosperous middle-class family with ancestors dating back to colonial America. The Whittleseys were all too familiar with tragedy. Charles's older brother Frank Jr. died in 1887 at age four, and his younger sister Annie passed away in 1894 at age eight. Shortly after this tragic event the family moved to Pittsfield, Massachusetts. Charles's love of books helped sooth the discomfort that he must have felt in the midst of these losses and life changes, and his studious habits set him on the path to success.

Graduating from Pittsfield High School with good grades, approving teachers, and bright prospects, Charles transitioned easily to life as an undergraduate at Williams College. A gentle-humored, quiet young man who liked solitary nature walks, he was respected by his classmates and joined the Delta Psi fraternity and later the Gargoyle Society for college seniors. Charles's delight in reading blossomed into a passion for literature and learning. He put his talents on display as editor in chief of the college yearbook, and as editor and frequent contributor to the *Williams Monthly* and the *Williams Literary Record*. To some of his classmates Whittlesey may have seemed austere and aloof. His dignified bearing earned him the nickname "Count," and his designation as the "Third Brightest Man of the Graduating Class of 1905" looks like damning with faint praise.

Though Whittlesey liked people, he conformed only with effort. The interest in socialism that he expressed as an undergraduate at Williams clashed with the fashionable progressivism common among privileged young men of his day. Whittlesey thought deeply about the human condition. Although his ideas were informed by reading about rather than experience of hardship, his sympathy was genuine and hardwired into his nature. Even in repudiation he was gentle. Whittlesey didn't rant or judge but discussed his beliefs earnestly, and upheld them even if it meant separating from those who disagreed. Inevitably, he wondered if anyone understood what he believed or how he felt.

Studying law followed naturally after Williams. For Whittlesey, it offered an outlet for his personal sense of idealism in the pursuit of justice. Whatever his motives, Harvard Law School suited Whittlesey perfectly. He spent three quiet and hard-working years there and later became a member of New York City's Harvard Club. After graduating with his law degree in 1908, Whittlesey entered practice in the city with the firm of Murray, Prentice and Holland. Three years later he partnered in a private practice at 2 Rector Street with his friend and classmate J. Bayard Pruyn, and lived on East 44th Street.

As an attorney, Whittlesey was renowned for his preparedness, precise arguments, and above all honesty. Even as his youthful infatuation with socialism faded he maintained his humanistic idealism. While many lawyers kept emotionally distant from their clients, Whittlesey stood out for his compassion and absolute dedication to do his best on every case. This habit of giving to the point of personal sacrifice was ingrained, and eventually took a heavy toll. At first, though, it fed a passion for civic responsibility. This conviction led Whittlesey, the most unmilitary of men, to take a month's leave of absence from his practice and travel to camp at Plattsburg in July 1916.[12]

The officers running the Plattsburg camp worked Whittlesey's contingent far harder than their predecessors, and emphasized military activities. A few days after arriving the men hefted thirty-seven-pound packs for route hiking. Their days started earlier than at previous camps—4:15 A.M. instead of 5:45 A.M.—so the men could engage in early morning target practice. Daily free time was reduced to a mere twelve minutes. Five days after arrival the men were already learning skirmishing and attack techniques. A short time later Whittlesey's group was assigned to battalion combat war games. Three days before discharge the men were battling under temperatures reaching 111 degrees. Whittlesey carried on quietly through it all, meriting a final evaluation of his service as "honest and faithful."[13]

After Plattsburg closed up for the season that autumn, graduates joined with veterans of other civilian camps to form the Military Training Camps Association (MTCA). Flying in the face of naysayers who argued that the camps fostered militarism and made war more likely, the MTCA sought to expand into a vast program for national preparedness. When the United States entered the war in 1917, the MTCA changed its focus and successfully lobbied the War Department to convert the civilian camps into training camps for officers.

When the national draft kicked into gear in the spring of 1917, officer candidates from New York and across the country applied for entry into the camp at Plattsburg. Here, as at other camps, they would undergo ninety-day training courses that prepared and certified them for service as officers in the AEF, entrusted with the responsibility of leading men from Sacramento, Abilene, and Hell's Kitchen into battle under the same flag. There was no shortage of applicants. Many of the candidates had attended civilian camps in 1915 or 1916, and all were the same type of material: Ivy League graduates, successful businessmen, sportsmen, politicians, celebrities, and the like. Whittlesey reported for duty at Plattsburg on May 14, 1917. Two days earlier, the camp gates had admitted New York stockbroker George McMurtry, with whom Whittlesey was destined to share the most important moments of his life.[14]

McMurtry was eight years older than Whittlesey. He had grown up amid Pittsburgh's towering steel mills, where his father worked after arriving in America from Belfast, Ireland, in 1860, and eventually earned a fortune. Though he spent much of his youth among working-class men, George didn't experience real hardship. He did, however, imbibe a fierce work ethic, and a perfectionism similar to Whittlesey's. He went to private St. Mark's School in Southborough, Massachusetts, and excelled in both academics and athletics.

Unlike the fit but physically awkward Whittlesey, McMurtry was an athlete fully comfortable in his compact frame. He became St. Marks's middleweight boxing champion, and also stood out on the varsity baseball team. Combining these merits with a strong intellect, he won entrance to Harvard University. When the Spanish-American War began in 1898, McMurtry ditched the Ivy League in order to join Theodore Roosevelt's Rough Riders. He participated in the July 1 "charge" (really a cautious advance) on San Juan Heights in Cuba, performing well enough to earn Roosevelt's hard-won respect. A short time later McMurtry contracted malaria and left the service. He returned to Harvard and graduated in 1899 with a master's degree.

Though he might easily have followed Whittlesey's path and moved on to study law or enter politics, McMurtry instead plunged into the hurly-burly of New York City's stock market. He stood out in a city of men on the make. A year after graduation, McMurtry became a full partner in the brokerage firm of Benjamin, Ferguson & McMurtry. Three years later he settled on Fifth Avenue. By 1906 McMurtry was a thirty-year-old millionaire, and his career had hardly begun. McMurtry's success boiled down to native ability, regular habits (he jogged every day), and a fierce energy and drive.

Unlike some self-made men, McMurtry did not renounce his roots but cherished them. Brawny and ruddy faced, he embraced the role of the stereotypical hot-tempered Irishman, quick alike with his fists and with sympathy. McMurtry loved New York City from top to bottom, as he loved America. He felt comfortable with everyday people, including immigrants, and was at home on the streets. Friends would remember him in his prewar days as a likeable, talented, gregarious man—a natural leader with a common touch. McMurtry also had the humility that comes with self-knowledge. He knew he was a leader, and that as such he could best render service to his country. Though forty-one years old in 1917, he eagerly reentered military service, joining the Officers Training Corps at Plattsburg on May 12.[15]

Whittlesey's and McMurtry's motivations were simple: patriotism and duty. Neither had anything to prove or yearned for adventure. They were comfortable men who believed that civic responsibility accompanies success. McMurtry had already shown his capacity for commanding men in the field. Whittlesey may not have thought of himself as a natural leader, but he knew that he could do his duty. If they met each other at camp, as they likely did, they probably found much in common.

Camp life in the spring and summer of 1917 was every bit as grueling as it had been the year before. This time it lasted three times longer, from May to August, but otherwise the details were the same. Officers in training got up before sunrise and spent long hours of hard activity in all weather. They experienced the same drill, target practice, and calisthenics that they had in 1916, but with longer and more thorough lectures on military theory.

The lectures reflected General Pershing's desire for his officers to learn aggressiveness and initiative. Condemning the practices of Europe's massed armies, American military theorists declared that individual rifle-bearing soldiers would determine success, or failure. Plattsburg cadets were taught not to depend on support weaponry, least of all artillery, grenades, poison gas, and machine guns. Instead, they were encouraged to cultivate superior patriotism and vigor—essentially, guts—and seize control of the battlefield from the enemy.

Instructors said that the Europeans had become demoralized from years of trench warfare. American officers must ensure that they and their men did not become infected by apathy and defeatism. United States servicemen would cast aside the prejudices that confined Europeans to their trenches, assert their inherent superiority, defeat the enemy, and go home. For the diverse troops drafted from New York City and its environs, many of whom still considered themselves Europeans, the challenge was obvious. Their officers must ensure that they fought in the American way.

McMurtry understood some of the complexities of the battlefield, but knew nothing more of modern warfare than any of his camp mates. Whittlesey, a total greenhorn, absorbed every idea that the instructors threw at him. He didn't do so unthinkingly—he had a reputation for asking the instructors for thorough explanations—but reasonably presumed that the professionals knew what they were talking about. That was what made them who they were, just like successful businessmen. Whittlesey listened attentively to lectures and precepts without knowing how empty they were.

While Whittlesey, McMurtry, and the first batch of ninety-day wonders trained at Plattsburg beside beautiful Lake Champlain, gangs of civilian laborers from New York City followed their military guides to a nondescript patch of pines and weeds on Long Island. The place was called Yaphank, and nobody had ever heard of it before. Soon it would become Camp Upton. The name came from Union general Emory Upton, who had distinguished himself in the Civil War for successfully directing his troops to storm Confederate entrenchments using only their bayonets and rifle butts. As an army reformer, Upton had also promoted rifle marksmanship and individual initiative—concepts dear to Pershing's own heart, and which the enlisted trainees at Camp Upton would be expected to learn.[16]

Located about sixty miles from the city—out of reach of temptation, in theory if not in practice—and midway between Long Island Sound and the Atlantic shore, the camp took up about ten thousand acres of sheer nothing. That is, before the construction workers, representatives of the Thompson-Starrett Company, which had won the contract from the army Quartermaster Department, arrived in June 1917. Foremen grasping plans and blueprints directed the workers in cutting down trees, laying light railways, digging ditches, stringing electrical wire, and stacking bricks while vigilant guards watched for German agents lurking in the woods. (The *Brooklyn Daily Eagle* obligingly printed a full-scale map of the camp, including locations of headquarters and other sensitive points, for anyone seeking convenient access.)

Within days of their arrival, the workers were confronted—and routed—by a sinister enemy. "Mosquito Pest Delays Work," screamed headlines on the *New York Sun*, "Laborers Flee from Long Island Cantonment to Escape It. Worst Plague in Years. Fate of Soldiers Now on Guard Augurs Ill for Comfort of Conscripts." The slaughter that followed became the stuff of legend. Teams of workers threw down their tools and quit. Guards boasted to reporters that they would "cheerfully endure any 'frightfulness' after meeting the mosquitoes' bayonets" but swatted miserably as soon as the newspapermen departed.[17]

Only the strong and the well paid survived (workers were tempted back with ransomlike wages). The army worked hard to keep up their morale. YMCA volunteers did their bit and so did roving preachers, who exhorted the workers to resist their tiny tormentors. By the end of August ten thousand workmen toiled at Camp Upton to erect barracks designed to house four times that number. The buildings were arranged in orderly fashion, stiffly constructed, and well lighted. They adjoined support facilities and drill and exercise fields, enough for subsistence and training, nothing more. By the time the first troops arrived at the beginning of September, however, only a third of the camp had been completed. And nothing could be done to alleviate the seas of mud and masses of mosquitoes.[18]

The national draft moved forward swiftly. Thousands of men in and around New York City learned by July that they were destined for service. The identities of those assigned to Camp Upton remained hidden from the public, however, until mid-August. The first general officer assignments were announced then, and the press reported that draftees from the city and surrounding counties would all go to the mosquito pit in September. To prepare for their arrival, the army ordered liquor stores closed within a five-mile radius of the camp. Camp officials also established provisions against "dope" smuggling, and warned female visitors to expect close inspection. Of course, contraband found its way into camp anyhow.

The army announced that the unit training at Camp Upton would be the 77th Division of the so-called National Army, a designation that meant it would be composed not of regulars or

National Guard troops but draftees. The division's commander would be sixty-one-year-old Major General James F. Bell, a Kentuckian and Medal of Honor recipient who had fought in the Indian Wars and the Philippines. An old-fashioned but no-nonsense career soldier, Bell had managed officer training camps at Plattsburg and elsewhere with the help of his aide, Captain George C. Marshall.

After learning that he would take command of the 77th Division and presumably lead it into battle, Bell told reporters at Camp Upton that "I am anxious to have this camp become well known as one of the singing camps of the army, not only because singing men are fighting men, but because . . . Nothing will so aid in unifying them in mind and spirits as their frequent singing together in large groups." He established a fund to ensure that no soldier would go without sheet music or a musical instrument if he so desired.[19]

By the end of the summer, New Yorkers could no longer avoid facing the reality that the country was at war and would remain so for the foreseeable future. Mayor Mitchel kept pushing unity. Flags, posters, and placards decorated city streets, including in the tenement districts. Newspapers updated readers on events in Europe, where terrible battles were raging. Patriotic songs filled music halls. Police sought out traitors and slackers. Average New Yorkers, though, seemed unable to overcome a sense of bewilderment at all the commotion. There was plenty of hubbub on the streets, but still little passion.

President Wilson declared September 4 "National Draft Day," as if compulsory service was something to celebrate. In New York, army and city authorities marked the occasion by staging grand parades of draftees through Manhattan and Brooklyn. This way the people could pay the men tribute before they set off for Camp Upton. Similar events took place all over the country, often to hordes of cheering civilians. In Washington, DC, President Wilson watched a parade of draftees and some Civil War veterans, and released a letter saying that he envied those who had been forced to enter the armed forces and wished he could join them on the battlefield. In New York, though, the mood was noticeably somber.

Young men began gathering at street corners just after dawn, and at around eight in the morning they unfurled draft board banners at assembly points in the various boroughs. Officers fresh from Plattsburg, likely including McMurtry and Whittlesey who had both graduated with the rank of captain at the beginning of August, met their men for the first time and hectored them to assemble in formation. The draftees shuffled back and forth willingly enough, but controlling them was like trying to straighten out a blob of Jell-O.

In central Manhattan, groups of men formed in side streets around Washington Square. Mayor Mitchel arrived at nine thirty, and they swung out behind him in something like unison. A genial mob of men still dressed as civilians, many of them sporting tattered clothes that identified denizens of the tenement districts, ambled down Fifth Avenue in front of growing crowds of onlookers. Among the watchers were dozens of journalists, including a hyperkinetic man with a piercing gaze named Damon Runyon.

Nobody except journalists studied the marchers carefully, which may have been just as well because they were not much to look at. Instead, spectators chatted with each other or craned their necks to catch a glimpse of former president Theodore Roosevelt, who stood at a reviewing stand alongside a group of generals and city officials. Even the marchers seemed more interested in him than in each other. As one group of draftees wandered past the stand, a recruit in a yellow flannel shirt pulled back with several of his friends and shouted, "Hey you, Teddy!" For a few moments the parade paused as the recruits serenaded the ex-president. He in turn "shouted, snapped his teeth, and flapped his hat lustily." Elsewhere, the new soldiers just bantered light-heartedly and smiled at the buildings and the crowds.

After the disjointed parade reached its finish line at Fifth Avenue and 50th Street, the crowd broke up and the real fun began. Hearing that their "N.A." (National Army) brassards would get them free admittance to a ball game, several thousand sports-hungry draftees made their way uptown and surged to the Polo Grounds to see the afternoon match between the New York Giants and the Boston Braves.

The men assembled in the upper grandstand, watching the players warm up and chatting furiously. Everyone looked forward to the game, but during the opening ceremonies the usual show-offs demanded their time in the sun before a captive audience. First among them was the mayor, who strode out to home plate and gave a short speech. He coaxed some applause from the still-patient crowd by turning to the players and soldiers and shouting, "Fight clean, fight fair, fight hard, and win."

Then came burly, balding, and bustling Harry Barnhart, leader of the Community Chorus and a favorite of General Bell. A collective groan wafted through the stands as Barnhart impetuously demanded that everyone sing. Strutting back and forth on the ball field with baton in hand, he led the crowd in one patriotic song, then another and another. Each one seemed like it might be the last, and by the time they got to the "Star-Spangled Banner" the crowd lost interest. The ballplayers—among them five future

Major League Baseball Hall of Famers including Giants manager John McGraw and a thirty-year-old Native American pinch hitter named Jim Thorpe—hung around looking bored.

But Barnhart was just getting revved up. Annoyed with the weak response, he turned to the players and demanded, "Now, you look like very good singers. Come here, all of you." The slow-witted among them shambled obediently over, but the smart guys caught the glint in his eyes and disappeared into their bullpens. Barnhart shepherded the slowpokes into the practicing cage, and then dove into the bullpens to rout out the other players while the crowd (misery loving company) shouted encouragement. Finally, he drove fifty players on the field and verbally whipped them and the crowd into one song after another and another. It was entertaining at first, but pretty soon it became excruciating.

Barnhart was delighted. This could go on forever so far as he was concerned. Eventually, rising from the backdrop of an increasingly feeble chorus while the players panted in exhaustion under the afternoon sun, a rhythmic shouting became audible from the upper grandstand and spread through the crowd. Barnhart heard the shouting and assumed that everyone was so thrilled with singing that they wanted more. "I'll give them whatever they want," he yelled, and scurried gleefully over to the stands with his hand cocked to his ear. But they didn't want more songs. The draftees had been gobbling free ham sandwiches all day and singing, and had become thirsty. They were chanting, "We want soda!"

That finally shut him up. Boy Scouts were dispatched to the stands with baskets brimming with bottles of soda pop. Quiet reigned for a while as the draftees mobbed the Boy Scouts, who escaped looking "badly ruffled" with empty baskets, and slaked their thirst. Maybe the game could begin; but no. Some bozo had decided that another patriotic display was just what the people needed, and that was what they got.

A half-trained batch of men styling themselves "Boyce's Tigers," who had been camped out for weeks on Governor's Island learning how to become noncommissioned officers, strutted onto the field and started marching around and charging back and forth across the field. By now the draftees had entered into a full-on state of New York City sarcasm. They let the wannabe noncoms have it, shouting quips like "Steal third!" and "Come on home!" Eventually the Tigers withdrew with their tails between their legs.

Finally, the game began. The Giants seemed limp—understandably, maybe—and when a Braves slugger hit a home run in the sixth inning one of the many brass bands that Barnhart had brought to the stadium erupted into a rendition of "Smile, Smile, Smile," causing the Giants players to glare at the bandmaster with a hatred usually reserved for umpires. When the Giants scored a run off a double in the eighth, leaving them behind 2-1, the crowd really got into it. Life was good.

But then, at the end of the eighth inning, General Bell walked onto the field. He was in fine fettle. During the parade that morning, he had been heard to mutter, "Splendid, splendid"; and as commander of what he hoped would become the finest singing division in the AEF he had loved how Barnhart got the men warmed up. With the men relaxed and the game on the line, he decided that the time had come to give the men a speech about mosquitoes and how he planned to eradicate them from Camp Upton.

By the time the general wrapped up his speech on pest control and departed the stage he had killed the game. It was hard to get excited after that, and the Braves drove the final nail in the coffin with another run. As the match ended with New York falling to Boston 3-1, the men staggered out of the Polo Grounds, tired and thinking not of baseball and ham sandwiches but of the billions of buzzing bloodsuckers that awaited them out on Long Island.[20]

Thousands of draftees had paraded in Brooklyn too. A reporter for the *Brooklyn Daily Eagle* commented on their headgear, which included straw hats, gold caps, and "felt hats of an ancient vintage," and marveled at how draftees and onlookers alike seemed "too serious for cheering." At times, all the reporter could hear was the tramp of boots and "the snapping of the flags in the sharp September breeze." Even attending Civil War veterans were solemn, and some of them cried. The mood fell even further when word got around that a young girl had jumped out from the police line and been run over by a car. The only good thing was that the men got to go to Ebbets Field afterward to see their beloved Brooklyn Dodgers play the Philadelphia Phillies—without interruption. But even that turned sour; the game ended with darkness after fourteen innings, and no score.[21]

As evening fell, Damon Runyon walked to his office across from city hall and sat down to tell his typewriter about everything he had seen and heard on National Draft Day. As he did so, draftees wandered the streets in search of something stronger than soda pop, and of more comfortable accommodations than hard bleachers at a ball game. The unthinkable lay ahead. None of them knew a thing about war beyond what they had read in the newspapers. At the Polo Grounds and Ebbets Field they had dropped newspapers emblazoned with rambling columns about European battles. Most of them probably hadn't pondered the details too deeply. The only thing certain was that they were no longer private citizens. In a few days they would leave for Camp Upton.

(CHAPTER TWO)

WAR'S STORY

Damon Runyon didn't watch the first batch of draftees depart for Long Island. There was too much happening at the Polo Grounds. The season wouldn't end for another month, but everyone, Runyon included, expected the National League's Giants and the American League's Chicago White Sox to meet in the World Series. A meeting between the Giants and the White Sox would be "the greatest series in the history of the game," he proclaimed. White Sox pitchers like Eddie Cicotte had become formidable masters of the "jazz ball"—the recent invention of an alcoholic Pacific Coast League pitcher named Ben Henderson—and Runyon wasn't sure what Giants manager John McGraw could dial up to stop them. Still and all, the reporter had to favor his hometown Giants "because of the superior drive of the big-town men; especially do we like them on the old hometown heath, where the instruments of amusement are more carefully cloistered than in the American league, but we would like them a lot more if the jazz-ball is completely barred."[1]

But jazz ball wasn't barred. Chicago ended the season with a league-best 100–54 record, and won games one and two of the series at Comiskey Park on October 6 and 7 by scores of 2–1 and 7–2. Game three was supposed to return to the Polo Grounds on October 9, but Runyon was not optimistic. He rode with the Giants players on the train back from Chicago and thought they looked demoralized. New York fans wondered whether to dub the series "tragedy," "comedy," or "sheer farce," but Runyon held out hope that "a good, funny fall of the Chicago White Sox would undoubtedly tone up the finish for Broadway."

The city proved loyal. Giants stalwarts packed the Polo Grounds, and even when a downpour began the fans just sat and held newspapers over their heads in traditional New York style. Unfortunately, the rain kept falling, the newspapers were reduced to sodden pulp, and the fans fled under the stands in ignominy. The baseball commissioners called the game and departed to the Waldorf hotel in "deep sea-going cabs."[2]

Giants fans were unfazed as they filed into the Polo Grounds for game three on October 10. The city was in a war mood, and for a day the White Sox were the enemy. For his postgame column, Runyon borrowed language from recent headlines about the Western Front. The Giants had been "driven back on their own reboubts," he wrote triumphantly, "and were fighting in the last trenches," but this time they came through. "Lash-like, the left arm of [Giants pitcher] 'Rube' Benton rose and fell before the eyes of the Chicago White Sox . . . and, echoing the desperate swings of their bats, was a steady, machine-gun-like pop-pop of a baseball thudding" in the catcher's mitt. The White Sox proved helpless against this "barrage fire," and fell 2–0.

The following day dawned clear and mild, perfectly fit for baseball. Strangely, though, the New York fans suddenly deflated as if their minds were elsewhere. Before the game the bands fired up their instruments for a patriotic display that would put the spectacle of September 4 to shame, and manager McGraw and several of his players marched to second base carrying the flags of the Allies. Thousands of seats remained empty as the second inning began, however, and sportswriters grumbled that "the assemblage of fans remained more or less apathetic except at critical or exciting moments of the play." Still, "swinging their war clubs like the cavemen of old, the New York Nationals battered their way to victory over the Chicago Americans" by a score of 5–0.[3]

The next game went back to Comiskey Park, where the Sox drubbed the Giants 8–5 on October 13. Shamed by the press for not supporting their team, Giants fans returned to the Polo Grounds in droves for game six on October 15, but it was all for naught. The Giants fell 4–2, a result Runyon blamed firmly on Giants infielder Heinie Zimmerman, whose German ancestry made him doubly suspect. Maybe overdoing his effort, Heinie tried and failed to beat speedy Sox batter Eddie Collins in a race to home plate for what proved to be the winning run. "Well," Runyon mused bitterly, "it has been a tough era for Teutonic thought one way and another. . . . The Kaiser thought he could lick the world. Heinie Zim thought he could outrun Eddie Collins."[4]

This anticlimactic end to Gotham's biggest week left Runyon at loose ends. For a while he covered boxing and horse racing, but his writing lacked its usual vim. All around him big men—Ivy leaguers, star athletes, millionaires, and journalists—were donning uniforms. There was T. L. Huston, millionaire co-owner of the Yankees, now an army captain; multimillionaire Cornelius Vanderbilt III, now commanding the New York National Guard's 22nd Engineer Regiment; wealthy New York estate owner and adventurer Cushman Rice, now an airman; and even Percy Edrop, another newsman with the *New York American* who was now an army chaplain. And then there were guys like "Broadway Grenadier" Kid Bebee, a hard-nosed gambler whom Runyon caught watching the races at Belmont Park with a "languid eye." "This town and this country has been pretty good to me," Bebee told Runyon; "the least I can do is to fight for my country when it has a little fighting to do."[5]

A couple of weeks later, Runyon read that five hundred Yale undergraduates did or would hold commissions in the AEF, and decided to write a poem about the gridiron's best athletes taking it to the Hun on the Western Front:

> There's a mud-clogged field in Flanders;
> There's a trench by shrapnel flayed,
> Where the doughboys blink at the dawn's first wink,
> On the day that The Game is played.
> "Hup!" The signal passes!
> "Let's go!" The light turns blue!
> There's a splash and a crash,
> And a long, long smash
> As the lean-flanked backs drive thru!
> Hark! That's a song of triumph!
> Hark! That's the old, old hail—
> "Bulldog! Bulldog! Bow-wow-wow! Eli Yale!"[6]

To Runyon the autumn days felt like the final ticking moments before the ringside bell, but they seemed to stretch on forever. With every tick, the thrill became more unbearable. A big game, the world's biggest, attracting America's best, was brewing over there in Europe. In a few weeks, months maybe, American ears would hear the first "Let's go!" And all Runyon could think of was how he remained stuck over here.

The man who would become known as the "Voice of Broadway" grew up to a slow cadence of violence. He was born Alfred Damon Runyan on October 4, 1880, in Manhattan, Kansas, to what he called a family of "Huguenot horse thieves" and drunks. Seven years later his family settled in the bustling frontier town of Pueblo, Colorado, a protocity just outgrowing a legacy of conflict between miners and ranchers. Damon's mother died when he was eight, leaving his father, Alfred Lee Runyan, to raise four children alone. Alfred, an ex-cavalryman who had served briefly under Custer, spent part of his time writing for local newspapers and most of it drinking liquor. His writing was good but booze didn't help pay the rent, and the family lived close to poverty.[7]

Damon took refuge from his dismal home life in equal measures of reading and fighting. By the time he was nine he smoked and drank too. At the local library, he discovered the works of Rudyard Kipling, glorifying the bold men who adventured and built empires. More often he reveled in penny western tales of gunmen, outlaws, and Indians. Damon hated school, and left it after sixth grade without an ounce of regret. It did not take long to learn life on the streets and become convinced that most people didn't give a damn. "Everyone whose path I crossed" gave him "a swift kick in the little panties just as a warning not to do whatever it was I contemplated doing." Damon was a short child, but rattlesnake mean. He became a proud member of Pueblo's East Side Gang, acquired a complete vocabulary of swear words, and learned the dirty tricks necessary to hold his own in a street fight. By the time he hit puberty, and maybe a little earlier, he was womanizing too.[8]

Runyan blossomed as a writer before even reaching his teens. He began working for the *Pueblo Evening Press* at age twelve. His first assignment was to describe how a lynched bandit's swollen corpse had come to end up dangling from a telegraph pole behind Pueblo's Grand Hotel. After that he moved to general interest stories about puppy dogs, homicides, children's birthday parties, and armed robberies. Sometimes he wrote poetry, and he always followed baseball.

As his star rose, Runyan bought natty clothes and spent his free time bragging, fighting, and boozing in saloons like the Bucket of Blood. Always one to gain firsthand experience, Runyan didn't just watch but actively participated in another lynching, this time of a man who had stabbed a rival after an argument that began in one of the reporter's favorite saloons. The newspaper story he wrote afterward thrilled his boss and further established his career.[9]

For a lover of violence there was nothing more attractive than war. Runyan's dream seemed to come true after the battleship *Maine* blew up in Havana Harbor on February 15, 1898, and the United States went to war with Spain. Although still undersized and several months too young, Runyan managed to sneak into the army as a bugler with the 13th Minnesota Volunteers. That regiment went to join the American army of occupation in the Philippines, and he later claimed to have seen combat during the ensuing insurrection and been wounded twice. In fact, Runyan spent most of his eleven months overseas in a camp near Manila's red-light district, nursing a bad case of "dobie itch," or boils caused by ringworm. He passed his time by writing for an unofficial military newspaper named the *Manila Freedom and Soldier's Letter*, concocting stories based loosely on gutter tales and camp gossip.

Runyon was a brilliant caricaturist who understood how to capture moods. Men talked all the more freely knowing he would listen. They loved how he embellished their stories with elements culled from adventure literature, and how his pen transformed them into larger than life Kiplingesque heroes. Runyan lived as they lived, earning his barracks-room credentials by getting drunk and carousing whenever possible. For perhaps the first time in his life, he felt like he belonged to something important. Runyan cherished these memories until the end of his life. In later years he hung his old Spanish-American War uniform behind his door, and gleefully showed visitors a machete and .45 pistol that he had used in the Philippines.[10]

Denied the combat he craved but still feeling himself a soldier, Runyan boarded a ship and went back to San Francisco, where he was discharged on October 3, 1899. He celebrated by getting drunk and spending all his money. Readjusting to peacetime was difficult. Emulating his father, he wandered Colorado and other western states as an itinerant newspaper reporter, drinking heavily. Somewhere along the way a typo changed his last name to Runyon, and he kept it, also dropping his original first name Alfred in favor of Damon.

The liquor habit finally wore out the patience of his editors, who moved him to sports writing. This was fine with Runyon, who gravitated naturally to boxing and found catharsis in watching bare-knuckled brawlers slug each other into bloody pulp. Still thinking wistfully of the war, he developed a full-fledged military fantasy life, writing stories and verse about soldiers and even concocting a tale that he had served with American military instructors in China. In this kind of writing Runyon discovered a sentimentality he had never displayed before, for example in a poem titled "The Spirit of You" about a dying soldier, which ended:

We laid him out there as he wanted—McSweal, of the Battery, dead;
With a blanket of perfumed blossoms, and the guidon under his head;
With the locket still clasped in his fingers—we gave him a volley or two,
And we left him out there as he wanted—to talk with the Spirit of You![11]

Nobody except Runyon knew why he abruptly decided to change his life in 1910 and move to New York City. By then his wanderings had brought him to Denver, and his drinking and gambling had gotten him in no end of trouble. Somewhere along the line he hit rock bottom to the point of complete physical collapse. After this scare Runyon picked himself up, quit drinking (which he replaced with compulsive smoking and coffee habits), and looked for a change of scenery. Over the past several years he had become an excellent sportswriter with a keen knowledge of the major sports and an eye for scenery and drama. He also had begun selling literary odds and ends to New York magazines, mostly stories and poems about soldiers and hobos. When fellow sportswriter Charlie Van Loan offered to put Runyon up at his home in Brooklyn until he could catch on with a city paper, he jumped at the chance.[12]

Like the immigrants swarming ashore, Runyon started in New York City with nothing except talent and ambition. Shortly after arriving he would have crossed the Brooklyn Bridge to walk along Park Row, the heart of the city's newspaper world. They were all here: the papers owned by Joseph Pulitzer, Hearst, and the others, inhabiting skyscrapers that competed for prominence just like the papers themselves. These included Horace Greeley's New

York Tribune Building of 1875, once the second-tallest building in the city after Trinity Church, and now flanked by the taller 1889 New York Times Building and the sixteen-story 1890 New York World Building. Everyone made fun of the squat, troll-like New York Sun Building next door—but then, each paper hired architects to call rival buildings ugly. By the time Runyon arrived, however, the Times had picked up and moved to Times Square.

City journalists led crazy, hectic lives, just as they had for decades, competing to outdo reporters from other papers and colleagues from the same paper. They raced from teeming, smoky newsrooms to teeming, smoky streets and back again, bawled at by managers and bawling out copy editors. Everything that happened in the city entered print somewhere. But journalism was in a transitional period. Newish technologies like typewriters and telephones settled in as brand new technologies like radio or wireless telegraph changed the way reporters gathered information and sent it out to the public.

In recent years an entirely new breed of reporter had come to the fore: the war correspondent. Foremost among them was the great Richard Harding Davis. By 1910 he was big time. While Runyon scraped stories off barracks-room floors for an obscure soldiers' paper in 1898–1899, Davis wrote for Pulitzer's *New York Herald* and *Scribner's Weekly* about Roosevelt and his Rough Riders on San Juan Hill. From there he had gone off to cover the Boer War in South Africa and conflicts in southern Europe that presaged the Great War. He earned top salaries, and was also a successful novelist and playwright; in short, everything Runyon wanted to be. Some accused Davis of sensationalism, but his prose couldn't rival the kind of things Runyon eventually wrote.

For Runyon, New York was the life. Despite the years he had spent wandering the Rocky Mountain West, he and the city matched perfectly. Before long he landed a job with Hearst's *New York American*. The newspaper occupied a seventh-floor office across from city hall. The city room presented a haphazard collection of lights, electric cords, and green lampshades surrounding a horseshoe desk occupied by frantic copy editors. Reporters shoved and snarled at each other and threw caustic remarks. Copy hurtled through a series of brass pneumatic tubes lining the ceiling. The night editor hovered impatiently for news of murders and disasters that would make great morning fare (the Black Tom explosion thrilled him). Hearst inspected everything with his steely eyes and demanded perfection.

Runyon's first city job was as a sportswriter. These were a special breed. Though they wrote about entertainment, they behaved as if they were war correspondents, immersing themselves into the blow-by-blow of a pitiless world where only the fit survived. Runyon's writing brought a new style to the trade, though, moving beyond the purely descriptive to humanize not just athletes but fans too—just like he had with soldiers in the Philippines. Athletes and fans were all storytellers, and Runyon used the same keen ear to record, elaborate, and spin yarns that transformed them into characters in some epic novel, with equal parts violence, humor, whimsy, and pathos. Readers loved it. By 1914 he had his own daily column, "The Mornin's Mornin."

The work kept Runyon where he loved most: on the streets. He spent much of his time at the Polo Grounds, where he became the Giants beat reporter. But he didn't just sit down to watch and report the games. In fact, his columns suggest he didn't watch some games at all. Instead he walked the lots and roamed the stands to chat with fans. He talked up cops and vendors. Runyon stalked locker rooms to interact with athletes, and joined them on trains to cover away games. He had a knack for digging out family stories, jokes, anything he could build upon to give readers a sense that they were there too, sharing ideas and swapping gossip. Every man, woman, and child in his telling, from the middling ball player to the bored cop to the overweight middle-aged fan, became some oversized, fantastic figure straight out of a comedy or adventure story.

It was in the process of hunting down some of these characters where they were most themselves—in their homes—that Runyon became a part of the city. The reporter looked up Bat Masterson, the former western lawman who had moved to New York and become a newspaper columnist and sportswriter, and the two men became regulars at the Metropole on West 43rd Street. From there Runyon explored Broadway and Times Square and the area around mid-Manhattan and discovered all the action going on there—with so many stories! Soon he was spending most of his time in the district, day and night, watching and recording and spinning.

By the time he got his daily column Runyon had become a city celebrity and acquired his trademark style. Since his youth he had filled out vertically but not horizontally. He stood five foot nine and a half, but was a thin man with small feet encased in 5.5B shoes. His eyes were pale blue, unblinking and penetrating, magnified by wire-rimmed glasses. They stayed fixed on his interview subjects with absolute attention, but only enough to show that he was listening. He had a way of making people feel at ease, head cocked at a perpetual angle with his heavy brow, long chin, and pouting lips, hands clasped in his lap with a burning cigar or cigarette. Hidden behind his firm look, though, lurked the barest hint of a smirk that broke easily into a wry, self-deprecating smile.

The hard edge dwelt there too, that of a man who had grown up amid violence and knew what it meant. In 1911 Runyon married society reporter Ellen Egan, whom he had met in Denver. That was a mistake, for he was not at all the domestic type. He womanized constantly and neglected his children. When this brought his home life on West 113th Street (not far from the Polo Grounds) deeper into misery he responded by spending more time away, where he felt comfortable—at the ballpark or on the streets. Hearst rewarded his habits by letting him relegate sports writing to a part-time occupation. Runyon enjoyed the freedom to write about anything that he could gather from the streets.[13]

When the European war broke out in August 1914, Davis was one of the first reporters to go. He demanded, and received, the incredible annual salary of thirty-two thousand dollars for his war correspondence. And he delivered with his usual top-notch war reporting, even managing to get himself arrested for a time by the Kaiser's troops. Davis returned the following year, however, in a huff about Allied restrictions on the press. Everyone assumed his absence would only be temporary—he was the best war reporter America had.

On March 9 of that year, Mexican bandit Pancho Villa led a raid on the New Mexico border town of Columbus, killing several American soldiers and civilians. President Wilson retaliated by ordering General Pershing to organize an expedition to pursue Villa into Mexico. The ultracompetitive New York papers understood that they would need to get their best men into the field immediately, if possible scooping Davis, who would be certain to demand a huge contract before he moved anywhere. Hearst stalked into the *New York American* offices one morning wondering why Runyon was still writing about boxers and Broadway.

"War is the number-one newspaper seller of all time," the newspaper mogul snarled. "Get Runyon to war."

But there was no need to send Runyon anywhere. On the day that Villa crossed into New Mexico, the reporter was in Texas reporting on the Giants' training camp. And he had already encountered the bandit leader. Five years earlier, at another visit to training camp, he had heard something of the Mexican's exploits and gone off to meet him in Juarez across the Rio Grande from El Paso. Fortunately, Villa admired Hearst, and shared with Runyon a common interest in baseball, horse racing, and women. The meeting was friendly and made good copy; afterward Villa sent Runyon a gold cigarette lighter studded with a ruby, a gift the reporter would cherish for the rest of his life right alongside his Spanish-American War memorabilia.[14]

The day after the Columbus raid, Runyon packed his bags—he always had a huge trunk and at least two suitcases—and took a train for the border. The thought of meeting Villa again under new circumstances thrilled him, but so did the opportunity of reporting a new war firsthand. When Pershing's men crossed the border with several thousand cavalry and infantry Runyon was right there. Knowing that his best chance for favored treatment was to cozy up to the top brass, Runyon didn't complain about censorship. In fact, he saved the army censors trouble by censoring his own writing. He won Pershing's confidence by writing about him with undisguised admiration. Pershing rewarded the reporter by letting him near the front. By April, news arrived that Runyon would be the undisputed star of the show—Davis had died of a sudden heart attack on April 11, not yet fifty-two years old.

Other correspondents would have, and did, race to report on every detail of the undeclared war's first skirmishes. But Runyon was not like other correspondents. Although he reported dutifully on military encounters, he did not seek out combat per se. He was interested in the men, how they lived, what made them tick. He wanted, and found, stories. Among them was a brash young lieutenant named George Patton, who bragged about killing a Mexican bandit in front of his family and then throwing the body on the hood of his car along with two other dead Mexicans and driving to camp with the trophies. Runyon found four Japanese civilians arguing with some soldiers about a dog and wrote about that too. There really was nothing to censor. Branding the just-named "doughboys" the "greatest of all the world's foot soldiers," Runyon spent his time writing about them. Villa was never found, but when Runyon packed up to return to New York City in May he had added another to his long list of talents, all of which boiled down to writing sympathetically about people in all situations.[15]

Runyon's Mexican border dispatches made him a national journalistic celebrity, so much so that Hearst dispatched him in June to cover the Republican national convention in Chicago and the Democratic convention in St. Louis. Small papers across the country bragged when they struck deals to print his articles in syndication. Back in New York he returned to his city beat, covering sports and events on the streets. But Mexico had not sated his fascination with warriors—athletic and military—and with war. He continued to write stories, verse, and even songs about soldiers, leading some—no doubt to Runyon's deep satisfaction—to compare him to the Kipling he admired. Had he known it, his coverage of the 1916 World Series between the Robins and the Red Sox would mark the end of an era for himself, and his country.

The declaration of war found Runyon on the road in Oklahoma and Kansas, covering spring training and exhibition games, and increasingly aware that he would no longer be able to write about sports in the same way. "The spectacle of a bunch of trained athletes practicing an amusement when their country needs men of just their physical type, would be intolerable," he told his readers. "The time is probably not very far distant now when a baseball bat, a golf stick, or a tennis racket in the hands of a man of serviceable age and physical ability will be an insignia of discredit."[16]

At the end of June Runyon joined the swarms of reporters at Plattsburg, observing the ninety-day wonders destined to lead New York's contribution to the American Expeditionary Forces. To his frustration, he was not permitted to provide specific information about individual officer candidates, though he did notice a "tall and dusty looking young man," earnestly preparing maps, who might well have been Whittlesey. Blocked from personalizing his writing, Runyon left Plattsburg after only a day or two.

The Draft Day parade of September 4 was an entirely different kind of event. Its participants represented the kind of everyday men he respected. Like him, they started from the bottom. There was "no odium" attached to the word "conscript," Runyon insisted. In his mind, draftees still represented America's best and brightest, and they deserved a grand send-off. "Send 'em away with a cheer!" he enthused.[17]

"'The Melting Pot' tipped over yesterday and spilled a stream of pure 22-karat Americanism through the streets of little old New York," Runyon wrote in the *New York American*'s lead column about the parade. He noticed the draftees' shifting hands and awkwardly shuffling feet as they struggled to keep time and formation. Even so he regarded the parade as the "most impressive spectacle to be witnessed on this earth."

Runyon stood at the corner of 42nd Street and Fifth Avenue with Jack Doyle, "who knows many things about Broadway."

Together they picked out the characters, including a guy in a barber-pole shirt who was "the best one-stepper in this town! He's what you call a Jazz-spider, which is the same as what a tango-lizard used to be." They also identified "a waiter from Jack's and a Greek hat-grabber from Rector's," among others. They were "all of them the children of old New York," Runyon thought, "and all of them the sons of Uncle Sam."[18]

Runyon never forgot his western roots. As he watched star athletes and big-town men suit up for war, his mind embraced the millions of rural and small-town Americans across the country who were doing the same. In his ramblings, and in his coverage of sportsmen from all backgrounds, Runyon had developed a sense of America's growing diversity—and never more so than in the military, as he had seen in the Philippines and on the Mexican border. When he eventually did get overseas, he would start by seeking out the New Yorkers in uniform. Soon, however, Runyon followed the scions of rural America too—men like a Bible-believing farmer from Fentress County, Tennessee, who agonized over whether to answer his country's call for his service.

(CHAPTER THREE)

THE COUNTRY AWAKENS

New Yorkers heading south—as Damon Runyon often did when he went to Texas to attend the Giants' spring training—took trains from Grand Central by way of Philadelphia and Baltimore to Union Station in Washington, DC. From there they had several options. The railway toward Richmond opened the gateway to the Carolinas and the Deep South. Another route ran southwest through Virginia to Salisbury and Asheville, North Carolina, and across the Smoky Mountains to Knoxville, Tennessee. Passengers on locomotives laboring across the Smokies entered a different world, one foreign to the low-country Dixieland Confederacy. The mountains were rough, misty, remote.

Most travelers forgot the mountains and continued west, but some exited the train at Knoxville. Every now and then, somebody rented a car and drove west about seventy miles to Crossville, and then north toward the Kentucky border. After about fifty miles the macadam road ended at Jamestown. From here, travelers who were adventurous enough or had kinfolk up that way could get horses or mules, or hitch rides on wagons over bumpy, deeply rutted dirt roads farther up into the mountains toward the region of the Upper Cumberland.

The route traversed a slowly rising grade over increasingly narrow roads. After a few miles the hills rose suddenly; the trees were uncut except in patches where farmers scratched away on tiny plots. There were no signs. Visitors could stop and ask for directions at smithies, farms, and country stores from lean, closed-lipped, serious folk. Those who took on airs—locals called them people with big heads—might cadge simple provisions or animal fodder but otherwise wouldn't get much. But those who were humble, good listeners like Runyon, or best of all, God fearing, could expect easy smiles, directions over the hill to the next holler, delicious food, and lots and lots of stories.

Thirteen miles from Jamestown the mountain path reached the little town of Pall Mall. A place more different from New York City would be hard to imagine. It had a country store, a mill, and some clapboard houses but that was about it. Most people lived not in town but in the surrounding hills, often in family clusters like clans. The rough spots, where hard men drank hard liquor, were out there too.

Riding dirt roads and paths among the farms in this region, visitors sensed differentness. These were not the lowland farms and plantations of the Deep South, with poor whites and black sharecroppers, where the Ku Klux Klan reigned. Nor were they the mining towns of east Kentucky, with soot-caked miners struggling to make a living in company housing. The people here still lived much like eighteenth-century pioneers, or their ancestors from the highlands of Scotland. Violence defined life here as it did on the Lower East Side. If you wanted a fight, you got it and then some—a knife fight between one of these and a Bowery bum would have been evenly matched. Still, folks here were not unfriendly to strangers—you just had to know how to sit, maybe take up a whittling stick along with your sharp-edged knife, and listen.

When front-porch conversation among the hard-flint mountain farmers of East Tennessee and Kentucky turned to violence and war, someone always mentioned Champ Ferguson. During the Civil War—or the War Between the States, depending upon which side you took in this deeply divided region—Ferguson and his raiders had terrorized Yankee soldiers and sympathizers alike. No one anywhere in the Upper Cumberland could rest safe; once Ferguson decided to get you, he would find you. Union guerillas such as "Tinker Dave" Beaty tried to keep up, and committed their share of atrocities against Confederate sympathizers. But they lacked Ferguson's knack for war, if not his ruthlessness.

Born about fifteen miles northwest of Pall Mall near Albany, Kentucky, on November 29, 1821, Ferguson was like most people in this area of Scots-Irish descent. Their ancestors had arrived in America a century earlier and trod Virginia's Wilderness Road to the Appalachians, but they never forgot their roots. They took friendships, and enmities, deadly seriously. In Revolutionary War times, people from these parts were called "Overmountain Men." When British major Patrick Ferguson tried to bully them in 1780 by threatening to "march his army over the mountains, hang their leaders, and lay waste the country with fire and sword," they came over the mountains instead and destroyed his army—killing him in the process—at the battle of King's Mountain.

The land the mountaineers tried to farm was bleak and unforgiving, with rocky soil that barely surrendered enough nutrients to keep them alive. Well into the twentieth century this would remain the most impoverished region in the entire United States. It took a special kind of man, or woman, to stay here and fight for a living. City folks might scoff from the safety of their drawing rooms, but no one would be fool enough to call a man from these parts a hillbilly unless he knew how to handle a gun or was quick with a knife.

Ferguson was a "gambling, rowdyish, drinking, fighting, quarrelsome man," but then so were his enemies, and indeed many young men in the mountains. They could till their hardscrabble farms that barely provided enough for a living; they could drink hard liquor; and they could fight. Just before the war began, Ferguson got in a brawl at a mountain camp meeting in Fentress County, Tennessee, and knifed a constable. Tennessee's secession in 1861 gave him an opportunity to join the Confederate army and so avoid prosecution. Enlisting was a mere formality—in effect, he could do what he wanted, so long as it hurt the Yankees. He also settled personal scores.

On one occasion early in the war, Ferguson tracked down a man named William Frogg who had returned home to Clinton County after catching measles in Union camp Dick Robinson, and lay sick in bed. Ferguson knocked on Frogg's door, which was opened by William's young wife, Esther. Trembling in fear, she offered him a chair.

"I don't have time," Champ brusquely replied. She then pointed to some apples she had just peeled.

"Have some apples," she said.

"I've been eating apples," he replied, and pushed past the woman into Frogg's bedroom, where he lay sick next to his five-month-old child.

"I reckon you caught the measles at Camp Dick Robinson," Ferguson drawled, and promptly shot the man dead.

At about the same time, according to mountain lore, Tinker Dave Beaty caught one of his own enemies, and finished him off by crushing the man's face beneath his horse's hooves.¹

The spoils of war—and revenge—go to the victors. Ferguson and Beaty never met in combat, but the Confederate guerilla ended his life in a hangman's noose while the Union raider went free.

The mountaineers of the Upper Cumberland loved storytelling, and so the legends of Champ Ferguson and Tinker Dave Beaty were still fresh when Alvin C. York was born on December 13, 1887, in Fentress County, Tennessee, near Pall Mall. His grandfather Uriah York had died after contracting an illness while fleeing Confederate raiders. His parents, William and Mary Brooks York, were small farmers with a typically large family of eleven children (Alvin was the third) wedged into a one-room cabin. Everyone worked just as soon as they could walk, not least the York children. Alvin was cutting weeds and shucking corn by age six, and learning how to care for horses, mules, and dogs.

Upstanding churchgoing men like William York took their pleasure hunting turkeys, raccoons, foxes, and other small game. Guns were part of everyday life, especially muzzle-loading rifles for hunting and revolvers for target shooting. After the war, storytellers seeking to portray Alvin York as a latter-day Davy Crockett had a field day with the image of father and son, guns in hand and dogs in tow, roving the back country in search of coons and turkeys. They imagined Alvin becoming a deadeye shot as if in anticipation of his exploits in the world war. The first book he read, they said, was about celebrity outlaws Frank and Jesse James.²

But life in the mountains meant a lot more than playing Buffalo Bill and toiling in the fields. There was eating—and drinking; whittling—and storytelling. There was school, now and again, in tiny one-room schoolhouses. There were family friendships and rivalries. And there was God.

The Upper Cumberland was the domain of Bible-believing, evangelical Christianity. Baptists dominated, but itinerant "saddlebag" preachers of all known, and many unknown, denominations walked rugged mountain roads, visited families and schools, and held revival camp meetings deep in the hills. The region was isolated from the surrounding lowlands of Kentucky and Tennessee, and from cities like Knoxville, not just geographically but culturally. As in any small towns in rural America, plain, straight-arrow, Bible-believing folk abounded; but there was also sexual misbehavior, domestic violence, substance abuse, and just plain rowdiness. Prostitutes dwelt in ramshackle but well-visited mountain cabins. As any preacher would have said, the church housed saints and sinners; and while the threat of fire and brimstone beckoned, so did the angel of redemption.

York fell. Though his parents were by all accounts simple Christian folk, never evidently short of consideration and compassion, young Alvin found peers who promised easy shelter from the storms of everyday life in good times and moonshine. Liquor laws could be stringent, but enforcement was nonexistent except when a stray constable wandered through town. And even then, a gray area of authority existed along the Kentucky-Tennessee border where illicit dens known as "blind tigers" peddled moonshine, gambling, and women. Just like in Champ Ferguson's time, these places became the resorts of all sorts of desperate characters swift with knives and quick with guns.

The rowdy elements did not stay on the fringes. Drunk, well-armed young men frequently hung around tent revival meetings and sometimes broke them up just for the hell of it. They enjoyed taunting converts into abandoning their newfound godly ways.

Hair-trigger tempers, acquired in violently abusive homes and schoolyard or back-road brawls, suckered many a God-fearing man back into the gutter, and provoked despair leading to drink. York participated in a good number of fights, and saw men badly hurt or killed. His experiences were not at all unusual for the place and time.[3]

If his later memories were correct, York's "bad" period lasted from 1911, when his father died at age forty-eight from a heart ailment, until 1915, when Alvin was twenty-eight. Those four years and the tough-guy culture they embodied left their scars, even after York renounced them. Every day of his life he would choose afresh between the call of God he eventually embraced and the temptations of a world in which men lived and fought hard. In some ways, this everlasting tension crafted him into an ideal soldier.[4]

The journey toward personal faith was neither quick nor easy. Only York knew how and why it happened. According to the storybook version later peddled for public consumption, Alvin took his first steps toward God when the Bible-believing father of the girl he loved, blue-eyed blonde Gracie Loretta Williams, refused to let him court her because of his bad habits. He could only see her when they both went to church. Guilty feelings about the admonitions of his dead father, and the living admonitions of his mother, tormented him. There are also unpublished accounts that he renounced his hard life after becoming involved in a drunken brawl in which a friend and near relation was killed.

Whatever the true cause of his conversion, the final stage apparently occurred during the week leading up to New Years' Day, 1915, when York attended a camp meeting led by saddlebag preacher Rev. Melvin Herbert Russell. York attended over several days, finding his temptations to sin gradually slipping away, replaced by a yearning for salvation and peace. On New Year's Day, finally, "it was as if lightning struck my soul"; and he stepped forward to accept Jesus as his savior.

Like many converts, York furiously rejected anything smacking of inconsistency and weakness. Offended by the continuing presence of unrepentant sinners, including some of his old rowdy friends, in the church he initially attended, he joined a Pall Mall congregation of the Church of Christ in Christian Union (CCCU) as a deputy pastor. The pastor, Rosier C. Pile (a cousin of York's), took Christian living seriously, and monitored and chastised deviation. He and his Bible-focused congregation interpreted the "Good Book" literally, including the commandment "Thou shalt not kill"—a direct rebuke to the activities of Champ Ferguson, Tinker Dave Beaty, and their twentieth-century heirs. York felt content, not least when Gracie Williams and her family joined the CCCU, and especially when she consented to marry him in June 1917.

When Alvin proposed to Gracie the United States of America had been at war for two months. News arrived slowly in the mountains, though; hardly anyone had a radio, and local newspapers covered local news. Much of what people learned came by word of mouth from travelers wending their way over dirt roads and trails. Up to that time York had thought little of the troubles in Europe. When news of the war did arrive, it found the mountaineers intensely patriotic but baffled at all the fuss. Soon afterward postcards began arriving on cabin doorsteps telling the occupants to register for the draft. Most men went uncomplainingly, whether married or single, young or middle aged. But York believed in the Bible and didn't know whether he believed in war.

York's card arrived on June 5 after being sorted by the postmaster, Reverend Pile, at his store in Pall Mall. It directed York to go to town and register, with Reverend Pile, who served as the town's de facto mayor. York submitted his registration card as the law required, but wrote "I don't want to fight" at the bottom. He also pleaded with the reverend to help him find a way out of joining the army if he was called up in the draft. To him, war presented a temptation to turn back to his old ways, along with the violence that had defined the history of his people. York also struggled to decide what this war against Germany was all about.

After several discussions, Pile agreed to help York write a letter to the Fentress County draft board. In it, York requested exemption on the grounds that he belonged to a "well-recognized sect or organization" whose "existing creed or principles forbade its members to participate in war in any form." But the letter did no good. In its reply, the draft board rejected York's application on grounds that the CCCU did not represent what he claimed. "We understand," they wrote, that "it has no creed except the Bible, which its members more or less interpret for themselves, and some do not disbelieve in war—at least there is nothing forbidding them to participate."[5]

It was a gut-wrenching message. In a couple of bland sentences, the draft board simultaneously quashed York's application and questioned his church's consistency of purpose—the very thing that had led him to join it in the first place. If some of his brethren chose to fight and others didn't, where did that leave York? Faith might give security, but there would still be times when he had to make tough decisions on his own, regardless of what people told him was right or wrong. He prayed on it long and hard.

York appealed the Fentress draft board's decision to the State of Tennessee, and lost. Defeated, but with undaunted patriotism, he submitted to God's will and prayed that he wouldn't be called up. Many eligible men never received the call. On November 10, 1917, however, York received notice to report to Jamestown for duty. Pastor Pile worked to convince him to bow to necessity, but it was with a heavy heart that York walked over the mountains to Jamestown on November 14. Still unconvinced that he could fight, he hoped for inclusion among the majority of soldiers never asked to do so.[6]

After several days for processing, York went to Camp Gordon, Georgia, for basic training. Being around other men of varied backgrounds didn't bother him—he had mixed with all kinds in his day, and determined to set a quiet but firm example of prayer and integrity. He may have enjoyed the sense of discipline and common purpose instilled by parade ground exercises, and his lean body easily endured long-route marches through pine woods, and manual labor. Target practice must have seemed silly to York, who was already a marksman. Bayonet practice, though, sickened him as he imagined a human being substituted for a straw dummy. With each lunge he wished himself a thousand miles away.

In February 1918 York was assigned to the 82nd Division, also based at Camp Gordon. Originally filled with southerners, the division had been reformed and diluted with draftees from almost every state in the union, including large numbers of recent European immigrants. This presented an education for the humble mountain farmer. New comrades attempted to call York back to the sinful days of his youth, urging him to overstay his leave with them in the taverns and brothels of Augusta, or even skip out at night. He stood strong, however, and sought out fellow Christians to share quiet spaces in the barracks or under the trees to study the Bible, or discuss it while on the march.

Training intensified. Route marches lasted longer and came more frequently. The men sang as they slogged, York refusing to join in bawdy lyrics improvised on the go. His doggedness and strict obedience earned him the designation of "a good soldier, being willing and quick to pick up work and obeying all orders." On the firing range, York showed calmness and accuracy—to him, the rifle was a true friend. With each shot he fired, however, the Tennessean fell more deeply into war's embrace. He was too good, too instinctively a warrior, to be kept out of the fight. Still yearning for escape from the moral chasm, York asked God to lead him. He could not run any longer. He would have to decide.[7]

One day, York went to visit his captain, E. C. B. Danforth. A Georgian who had made good at Harvard, Danforth was hard but fair and, as York knew, a Christian. In open conversation that broke all the rules of military etiquette, each man laid it on the line. York said he had prayed but without reaching resolution. Danforth asked him if he objected to fighting. "No, that's what I'm here for," York replied. "But I wish you would tell me what this war is about." He would kill Germans if he had to, but couldn't motivate himself to desire combat. The two men ended at a respectful impasse. Unwilling to lose one of his best soldiers, Danforth passed York on to his battalion commander, Major G. Edward Buxton.[8]

Another Harvard man but unlike Danforth a New Englander, Buxton was a forthright Christian and fervent patriot who had no doubts as to which side God favored in this war. But his faith was far from shallow; he had studied every page of the Bible both as an intellectual and a believer, almost as if he anticipated having to justify his stance to nonbelievers on the one hand and well-meaning conscientious Christians on the other. When York trudged into his office carrying his "old Bible," Buxton was ready for him.

Like his captain, the major did not try to pull rank over the earnest private. Instead, York and Buxton sat and swatted Bible verses back and forth like a tennis ball. York was earnest but his faith young; and in intense debate with the Harvard officer he stood less chance than a high school prodigy against a Wimbledon champion. In a final crushing volley, Buxton expounded the Christian "just war" principle, backing it up with one Bible verse after another until York, caught flatfooted, admitted defeat by begging for time to go and think it over.

But time was running out. Back in barracks York recovered somewhat the courage of his convictions, only to end up in a heated argument with one of his comrades, a former Irish bartender, who threatened to kill York if he went on with his nonsense about not wanting to fight. Finally, York received a ten-day leave of absence that coincidentally began on March 21, the same day that the Germans launched their final major offensive on the Western Front. York could not have been unaware of the Allies' increasingly desperate plight on the Western Front as he wandered the mountains of home to try and make up his mind.

As storytellers speaking on York's behalf later described it, the final decision came as an epiphany. God filled him with a "peace which passeth all understanding" and he returned from the hills as a witness to the Transfiguration. "I am going to war with the sword of the Lord and of Gideon," he explained to his mother. "I have received my assurance. I have received it from

God himself—that it's right for me to go to war, and that as long as I believe in Him, not one hair of my head will be harmed."

Whatever the cause of his change of heart, as he returned to Camp Gordon York seemed like a new man—on the outside. Inside, though, his soul recoiled from demons whispering of betrayal and guilt. The anguish they fostered, not enemy bullets, would not long remain buried, and marked the true threat to his hopes for redemption. Six months in the future, in the aftermath of what others called victory, York's life would lie in the balance.[9]

Like Alvin York, millions of Americans prepared that spring and summer to face the unfathomable, populating the eternal scene: packing bags, one more spree, one more ball game, and hopefully not final farewells. Men closing farm gates, walking down the front steps of suburban houses, catching buses and subway trains, or saddling the family horse. In a country evenly balanced between urban and rural (the 1920 census would record a population just tipped to fifty-one percent urban), they came from all backgrounds. York's fear of committing to military service set him apart from most of his peers. Volunteers joined up out of a mixture of idealism and thirst for adventure, but even draftees felt a mixture of resignation and enthusiasm. Almost no one spoke out against conscription.

Rural America was still mostly composed of small farmers—in much of the West, a barely tamed wilderness inhabited by sodbusters, cowboys, and prospectors—and Native Americans struggling to learn how to live in a world they did not invent. Most were only a generation or two removed from the East, and recent immigrants had settled in places like Minnesota and Wisconsin.

Though patriotic, people were just learning how to put down roots, form communities, make a living on the margins with only dreams of future riches to feed upon. Now Uncle Sam called them to leave their new homes, return to Europe, and fight there to prove they were Americans.

None of those leaving their homes knew what they were getting into, but the idea of violence did not frighten them. Most people experienced it in one form or another in their daily lives, much more so than average Americans would a century later. Violence existed everywhere: at home, in the workplace, on the streets, in entertainment and literature, and sometimes in religion. Rural Americans carried and used guns frequently, especially for hunting, though most could not afford modern equipment. Lynchings and private gun feuds still took place in the West, as Runyon had witnessed, and the Klan approached the height of its popularity through much of the country, especially in the South and Midwest.

In the cities too, men, especially from poor and working-class districts, encountered violence every day. Cornelius Willemse, who served as a New York Police Department (NYPD) patrolman and detective from 1900 to 1925, later wrote that he and his fellow cops did not hesitate to use the "third degree" against criminals. "I've forced confessions—with fist, blackjack and hose—from men who would have continued to rob and kill if I had not made them talk," he admitted.[10] Criminals, of course, were far more ruthless, and the era of the gangster was already under way. Most citygoing Americans simply took this for granted.

Patriotism also took violence for granted. Every American schoolchild knew that his country had been founded, built, and maintained in war, from the Revolutionary War to the War of 1812 to the Civil War to the Indian Wars and to the Spanish-American

War. People believed that there was a special American way of war superior to any on earth. Teddy Roosevelt's "big stick" diplomacy was a recent memory. Though Americans were reluctant to become involved in European wars, and even hesitated to enlist voluntarily, they felt complete conviction in their ability to fight and win when well and truly roused. Still, the popular idea of a "fight" was individual: the western gunslinger, the backcountry sharpshooter, and the urban "hard-boiled egg" being the national ideal who always won a square fight.

Total war, however, presented a new kind of monster. British civilian audiences encountered it visually for the first time in August 1916 with the release of the film *The Battle of the Somme*. Moviegoers thrilled and sometimes cried to see live-action scenes of artillery firing, explosions, demoralized German prisoners, and even—in one chilling sequence—an exhausted and probably shell-shocked British soldier carrying a mortally wounded comrade on his shoulders through a trench. Americans, though, didn't get to see even this sanitized movie until a year after its UK release. Instead, people in New York and other cities attended screenings of expurgated film clips, such as "With the British and Canadian Troops in France" shown at the Brooklyn Academy of Music, along with a lecture by a British officer who dwelt "more on the humorous and cheerful side of the war, than upon the tragic, which was more easily imagined."[11]

Until the spring of 1917 there simply hadn't been much popular demand for information about the war. Newspapers printed official dispatches from both sides, but after Richard Harding Davis's departure from France in 1915 few American war correspondents operated anywhere near the front. Freshly minted American soldiers, then, left their homes ready to fight but in complete ignorance of how they would come to grips with and thrash the enemy.

At Camp Upton and places like it, men like Charles Whittlesey, George McMurtry, and Alvin York would get their first inklings of the future, all under the penetrating eyes of men like Damon Runyon. At home, meanwhile, the desire for knowledge—and for heroes—would soon become an all-consuming hunger.

(CHAPTER FOUR)

THE ADVENTURE BEGINS

Alvin York was still working his farm and wandering the hills of Fentress County, wondering when he would be called up, when Boyce's Tigers, the feisty noncoms in training who had braved the crowd's derision at the Polo Grounds, slouched into Camp Upton trailed by a rolling cloud of mosquitoes. The Tigers were supposed to be picked men, but when Pershing ordered his Regular Army officers to select candidates from their units to go to Camp Upton as noncoms and train draftees, the officers exploited the opportunity to get rid of soldiers noted for indiscipline and stupidity. Some privates—or busted former noncoms—were "rewarded" with promotions for this purpose. Officers such as Captain Charles Whittlesey and First Lieutenant George McMurtry (who was promoted to captain in September) would have to rely on them to help whip the 77th Division into shape. Both officers and noncoms would need every ounce of skill and luck at their disposal.

If Charlie Chaplin's "Little Tramp" had served in the American Expeditionary Forces, he would have gone through basic training at Camp Upton: it was that kind of place. Camp graduates told their grandchildren about the madcap moments they experienced there before they got to routine things like fighting the Germans. The truth emerged the moment the first draftees lined up in front of their noncoms and officers on September 10 "wearing Panamas, smashed derbies, and top hats that looked as if they had been stolen from corpses" as well as "dinner jackets, Palm Beach suits, starched collars, silk stockings and Sunday-go-to-meeting outfits." When the men began trying to play soldiers, drill sergeants groaned and wondered whether they should all just quit and go home.[1]

The first days at Camp Upton were like a slapstick circus, except for the mud and mosquitoes. Barracks evenings echoed with laughter as men told of their first experiences working for Uncle Sam. Some of the more literary-minded men wrote down the best anecdotes for posterity. Many of the episodes happened at the initial roll calls, where the draftees eyed their officers, as one of them recalled, "with expectant curiosity, with friendly amusement, with critical displeasure, or with apathy, according to their nationality or mood—with any and every emotion save military respect."

One officer called roll for the first time and struggled to pronounce "Krag-a-co-poul-o-wicz, G." His attempt to utter this tongue twister was firmly ignored and he had to repeat it until a sullen Polish private grumbled, "Do yuh mean me? That ain't the way tuh say my name. Me own mother wouldn't recernize it." "Quiet," the officer barked, "say 'here,'" provoking Private Kragacopoulowicz to whine, "Then I ain't here. That's all. I ain't here." Another officer called out, "Morra, T." A man responded, "Here."

Next, "Morra, R." The same man responded, "Here." Annoyed, the officer demanded, "Does your first name begin with a T. or an R.?" "Yes, sir." "Is your first name Rocco?" "Yes, sir." "What is your first name?" "Tony."[2]

The division's almost ridiculous diversity emerged at the beginning. Every element of New York City was present. There were Jews (one out of every four men, according to a census), Chinese, Poles, Italians, Irish, Greeks, Russians, Germans, and Anglo-Saxons. There were street toughs, urchins, bartenders, grocers, cops, streetcar conductors, writers, baseball players, stockbrokers, drifters, and blue bloods. The only people who weren't there—which was a shame for many reasons, not least for the special ingredient pre–Cotton Club Harlem would have added to the mix—were the blacks, who were restricted from serving alongside whites because of racist segregation policies. Many of them went on to serve with distinction in the 93rd Division's 369th Regiment, the "Harlem Hellfighters," under French command.

The men of the 77th Division—organized into the 305th, 306th, 307th, and 308th Regiments in the 153rd and 154th Brigades—did have some points in common. Like all New Yorkers they were champion-league talkers—it went with the territory, where a man could walk down the street any day and hear seven languages being spoken—and cussed and argued like no one else on earth. The white-collar men among them knew how to handle pens and typewriters, and would later write company histories and memoirs. Some of the soldiers preferred to let switchblades and blackjacks—or bayonets and bowie knives—talk for them. Whatever their origins, they navigated sidewalk crowds like ski slopes, and thrived in competition. But they also understood each other. They all knew baseball, even if they didn't root for the same team. Sharing complaints about the home neighborhood forged instant friends out of strangers. In times of crisis they pulled together to face down enemies, or just make things work.

The Tigers pounced on the first sorry lot of draftees who slogged into camp, wreaking revenge for their humiliation at the Polo Grounds by working them savagely. The bossing and bullying receded somewhat after September 20, when a contingent of street toughs from the Gas House and Hell's Kitchen districts swaggered into camp. Noncoms who tried to push these men around paid the price if they were foolish enough to stroll around barracks alone after dark. All of the draftees, however, bowed down before "the Needle," wielded by merciless doctors who administered inoculations for several days running until the men could hardly lift their arms. Every man likewise endured the mosquitoes and seas of mud as they trudged around a camp that had the appearance and all the charm of a half-finished construction site in the middle of a swamp. A sense of collective suffering brought the first hints of unity to the 77th Division.[3]

Once the men were processed and inoculated, basic training began in earnest. There wasn't much to it at first except intensive exercise and repetition. Men learned how to keep bunks, dress properly, eat fast, salute, drill, shovel dirt and coal, haul wood, and do KP. They performed calisthenics, and marched on dusty roads and through squishy swamps. This at least accustomed them to discipline and made former city desk jockeys physically fit. After a few weeks of this, men learned techniques of physical combat and bayonet drill and, as rifles became available, tried their hands at target practice.[4]

Officers lacked the knowledge and experience, however, to give basic training much focus. Some of them had arrived at Camp Upton in late August, and then sat around for days with nothing to do except riffle through training manuals and swat bugs. The rest entered camp at the beginning of September after helping to conduct the Draft Day parade. For the most part, the noncoms were all strangers to them. So were the basic elements of tactics. Despite their experiences at Plattsburg through the spring of 1917, the officers had learned very little about the attributes of war on Europe's Western Front or how the AEF intended to address the challenges it would face there. Because Wilson's administration and American military leaders had not thought deeply over the previous few years about the consequences of American entry into war, the Plattsburg regime had emphasized physical fitness, mental readiness, and the lessons of America's military past rather than modern realities. Life at the school had taught them little about men, barracks life, or training, let alone the challenges of twentieth-century warfare.

Whittlesey, appointed to the headquarters company of the 308th Regiment, had never given an order in his life outside his law office and struggled to acquire the confidence of command. His first duties were administrative—exceptionally important work, for the division needed proper organization—but not designed to give him practical experience. On first glance, the men who worked with Whittlesey must have hardly noticed him. Despite his prosperous law practice, his celebrity to this point consisted in appearing on a list of reserve officers published in the *New York Herald*. If the nicknames he eventually acquired are any indication, the noncoms and men viewed the quiet, awkward officer with amused puzzlement if not contempt.

The first question—what to do with the men—was the hardest for Whittlesey to answer. School at Plattsburg had provided only minimal guidance. General Bell was a decorated professional soldier who understood how to build divisional cohesion and esprit de corps, and wanted his men to sing. His brigade and regimental commanders were all competent men. None of them had studied current military affairs in any depth, however, or would ever gain reputations as military innovators. In such circumstances, Whittlesey naturally turned to the regulation book for refuge. On Saturday breaks from camp, he could be found at a table in front of the grill at the Williams Club, reading, chatting, and joking quietly with friends and kibitzers.

In camp, he maintained a military bearing, although not yet very efficient. Like many new officers at Camp Upton, Whittlesey spent long hours studying the manual, drilled it into his noncoms, and ordered them in turn to impose it on the men. He lacked the personal touch, and indeed his own awkwardness made it difficult to lead by example. Still, the manual at least provided guidelines that he used to supplement his noncoms' experience of army life. As the autumn passed the troops acquired a good basic knowledge of drill and chains of military authority, while constant activity, including long route hikes with heavy packs through the Long Island pine barrens, melded them physically into shape.[5]

George McMurtry worked more directly with his men than did Whittlesey. Appointed to command Company E of the 308th Regiment's second battalion, he became known for his gruff good humor and high expectations. His mood depended on the recognition that the company received in drills and competitions. His men wanted to do their best for him. A decade later the regimental historian still remembered Company E barracks, with its "cement incinerator, gray painted walls, elaborately constructed gun rack, bronze fire-gong, and ever-polished windows and doors." When the regiment's colonel demanded that all of his company commanders spruce up their barracks, McMurtry promptly replied, "Surest thing you know, sir. We'll start work in E Company this red hot minute." In December E Company won distinction as the best in the regiment, earning McMurtry promotion from lieutenant to captain.[6]

Officers and men learned methods of overcoming the language barrier as training intensified in September and October. Many a second-generation American found himself acting as an interpreter between his company commander and comrades who had recently stepped off the boat at Ellis Island. McMurtry drilled Company E hard but also encouraged camaraderie through parties, amateur theatricals, and athletics. His lieutenant Jerry Mullin penned the company song "The Army, the Army, the Democratic Army" with the verse "All the Jews and Wops, the Dutch and Irish Cops, They're all in the army now"—roles performed respectively by Privates Goldberg, Ginsberg, and Perlberg; Del Duca, Petrissi, and Carucci; Schmidt and Leumann; and finally Curley, Fallace, and Sargeant as "Erin's representatives of 'New York's Best.'"[7]

As autumn passed, the 77th Division looked more and more like a quality unit. Bell and his staff and field officers did their jobs well, and gradually the draftees felt pride in belonging to New York's own.

But then the War Department tore everything apart.

When the war began, National Guard units and National Army units like the 77th Division were organized by state or region. They spent months training together at their respective camps, and slowly melded into cohesive outfits. In the winter of 1917–1918, though, the pressures of mobilization—actually, sheer administrative chaos—convinced the military authorities to break up nearly combat-ready divisions and merge their best-trained contingents into units that could be sent quickly overseas. This happened to the 77th Division that winter when it was partially gutted and thousands of enlisted men were dispatched to reinforce other units. This forced its officers to rebuild the formation from its remaining originals and a bevy of newcomers.

Lots of the new draftees who arrived at Camp Upton in early 1918 hailed from upstate New York or small New England towns. There also were swarms of draftees from the western plains states. What military genius cooked up that ideal combination remains unknown. In any case, it took a while before the originals—used as they were to people from every imaginable category—realized that some truly bizarre new types had entered their midst. Everyone knew men who had been farmers in the old country and tried to make good in the city. But who ever heard of a clodhopper farmer whose vision of paradise entailed going back to the country to milk his cow or swing his hoe? More than that, who could relate to men who spoke only English—slow, drawling English at that—went to tent revival meetings, and (so the city boys expected) stood flat-footed in a fight? The 77th had looked like a crazy mélange even before the army bureaucrats stuck their spoons into the stew—and their stirring just made it crazier.

Despite the personnel changes, the 77th Division remained intimately tied to New York City. Henry L. Stimson, Teddy Roosevelt's former secretary of war now serving as a lieutenant colonel with the division's 305th Artillery Regiment, invited the ex-president to Camp Upton to speak. Roosevelt, who had entertained the draftees during the march in Manhattan, arrived on November 18 to a rousing reception. With a keen instinct for his audience—in this case, including immigrants who aspired to a political voice in their new country—Roosevelt declared, "It is only you and your kind who have the absolutely clear title to the management of this republic. It is only the men willing, when the need arises, to fight for the Nation and to die for the Nation—it is only those who are really entitled to have a voice in the halls of the nation."

Roosevelt also delighted the soldiers by denouncing conscientious objectors as "male sissies." "To the man who dared tell me his conscience would not let him fight," he pronounced, clapping his hands together for emphasis, "I would say, your conscience won't let you fight and mine won't let you vote in a nation that can only be saved by fighting men." He also had a warning for immigrant soldiers who still felt loyalty to their former countries: "I've no use for the man with a fifty fifty allegiance. I've no use for the man who can say that he loves another nation as much as his own. That man is a traitor." His speech ended with a grandiloquent rendition of the "Star-Spangled Banner."[8]

The distraction provided by Roosevelt was fleeting. As military authorities had anticipated, New York City tempted tired soldiers with a mischievous bent, which applied to just about everyone in the 77th Division. Although the army had closed liquor-dealing establishments near the camp, and forced soldiers to sit through moralizing lectures by officers, chaplains, and representatives of organizations like the YMCA and Knights of Columbus, men still found access to alcohol and prostitutes. Soldiers also showed up in the city, where curious civilians begged them to reveal what it was like "out there at Yaphank."

The New York media also wondered about the goings-on at Camp Upton. The usual bunkum was always on tap. Bell and his officers gave lectures throughout the city, reassuring audiences that the men were happy, patriotic, and ready to fight the Kaiser. A training film of the 307th Regiment's machine gun company appeared in city movie houses, reinforcing the same happy and carefully edited image. Soldiers also wrote letters home that were censored before being published in local newspapers alongside third- or fourthhand anecdotes and official dispatches.[9]

None of this sufficed for the most sophisticated and demanding consumers of media and information in the world. The Wilson administration and the army placed heavy restrictions on media, but reporters and especially consumers remained determined to know the truth. They wanted to know how their boys lived, what they felt, what jokes they told, and even their misdeeds. They also craved updates on celebrities: not just the ones who dominated political, sports, and society headlines, but popular characters from Broadway or Fifth Avenue.

Damon Runyon shared his readers' curiosity, as well as a fascination with barracks life. Since the Draft Day parade, he had been writing daily editorial columns for the *American*, some of them patriotic poems but others vignettes of New York City celebrities turned soldiers. On September 10 he departed New York and arrived at Camp Upton. The first thing he did was to seek old buddies from the sports beat. These included athletes like Eddie Grant, who had retired in 1915 as a utility infielder for the Giants after a career with three different major league teams, and had played in the 1913 World Series. There were other baseball players, like Tom Owens, who had once played with Babe Ruth, and collegiate stars in football and other sports. Runyon wrote about them all.

Benny Leonard, lightweight champion of the world since beating Freddie Welsh at the Manhattan Casino on May 28, 1917, delighted Runyon by ensuring that the 77th not only sang but boxed better than any division in the army. Just twenty-one years old, he had been born in the Jewish ghetto on the Lower East Side, and could both deliver and take hard knocks. He boxed with every one of the officers, including Whittlesey and McMurtry, and let them take their best swings. He blocked most but also came down with a black eye or two. The men loved the spectacle so much that boxing became an epidemic at Camp Upton—each man boxed at least once and most wanted to do so all day. Leonard coached daily and carried them through regimental championships in six weight classes. By the time he finished he had boxed personally with thirty-five hundred men.[10]

But Runyon was a natural for the regular guys, and he made sure to hunt them down. He didn't look for spectacle but mixed with the soldiers as they went about their day-to-day activities. Runyon worked mainly with his ears, listening in on conversations and copying down, with his own embellishments, the inevitable jokes and stories. He spent nights in the barracks and observed the draftees' hilarious attempts to adjust to army life, starting with complaints about lumpy beds and snoring recruits. The man who snored the loudest was called "rat catcher," because he had actually caught rats on the Lower East Side. Runyon also focused on ex-tenement dwellers, who stuck together and adopted the war cry "It's a great life if you don't weaken!"

Runyon spent time with ex-policemen, college boys, high rollers, and the like. He chronicled the pathetic attempts of sad sack Steve Michalsuk to enter the army past officious clerks and skeptical doctors; and sampled canned salmon alongside the troops, who dubbed it "gold fish." There were bad moments—Runyon disgustedly reported a fight between soldiers of the Harlem-recruited 15th Regiment (destined to be segregated in an all-black division) and white construction workers—but he preferred to write about the light-hearted moments and build bonds of sympathy between his subjects and his readers. His efforts worked, thanks in no small part to his facility for recording their conversations and presenting them like short story characters.[11]

General Bell's dreams of marching to the front singing were dashed in December 1917, when army physicians discovered that he did not have long to live. Relieved with honor, he died in January 1919. A Brooklyn man temporarily took his place. Tall and slender, with a ramrod stiff posture, Brigadier General Evan Johnson had been born in Brooklyn in 1861 and lived a soldier's life, enlisting in the army as a private when he was twenty and working his way up through the ranks in the course of service against Geronimo's Apaches, the Spaniards, and Philippine rebels.

Johnson took post at Camp Upton a month before the soldiers arrived. He understood how they felt about being stuck in a Long Island swamp, and embraced their New York identity. The first thing he did after becoming acting division commander was to dub the 77th the "Metropolitan" Division and declare that it would be known as such from now on. His hometown paper declared that the division "is truly metropolitan in makeup and represents the most metropolitan of cities—New York.... [T]he new title strikes a responsive chord in the men. They like it."[12]

And they were almost ready to go overseas.

Several special trains from Camp Upton pulled in to Penn Station on the morning of February 3, 1918, carrying troops of the 308th Regiment. The soldiers alighted before applauding citizens and marched off to the Hippodrome on Sixth Avenue between 43rd and 44th Streets, where Harry Houdini had lately been wowing the crowds with his magical extravaganzas. Wartime had been big business for New York theater managers and nowhere more so than at the Hippodrome, which was one of the city's premier venues for public spectacle. This time the troops, highlighted by Captain George McMurtry's Company E, would provide the entertainment.

Four thousand spectators had taken their seats when the curtain rose to reveal a stage resplendent in red, white, and blue flags and bunting. To the tune of rousing martial music, Company E burst proudly upon the scene and marched back and forth in carefully choreographed "fancy marches" that would have done Busby Berkeley proud. After curtain-fall and a short break, the show shifted to a movielike stage play. First appeared the regimental chorus around a faux campfire "somewhere in France," the glow reflecting off the soldiers' faces as they sang patriotic hymns finishing with the "Star-Spangled Banner." Then the men dispersed across the stage to give a demonstration in camouflage and sniping, picking off six skulking "Germans."

The curtains closed, giving time for the prop men to work their magic. When they rolled back again, the audience gasped to see two lines of shell-blasted trenches separated by a no-man's-land replete with shell holes and tree stumps. A dozen khaki-clad doughboys appeared wearing white-rubber-soled "creepers," sneaking and dodging from one shell hole to another until they were within two yards of the German trenches. Several unsuspecting gray-clad Germans appeared. The scene paused in tense silence for a few moments until in all seriousness a tree stump that was really a doughboy in disguise shot forward, sending a German sprawling. At this signal the rest of the Americans rushed the German trench and subdued the enemy with gunfire, rifle butts, and bayonets. A single American was wounded and gingerly carried back to his own trench. The delighted crowd "yelled like mad" as choreographer Regnar Kidde, the regimental bayonet instructor and a second-generation Dane from Manhattan, took a bow.

Next, a platoon under First Lieutenant Louis J. Lederie Jr. of New York appeared in a mock trench with sentinels standing guard on a firing step. Suddenly a Klaxon horn sounded a gas alarm. Within six seconds every soldier had a fake gas mask on his face. A "real" attack followed by "enemy" soldiers, and the gas mask–clad soldiers stepped up and fired rapidly to beat off the enemy, while some of their comrades beat the poison gas out of the trench with sacks and overcoats. Sadly, one of the defenders was overcome by the gas and collapsed as the audience gasped in anguish, but his buddies carried the soldier to a "dugout," swiftly treated him, and sent him back to the hospital and the tender care of army nurses. "Here was the very stuff of modern warfare," enthused a reporter from the *New York Tribune*; "the smell and the thrill and the savor of it, in all its horror and its glory depicted by the men who are on their way to take part in it." Kidde would later be severely wounded, and Lederie killed in action.[13]

After the show ended to delirious applause, McMurtry, Whittlesey, and their fellow officers and men spent a freezing night in the armory at Park Avenue and 34th Street. On the following day, Monday, February 4 (the Sabbath Society put the kibosh on a Sunday march), they provided the city with its first military parade since Draft Day. The morning dawned cold and bright, and following drill and a presentation of colors at the Hippodrome the 308th Regiment marched up Eighth Avenue to 59th Street, and then across to Fifth Avenue. Turning with precision, they marched back down to 34th Street before cheering crowds. The 1st Battalion that Whittlesey would later command took pride of place behind the colonel, with the regimental band blaring music from thirty buglers and eighteen drummers under bandmaster

Herman Schoenfeld. A Long Island lawyer, Schoenfeld would later conduct funeral music for many of these men as they were carried dead out of the Argonne Forest.[14]

A weekend snowstorm swept through New York City on Friday, February 22, 1918—Washington's birthday—but that didn't stop half a million people from swarming Manhattan to watch their hometown boys converge in a grand parade. Crowds erupted in happy pandemonium as the 307th and 308th Regiments marched west along 57th Street with McMurtry and Whittlesey. At Fifth Avenue the two regiments turned left heading downtown, falling into step behind the lumbering British battle tank *Britannia*, whose bristling machine guns fired blanks overhead.

At 42nd Street the throng, "good-natured but obstinate," refused to budge when the NYPD tried to push them back, forcing the parade to pause for a quarter of an hour while National Guard troops herded civilians onto the sidewalks. Red, white, and blue flags and buntings fluttered from buildings and lampposts as program girls, oblivious to the snow in white gowns, purple sashes, and caps in national colors, danced alongside the merry doughboys. The divisional band marched at the parade's head, playing "Over There."

The troops marched in olive-drab long overcoats, light packs, and ammunition belts, crowned by winter caps, their heads and shoulders covered with snow. Spectators stood in awe at the change five months at Camp Upton had wrought in what had once been a crowd of undisciplined draftees. Now neatly uniformed, their boots moved in unison, slashing through snow and stinging wind. In September, the men had paused to greet friends and family members in the crowd, or to gawk at celebrities, but now they kept their eyes focused ahead. They sang lustily, as Bell had taught them, and passed under Johnson's gaze at the reviewing stand.

Still, their diversity remained evident. And though many of them were not native New Yorkers, the city embraced all the doughboys as its own. They symbolized a city that prided itself on being American, and wanted the rest of the country to accept it that way. Wrote one reporter: "The men in line were New York's own and they were typical of the great polyglot city. Swarthy Armenians strode side by side with fair-haired Scandinavians. Irish boys rubbed elbows with Jews. Italians trudged beside Poles. Here and there was a Chinese, and here and there a face that was typically Yankee. Sons of sons and daughters of the Revolution marched with boys whose fathers were immigrants a generation ago. But every one of them was a citizen of the United States, and they were soldiers all."[15]

A bigger headline overshadowed the march in many Sunday morning newspapers. At Camp Lewis near Tacoma, Washington, four draftees, all "enemy aliens," were accused of plotting to shoot their officers as soon as they arrived at the front in France, and to betray their fellow soldiers into enemy captivity. In response, a "general clean-up of enemy aliens" was initiated in that camp. The implications were clear for the Metropolitan Division—no unit in the army was more diverse. Was it reliable?[16]

Camp Upton became a hive of activity as final preparations were made for the division's move overseas. Only six divisions had been sent to Europe so far, and the 77th would be the first from the National Army. Rumors spread through camp as men speculated on what would happen next. Equipment was issued, checked, and rechecked. Officers worked frantically to ensure that essentials were packed and waste burned. Hitches were inevitable. Some valuable items were reduced to ashes while soldiers crammed useless geegaws in their already bulging packs. A few soldiers were court-martialed for going AWOL in Gotham after the march, and doctors sifted out men and officers who had contracted venereal disease or displayed physical or mental incompetence. The same went for some unlucky officers.

Up until the very last days officers still had to incorporate untrained men who had been detailed to their units. The army also pressured company commanders to send men to fill up units from other divisions still in training. Camp Gordon, where Alvin York's 82nd Division was training, had a particular need for men. Officers of the 77th Division got rid of their most incorrigibly wretched soldiers by sending them down to Georgia: "The man whose face seemed irreconcilable with a steel helmet, whose name on the roll call consisted only of consonants, or who had cast his rice pudding in the mess sergeant's face often completed his training there." Ironically, these same men would later be called upon to save their old 77th Division comrades in the Argonne Forest.[17]

The last paperwork and organization was completed—so much as could be managed, anyway—and the machine gun battalions and support personnel of the twenty-seven-thousand-man Metropolitan Division began leaving Camp Upton in sections at the beginning of March. The infantry regiments were certain to follow shortly. For Whittlesey, McMurtry, and the men of the 308th the feelings were bittersweet. On March 12, the regiment opened a theater, the only one in camp, in a frame building they had erected on a concrete foundation. It cost ten thousand dollars—raised from their show in the Hippodrome—and was replete with seats for fifteen hundred men with a stage, movie theater, gymnasium, and dressing rooms. Johnson and the regimental commander, Colonel Nathan K. Averill, presided over a packed house on opening day that featured eight boxing bouts, a movie, and vaudeville routines.[18]

At the beginning of April the 307th and 308th Regiments were put on thirty-six-hour notice. Amid frantic last-minute preparations the barracks were stripped of all their remaining amenities, including cots, forcing the men to sleep on the floor in freezing-cold weather. On April 5 the troops learned that the division would depart the following morning. The 308th Regiment, always taking the lead when it came to theatrics, arranged a torchlight procession that evening with drums beating and bugles blaring to serenade General Johnson and his staff. The men slept little that night.

Reveille blew at 4:00 A.M. on April 6 and the troops rolled their packs for the final time at Camp Upton. They marched out of camp past the now silent theater they had worked so hard to construct, and climbed on board waiting trains that took them to Long Island City. There they boarded ferries that carried them at sunrise around Battery Park. Crowds of people had gathered there to give them a cheery send-off despite the supposed secrecy of the movement. From there the ferries proceeded to the Brooklyn docks. Massive transport ships awaited them. The 308th boarded three ships by battalion: headquarters company with Whittlesey and the 1st battalion on the liner *Lapland*; 2nd battalion with McMurtry's Company E on the *Cretic*; and 3rd battalion on the *Justicia*.

On board, officers shouted and noncoms shoved men into bunk assignments as the doughboys filed into holds "like a file of ants entering its hole." They also tried to establish mess assignments, but in many cases there were none. It was a form of organized chaos—ship holds swelled to overflowing and units got mingled. As for the men, they hurled their packs down any old place and went to explore their vessels. Every porthole framed a curious head looking at coal barges loading on the docks or calling to men in adjoining ships.

The ships slipped away from the docks just as the New York workday came to an end. Whistle blasts and cheers announced the moment each ship departed. Officers and men crowded the decks to watch the New York skyline, Long Island, and Staten Island pass by as dusk gathered. The Statue of Liberty that had welcomed some of these soldiers and many of their parents, and endured the rain of shrapnel from Black Tom, bid farewell and the doughboys cheered her in turn. Ferries and tugboats blew their whistles and waved flags in tribute. The lights of Coney Island slowly faded, to be replaced by the lights of ships' signals that the troops puzzled to decipher, and the stars above. The troops fell silent, each man thinking his own thoughts. As the watery vista grew black the doughboys filed below.[19]

A week after the Metropolitan Division left New York City, a new contingent arrived at Camp Upton. The 82nd All-American Division, the second from the National Army, was next in line to head overseas.

The 82nd Division's journey to combat readiness had been even more challenging than that of the just departed 77th Division. It was also a misfit formation made up of draftees. Although a third of the officers were regulars with some previous experience, the troops came from all over the country with no regional focus whatsoever. Many, though, hailed from Greater New York and carried with them the same city spirit: the division's lightweight and welterweight boxing champions were both from

Brooklyn, and so was "little Brooklyn scrapper" Victor Vigonto, better known as Private Johnny Victor.

As with other AEF divisions, the war department repeatedly dissolved and reconstituted the 82nd Division with new men. In the process, it siphoned off three thousand "specialists," who were well-trained intelligent men, and sent them away. Those left behind were unwanted elsewhere. The All-American became a depot for rejects from other divisions. These included men who had traveled by rail from Camp Upton to Camp Gordon, only to board trains that carried their new division back to New York City.

Worse, in a mocking irony of its name, the division was filled with foreigners and suspected undesirables. Twenty percent of the draft of men who had arrived in Camp Gordon in November 1917 were of foreign birth. Several hundred of these were not even American citizens, and many could not speak, write, or read English. Worst of all, division officers were horrified to discover that a few thousand of their men had been drafted despite being "enemy aliens" from Germany, Austria-Hungary, and the Ottoman Empire.

Officers worried seriously about espionage and even sabotage. They could do nothing, however, except dispatch "suspicious cases" to the division's depot brigade while insisting that all men of foreign extraction undergo intensive English-language instruction in lieu of basic training. With a typically bureaucratic sense of timing, the War Department expelled fourteen hundred enemy aliens from the division just days before it entrained for Long Island, replacing them with untrained men from other camps.

The All-Americans, then, were rawer than the men who had preceded them at Camp Upton. Their training at Camp Gordon had consisted of the same routine of drill, exercise, target practice, and lectures that took place at Camp Upton. But their training was even more basic. Because of shortages of equipment, many of the men had used only wooden rifles. Machine gunners received obsolete weapons that would be discarded before they went overseas. Mortarmen never saw or fired a mortar. Men watched officers throw grenades once in a while, but were not permitted to do so themselves. For much of the rest of the time, as the official history noted caustically, training amounted to "road marching and organization singing." The division went through three commanders in one month from November to December 1917, and the man who commanded it when it went to Camp Upton would be replaced in turn before the All-Americans entered combat. No one ever fully took control.[20]

York received his first army rifle in March, and was disgusted to find it full of grease. A proud rifleman, he worked to get it clean and felt sorry for his buddies who knew nothing about guns or how to handle them. His platoon included every imaginable sort of soldier. His platoon sergeant was a big-voiced and hard-fisted actor from Brooklyn. One of the corporals was a bartender from Connecticut and the other a Polish iceman from "around Boston and New York." York's fellow privates had names like Saccina, Konotski, Swanson, Muzzi, and Beardsley—many of them also from New York City. He liked them all, but worried how they, and he, would do in battle.[21]

By mid-March York knew that a move was imminent and applied for leave to return home one more time. He took the train from Camp Gordon on March 20, and then hitched a ride to Jamestown. He walked the final twelve miles through the mountains alone, lugging his suitcase to Pall Mall and then home. He spent a week there with his family before bidding a tearful farewell to his mother and a heart-breaking goodbye to Gracie in a lane outside his farm. On the hike out of the mountains he spent most of his time praying. As he boarded the train to Camp Gordon, York felt a peaceful certainty that he would, in time, walk back into those mountains and return home.

The All-Americans began entraining at Camp Gordon on April 10—York's platoon left on the afternoon of April 19—and they arrived at Camp Upton in packets over the following days. There was not much there for the men to do but poke around the 308th Regiment's theater. The officers kept them busy drilling. In a sign that the division was still only half disciplined, however, hundreds of men went AWOL, and many did not return in time for departure. With no time for sightseeing and little for final preparations, the All-Americans boarded ships on April 25 and began their own journey overseas.

The departure was not as grand as it had been for the Metropolitans. York's regiment, the 328th, boarded trains for Boston on the evening of April 30. Immediately after arrival the following morning York's battalion boarded the liner SS *Scandinavian*. It departed in heavy rain, first to rendezvous with a convoy at New York Harbor, and then to head for Liverpool. It was the first time York saw the Statue of Liberty, or the open sea.[22]

Charles Whittlesey and his fellow passengers on the *Lapland* first sighted land on April 19. The destroyer escort slipped away, and the ship sailed into the River Mersey toward Liverpool's docks. Seeing river shipping and buildings on shore, the doughboys erupted into a frenzy of noise. Corporal Louis Ranlett remembered that they cheered "every tug and row boat, every floating log or orange peel." The band struck up, and for once the soldiers did not have to be ordered to sing—they even rendered "Over There" again and again, pretending they had not grown tired of it.

Much to their sorrow, the doughboys were not allowed to step ashore that night. Instead they spent all evening on deck studying the city skyline with its busy docks, warehouses, and tramcars. There were no obvious signs of welcome, but a massive billboard facing the harbor proudly promoted "Spratt's Dog Biscuit." Soldiers wondered if it signified the kind of rations they could expect in England. They were not far wrong.

The *Lapland* disgorged its troops and cargo on shore the following morning, followed by the 2nd and 3rd battalions on the other two transports. The men had burned off much of their pent-up excitement the evening before and curiously studied their surroundings. They expected to be welcomed by cheering crowds and bands, but saw just a few dour Liverpudlians eying them skeptically. When the doughboys marched into the city, however, they were delighted to see the stars and stripes displayed from almost every window along with Union Jacks. Corporal Ranlett, a former Harvard student, exulted to see his men, many of whom spoke only halting English, stick out their chests as they saw their national flag. Over the following days in England and France, Ranlett noted how the doughboys bragged endlessly that "their" country was better than anything "over here."[23]

The *Scandinavian* slipped into dock at Liverpool on May 16, and Alvin York's contingent of the All-Americans came ashore. The city didn't make much of an impression on York. For him the following days were just a blur of hiking and catching trains. His regiment followed the route that the Metropolitans had taken a few weeks before, riding trains generally southeast through the English countryside, which impressed the doughboys with its beauty and tidiness. Then the Metropolitans and All-Americans passed through London, which presented a dirty and gloomy appearance. The king and queen of Great Britain treated the division's 325th Regiment to an official review, but York, Whittlesey, McMurtry, and the majority of the doughboys only gained impressions of weak tea, fish sandwiches, and women wearing black mourning clothes.

By the time the Americans reached Dover much of their curiosity had faded. They bristled at the British Tommies, who noticed the New Yorkers' dark complexions and sneeringly called them "Indians." The dash across the English Channel was mercifully short, and the anticlimax of the 77th Division's arrival at Calais proved no disappointment. If anything, many of the doughboys felt a little closer to Gotham as they watched masses of troops, laborers, and civilians rushing about the filthy, impoverished, war-burdened coastal town. The crowds included not just French, British, and Australians but colonial troops and workers from places like India, Egypt, Senegal, and Indochina. There also were representatives of other Allied nations like Russia, Belgium, Serbia, Romania, and Italy. Poles and Greeks wandered about. German prisoners worked hard, glad to be out of the fighting. The scene did not differ from a typical day on the Lower East Side.

York, whose regiment came ashore at Le Havre, was in no mood for sightseeing. His channel crossing had been rough, and he felt homesick for his family and the Tennessee mountains. His disposition soured further when he was ordered to relinquish his Springfield rifle, which he had spent every day disassembling, cleaning, and reassembling, in favor of a British Lee-Enfield rifle—again, dripping grease. The Metropolitans had been through the same process. Next, the troops received helmets, gas masks, and brief instructions on how to use them. For York, the sight and feel of the mask brought the war a thousand miles closer. As he and his comrades marched inland at the end of May, American troops not far away entered large-scale combat for the first time.[24]

Damon Runyon would have liked nothing better than to walk alongside the doughboys as they landed in Europe and prepared for war. Given his druthers he would have shared their hardships in camp, and most of all listened to and retold their stories. The thought that they had gone without him tormented Runyon, as did the realization that other American pressmen already pursued assignments in France. For the most part, they simply loitered around army headquarters to hear official reports. No one provided updates on men like Eddie Grant, Bozeman Bulger, or the Broadway big shots, while Runyon dutifully reported on spring training, horse racing, and boxing. He had already decided that the war would not end before he made it "over there."

(CHAPTER FIVE)

FIRST BLOOD

On March 21, 1918, German forces unleashed a massive offensive on the Western Front, hoping to end the war before American troops intervened in strength. They nearly succeeded. Covered by morning mist, German *Stosstruppen*—highly trained storm troopers—infiltrated British positions in northeastern France and ripped them to shreds. By the end of their first phase of assault on April 5, the Germans had captured seventy-five thousand prisoners and captured twelve hundred miles of territory. British defenses collapsed under a renewed German onslaught on April 9, leading British field marshal Douglas Haig to tell his troops that "each one of us must fight on to the end." The next hammer blow fell on May 27, this time targeting a French sector in the vicinity of Soissons. Once again, the Germans broke through, sending thousands of blue-clad French soldiers known as "poilus" streaming to the rear.

Paris seemed to be in danger of falling for the first time since 1914. German long-range railway guns shelled the city, while Gotha bombers pummeled England. On June 13, a German air raid destroyed a primary school in London and killed eighteen children along with 144 other civilians. Public outrage availed nothing, however, and over a year after declaring war the United States still seemed unprepared to help. On May 28, the American 1st Division attacked and captured the small village of Cantigny, and on May 31 some machine gunners from the 3rd Division came into action near Château-Thierry. But this was mere window dressing. The first major American engagement did not take place until June 6, when US Marines and soldiers attacked German forces at Belleau Wood.

Officers and men of the Metropolitan and All-American Divisions knew about the brewing crisis, and felt embarrassed and angry at their inability to help. Only a handful of American divisions, not including the newly arrived 77th and 82nd, were prepared to help stem the German tide. Thanks to the emphasis that Allied leaders had put on shipping large numbers of men from the United States to Europe, the troop ships were crammed with soldiers but had no room in their holds for heavy equipment. But really that was just an excuse. As York and his comrades knew well from their days toting wooden rifles on the parade grounds at Camp Gordon, American industry lacked the capacity to produce much modern weaponry. AEF divisions arriving in Europe lacked machine guns, artillery, vehicles, and basic but crucial items such as grenades and gas masks.

The Metropolitans and All-Americans marched to training camps where they worked with the British. York's division was packed into troop trains that carried the doughboys east to the Somme River region. British officers provided the Americans with basic instructions on the use of British-manufactured machine guns, grenades, and mortars, which the doughboys finally received in quantity. The doughboys treated their instructors skeptically, especially when they were told to throw grenades cricket style. They preferred baseball.

York didn't remember British training so much as the endless hiking around rural France—not a problem for him because of his life in the mountains, but pure torture for the city boys in his platoon. While his friends rough-housed and caroused in local villages during their time off, York stayed in camp reading his Bible and praying. All-American troops began entering the front lines on rotation in July, but months would pass before the army authorities judged them ready for combat.[1]

The 77th Division's preparations passed more quickly. After organizing at Calais, the troops entrained for Flanders and a still-unoccupied sliver of Belgium that the British had held since the beginning of the war. Here the infantry worked to learn the ropes of war under British supervision. While they did so General Johnson, whose command of the division had always been understood as temporary, returned to take charge of the 154th Brigade. Major General George B. Duncan, a Kentuckian and West Pointer who had served with distinction in the Spanish-American and Philippine conflicts, took his place atop the Metropolitan Division. Duncan would remain in charge until the end of the summer.

In the shakeup following Duncan's arrival, Whittlesey was promoted to become the 308th Regiment's operations officer. This involved increased responsibilities for planning and managing movements behind and at the front, but did not often get him out of headquarters to interact with field officers and men. He was acting in this capacity when the division suffered its first battle death to German long-range artillery. Shortly thereafter, the Metropolitans were entrained and sent to work with the French in Alsace-Lorraine.

The new sector was relatively quiet, a land of rolling hills near the German border and far south and east of ongoing major combat operations. Even among these small villages, however, the New Yorkers discovered some familiar things. Entering the front lines, they relieved troops of the 42nd Rainbow Division, a National Guard unit that included the 165th Regiment, once Gotham's Fighting 69th, or the Irish Brigade of Civil War fame.

Father Francis Duffy, the regimental chaplain whose statue would later grace Times Square, watched the columns pass each other in the moonlight. It did not take long for the men to recognize fellow natives. Some good-humoredly broke out in song:

East side, West side,
All around the town,
The tots sang ring-a-rosie
London Bridge is falling down,
Boys and girls together,
Me and Mamie O'Rourke,
We tripped the light fantastic
On the sidewalks of New York.

Others traded sarcastic jibes and catcalls, or called to guys from their neighborhoods. "What are you givin' us," yelled a man from the Fighting 69th, "we was over here killin' Dutchmen before they pulled your names out of the hat" ("Dutchmen" being popular slang for Germans). Came the rejoinder: "Well, thank God we didn't have to get drunk to join the army." McMurtry, walking at the head of E Company, must have joined in the exchange. At one point two brothers back-slapped and arm-punched until their officers ordered them back into line. Duffy heard the lyrics "Herald

Square, anywhere, New York Town, take me there," as the passing columns faded into the dark.[2]

Entering the trenches on the night of June 21–22, the Metropolitans took pride in being the first representatives of the National Army to hold the front as a complete formation. The locale wasn't much to look at. The trenches had been built by the French years before and were filthy despite the efforts of the Rainbow men to clean them up. There hadn't been any serious fighting here for almost four years, and both sides used it more or less as a rest sector.

The Germans, though, learned that a new unit had entered the lines and decided to test it. Before dawn on June 24, an artillery and gas barrage landed on a sector held by the 308th Regiment's 1st battalion. German *Stosstruppen* followed close behind, rampaging efficiently through the American trenches and shooting or bayoneting seventeen doughboys to death. The Americans fought hard—no one fled—but they were shocked by the attack and uncertain how to respond. The affair ended in two hours and the victorious Germans withdrew with twenty stunned American prisoners.[3]

Whittlesey witnessed the raid from regimental headquarters, where phones rang, officers shouted, and runners sprinted before an ominous quiet descended. McMurtry got his first glimpse of action later that evening. Shouting, "Fall in!" and assembling his platoon leaders, he jogged forward with E Company carrying full fighting gear and extra ammunition to a shattered French farm under enemy observation. Here they remained all the following day under heavy artillery fire, suffering no casualties except for a corporal who blew his hand off while fiddling with a German detonator.

A few days later E Company pushed forward to the edge of no-man's-land, where it remained for a week. During this time McMurtry worked closely with French noncoms to give his officers and men opportunities to patrol the front line and trade shots with shadowy enemy patrols—all inconclusive, but valuable for green troops. The Metropolitan Division was about to embark upon its toughest test.[4]

The German offensive faded by mid-July. A final all-out assault along the Marne River on July 15 collapsed thanks to stout resistance by French forces and elements of the US 3rd Division—from then on called the "Rock of the Marne." Three days later the Allies turned the tables. French forces attacked alongside the US 1st and 2nd Divisions, pushing back the Germans beyond the city of Soissons. During these movements the 77th Division was transferred out of the Alsace-Lorraine region and to the Vesle River, where it arrived on August 10. For the first time the Metropolitans were to take part in offensive operations designed to begin driving the Germans out of France.

The 308th regiment's historian later remembered Alsace-Lorraine, where the 77th first entered the lines, as a "sleepy old lion." By contrast the Vesle front was "some sort of a monster hell-cat which scarcely for a moment ceased to spit and scratch, and whose very breath was death." French and American forces striving to eliminate a German salient had gotten hung up on the Vesle, where the enemy had destroyed all bridges and shown his determination to hold. It was the 77th Division's job to get them moving again.

Exhausted American 4th Division doughboys were in no mood to trade jibes as the Metropolitans moved in to replace them, and soon McMurtry could see why. Leading his troops forward to the lines at night in a column of twos along the side of a busy road, he passed clumps of ambulances, ammunition trucks, and supply wagons. Suddenly a shell landed in the midst of the column and McMurtry ordered his men to the ground. Someone screamed for "First aid!" One of his sergeants lay dead, with another sergeant and two privates seriously wounded.

Continuing forward, the men dodged and dove into funk holes (they were not called fox holes until World War II), taking gas masks on and off as shells landed intermittently. The men learned to recognize the sickeningly sweet odor of phosgene gas, and the smell of mustard gas like "rare, ripe onions." Ahead they saw enemy signals dotting the sky. Some were drifting flares like arc lights, and others caterpillar signals that resembled glowing strings of pearls. But there was little beauty here. The closer the Americans approached the front the more McMurtry could hear the pt-pt-pt of machine guns and cracks of rifles—and the more he could smell the stench of death.

McMurtry positioned his men in funk holes and hoped for the best. Within minutes, the Germans welcomed the Americans with a barrage of ghastly mustard gas that drifted and settled with seeming malevolence into any depression. The E Company men had shown off their aptitude with gas masks several months earlier on the Hippodrome stage. But they were not quick enough now. Several inhaled the acrid, burning poison, which even when not fatal could scar a man for life, and one coughed out his lungs and slowly died. They weren't yet at the actual front.

On August 15, McMurtry led his men forward to a railroad embankment along the Vesle near a French village. The men dug funk holes and hugged the earth while keeping watch for enemy attack. The Germans shelled E Company constantly with high explosives and gas, forcing the men to spend all day and night encased in masks during sweltering August heat. Fortunately, the masks also kept out the stench of the numerous putrefying German and American corpses. And the gas killed the flies that collected on every open surface, especially men's faces. McMurtry stayed with his men for two days before going back to take over temporarily for the 2nd Battalion commander, Major Kenneth P. Budd, who had been gassed and evacuated.[5]

There were other losses at the command level, and not all from enemy action. When General Duncan ordered the 308th Regiment to cross the Vesle by means of a bridge and reinforce two small bridgeheads on the northern bank, Colonel Averill discovered there was no bridge, halted his men, and reported the situation to headquarters. Duncan assumed the colonel was malingering and relieved him on the spot.

Meanwhile, some Metropolitans crossed the Vesle by swimming or shimmying across felled trees. On the north bank, doughboys held on grimly in half-shattered dugouts, fighting off several German attacks. On August 22, finally, the enemy launched an attack that they wryly code-named "Amerika" and wiped out the bridgehead, capturing thirty-three Americans and sending the rest diving into the river. The victory was short-lived. On the following day the 308th came right back across the river, ejected the Germans from their hard-won ground, and recaptured the bridgehead. They would not lose it again.[6]

All in all, it was not a bad showing for the first draftee division to enter combat. The Metropolitans had fought doggedly while enduring numerous casualties. There seemed to be a special determination to these men, as if they had something to prove—which they did. Duncan, however, displeased someone at AEF headquarters, likely Pershing, and was relieved. He would later take command of the 82nd All-American Division, which in early October helped decide the fate of his former division.[7]

Whittlesey monitored the situation at regimental headquarters. He regretted Averill's unjust dismissal, and did not get on well with the grouchy new regimental commander, Colonel Austin F. Prescott, who had been promoted from the divisional ammunition train. But Whittlesey did not let personal resentments interfere with his duty. Almost fanatically conscientious, he ensured that the 308th Regiment's frontline battalions received the best possible administrative and logistical support.

Exceeding his duties, Whittlesey haunted battalion and company headquarters in dugouts just behind the front lines, visiting them so often that he suffered from gas inhalation. Like many of his fellows he failed to appreciate the long-term debilitating impact of gas, and refused to be evacuated or report himself as a casualty. It was as if he had a premonition that his division would need him, and it did. At the end of the month Captain Lucien Breckenridge, temporarily commanding the 1st Battalion, was wounded. Whittlesey was promoted to major and assigned to take permanent command of the battalion in his place. For the first time, he would work alongside Captain McMurtry, still temporarily commanding the 2nd Battalion.[8]

Major General Robert Alexander took command of the Metropolitan Division on August 27 with all the brash self-assurance that characterizes both good and bad generals, and makes many of them so distasteful to others. Finding headquarters staff in agony over the terrible losses the men had recently endured, Alexander let it be known that he would run the division differently—and better. The general had little use for his brigade or regimental commanders, and they came to despise him too. Within two weeks this dysfunctional "team" would decide the fates of Whittlesey, McMurtry, and their men.

Alexander was not a West Point man, but had worked his way up through the ranks. Born in Baltimore in 1863, he geared up for a career as a lawyer by passing the bar exam and then abruptly decided to enlist in the army in 1886. After three years in the ranks he was commissioned a lieutenant in 1889. Alexander's first experiences of "combat" in command of army infantry were two sad episodes of ruthlessness: the crushing of the final Sioux Indian uprising at Wounded Knee in 1890–1891, and the breaking of the Pullman Strike in Denver in 1894. He then participated in the clearing of the last remnants of Spanish resistance in Puerto Rico in 1898 before going to the Philippines and helping to put down the native uprising there.

Though he never encountered serious resistance from a professional enemy, Alexander did receive citations for gallantry and a tribesman injured him with a bolo in 1902. After graduating from the Army Staff College in 1910, he served as an instructor with the Maryland National Guard. Promoted to lieutenant colonel in July 1916, Alexander commanded a regiment under Pershing on the Mexican border. In the summer of 1918 he commanded a brigade of the 32nd Division in action on the Marne, earning sufficient plaudits to win him promotion to major general and command of the 77th Division. Pershing liked confident, even arrogant commanders, qualities that Alexander had in plenty.

Alexander was a self-made military man who thought he had something to prove. His bearing said it all. Rotund, round faced, and apple cheeked, he seemed genial at first glance but made little effort to restrain his volatile moods. Lacking the precise professionalism of a career officer like Johnson—a type he hated—Alexander looked and behaved like a middle-aged barrister who could easily slip off his uniform, put on a suit, and walk with a commanding presence into a courtroom. Where other generals insisted on protocol or chains of authority, Alexander relaxed and chatted easily with enlisted men. This gave him an instinctive understanding of soldiers and what made them fight. But he had no experience with a formation as unusual as the Metropolitan Division.

With officers, though—especially West Pointers, possibly because he felt threatened by them—Alexander was prone to be a bully. He was the type of leader who liked to command obedience by overawing through force of personality; in effect, using his moods as carrot and whip. No one wanted to be the object of his temper, which could manifest alternately in shouting bombast or acid sarcasm. Ironically this style not only made enemies, but often caused critics to overlook Alexander's qualities in administration and logistics.[9]

Despite his confidence, Alexander did not institute any immediate changes as the Metropolitan Division stumbled through the first two weeks of September. After bloodying the Americans' noses along the Vesle, the Germans conducted a slow and fighting retreat to the Marne River while the 77th Division and others followed up the rearguards. Fortunately for Whittlesey and McMurtry, who were just getting used to their new commands, the 308th Regiment mostly remained in support during this period.

For the division as a whole, though, the strain was unremitting. When the Metropolitans finally departed the lines on September 14, they chain-smoked and their shoulders sagged. There was a severe shortage of officers too, and those who remained suffered from frayed nerves. While at the front General Johnson had decided to use a mustard gas–saturated cave for his brigade headquarters, and ordered engineers to clear it. They did so, at the cost of seventy gas casualties. When the officers moved in, they thoughtlessly brought back mattresses and furniture that the engineers had removed, and later jumped out of bed with gas burns, including Johnson.[10]

The 77th Division was relieved, appropriately enough, by an Allied Italian division. Just as they had with the 42nd Division weeks earlier, the New York boys found plenty of friends in the ranks of the new unit. Soon they were chatting amiably about Manhattan, where many of the Italians had once worked, and the old country, where some of the New Yorkers had been born.

Major Whittlesey, who had to coordinate the relief, had less positive experiences with the Italians. He encountered two Italian battalion commanders standing in the road, arguing about which should take precedence in the line. After a good deal of shouting and gesticulating, Whittlesey got them sorted out. That night, however, both Italian battalions showed up simultaneously and milled around chaotically in the dark. Instead of leaving them to settle their own mess, Whittlesey and a dozen noncoms took charge of the Italians and deployed them into the line. "It was a pretty discouraged Wop commander," he later remembered, "when we finally had to go away."

The horrors of war had not yet expunged Whittlesey's sensitivity. As he departed at dawn the next morning and walked through the shattered village of Fismes, he smiled at a roofless cafe with a sign declaring "Open for Business." He slept for a few hours in a cool forest, then walked along a scorching road until he reached "a fine rolling meadow country near a tiny town," where he washed off the filth of the front lines. Later he and his men boarded buses, which took off one by one along shell-pitted roads. As the buses tossed and jounced, Whittlesey marveled at the gorgeous moonlight, wondered at "gorgeous" plane and poplar trees, and admired passing ancient walls and gardens. During rest stops he sipped "pretty fine" coffee that a French soldier brewed with hot water siphoned off the truck radiator. Finally deposited in a small town near a forest called the Argonne, the major enjoyed a brief period of "fair peace," sampling scrounged delicacies like rabbit and duck.[11]

While Whittlesey, McMurtry, and their men enjoyed a brief respite, an official war correspondent named Frederick Palmer took stock of the Metropolitan Division. A forty-five-year-old mild-mannered Pennsylvanian, Palmer had spent almost his entire life as a journalist. He entered the world of New York journalism earlier than Damon Runyon, in the mid-1890s, but without much experience of life on the tough side of the tracks. Palmer had grown up in a peaceful (albeit poor) rural atmosphere, with a congenital heart condition that limited his capacity for hard living.

Palmer was a good writer. He began covering wars beginning in 1897 for a succession of newspapers including the *New York World*, *New York Globe*, and *New York Times*. From his mentor and competitor Richard Harding Davis he learned to write "bully stuff," rip-roaring articles that glorified conflict but without any innate understanding of what it meant. As such, Palmer earned the praise of men like Teddy Roosevelt. But he was a mainstream kind of journalist. In the Philippines, while Runyon hung around camp swapping stories with enlisted men, of whom he was one, Palmer consorted with generals.

Palmer earned repute in the first years of World War I by reporting from British headquarters, and in April 1917 the *New York*

Herald offered him the astronomical yearly sum of forty thousand dollars to cover American participation in the conflict. What the *Herald* could not offer Palmer, however, was power and prestige. Those were things Pershing held in his hands, and he offered Palmer twenty-four hundred dollars per year to serve as the chief of his press section. In this role Palmer could choreograph official censorship and make the final decision on accreditation of all journalists as war correspondents. Without Palmer's imprimatur, no journalist could make it anywhere near AEF headquarters, let alone to the front. Although he later presented this as a "sacrifice" that took him away from the troops, Palmer gratefully accepted Pershing's offer.

There was a cost. As Pershing's man, Palmer occupied a special room at headquarters with his name on the door. He learned about everything, from the headquarters level, as soon as it happened. And he lorded it over his peers. Although Palmer tried to liberalize standards for allowing reporters near the front, his efforts to target "experienced newspaper men" who would censor their own work backfired. His fellow journalists accused him of "going over to the enemy." Palmer visited the front, but only as Pershing's accredited representative. And he wrote press copy for the express purpose of bolstering the war effort.[12]

Palmer's appraisal of the 77th Division, then, toed the official storyline of city boys made good. In the city, he said, they had been puny specimens, but army life had given them a "robustness" and positive attitude that characterized any true American. "The spirit! Did they have that?" he wrote. "This was the right ingredient for the melting-pot under machine-gun fire. They were proving that they had under merciless test; and that they had certain qualities of ready adaptability which go with city life." But he never spoke to Whittlesey, McMurtry, or any of the doughboys.[13]

The summer of 1918 tested and blooded the AEF, with positive results on the surface. Germany's efforts to end the war with a supreme offensive on the Western Front had failed, largely thanks to British and French resistance with some help from the Americans. After the last German push along the Marne River sputtered out on July 15, Allied counterattacks had pushed the Germans back as far as the Aisne River. In the process, four American Regular Army and four National Guard divisions, and one National Army division, the 77th, had learned to fight. Their reward, in August, was the formation of Pershing's coveted First Army under his personal command.

First Army launched the first truly American offensive of the war on September 12. The target was a German salient centered on the town of Saint-Mihiel, north of the battered fortress of Verdun. The 77th Division did not participate in this attack, but the 82nd Division did, along with three other National Army divisions. The operation was a smashing success. The Germans had already planned to abandon the salient, but the American assault caught them by surprise. Over the course of four days, US First Army captured two hundred square miles. The Germans fled in disorder, leaving behind sixteen thousand prisoners.

For York and the men of his platoon, the affair didn't amount to much. The soldiers advanced aggressively, firing at everything that moved or didn't move, and captured one village and one German straggler. But they experienced no real fighting. Although his regiment incurred a few hundred casualties from German artillery, all York encountered was a shell that landed nearby as he plundered grapes from a vineyard, and sent him scampering to the rear.[14]

Some AEF senior officers were all for building on this success by pushing straight ahead through the hills of Alsace-Lorraine, past the fortress town of Metz and on into Germany. Pershing had other ideas. General Ferdinand Foch, the supreme commander of all Allied forces in France, believed that the time was right to strike a major blow against the weakening Germans. Few then expected the war to end any sooner than 1919, least of all Foch; but he believed that by attacking concentrically against the large German salient in northeastern France he could overwhelm the enemy and push him back toward the Rhine. The allies could then rest through the winter, and finish off the Germans in the spring.

Foch flattered Pershing's vanity by telling him that the American role in the overall offensive would be to attack through the Meuse-Argonne region toward a vital railway junction that supplied most German forces on the Western Front. This was a tall order, but Foch assured Pershing that he knew the doughboys could do it. Pershing readily agreed. "No other Allied troops," he said, "had the morale or the offensive spirit to overcome successfully the difficulties to be met in the Meuse-Argonne sector."[15]

Strategically speaking the Meuse-Argonne was a sensible choice. For the doughboys it promised hard work. Situated between the Meuse River on the east and the Argonne Forest on the west, the sector occupied part of the horrific battlefield of Verdun. The Germans held both flanks of the area in great strength, packing artillery respectively along heights above the Meuse River and in the eastern edges of the Argonne. In between, the ground was shell pocked and swampy on the south and rugged to the north where the main German infantry defenses were located. Advancing American infantry would have to attack through turgid, corpse-strewn swamps and into the teeth of German strongpoints rigged with trenches, barbed wire, and pillboxes, while taking fire from both flanks. To eliminate this fire, First Army must clear the heights of the Meuse and the Argonne Forest—and fast.

Logistical preparations for the offensive were a nightmare. Only ten days separated the end of the Saint-Mihiel offensive on September 16 and the start of the Meuse-Argonne offensive. Pershing had used the majority of his most experienced divisions at Saint-Mihiel, and it would take them time to disengage from that front. As a result, Pershing had to deploy almost entirely green divisions to launch the assault in the Meuse-Argonne. The only exceptions were the 4th and 28th Divisions, and the 77th Division, which was deployed facing the toughest terrain in the Argonne Forest.

General Alexander reconnoitered his division's sector five days before the offensive began. He went first to the soldiers' billets. Chatting with them gave the general a chance to show his sympathy. Alexander dragged one poorly clad doughboy to a supply officer and shouted, "Why the Hell can't this man have a decent pair of breeches to wear into battle?" The man got his breeches. The general had to shed his own clothes and don a French uniform afterward in order to maintain secrecy as he visited the front. What he learned there on a dark and rainy night unsettled him.

The Argonne Forest, Alexander surmised, was not so much a forest as a "wooded mountain." Along its southern rim the woods partially covered a heavily shell-pitted, noisome morass of bracken, broken trees, rotten stumps, and bogs. From there the terrain rose steeply, climbing the aptly named Dead Man's Hill to a plateau over six hundred feet above sea level. The Argonne was bounded on the east and north by the Aire River valley and on the west by the Aisne River valley. In dimensions, the forest was about six miles from west to east, and twenty-two miles from south to north.

Unlike other forests that had been obliterated by shellfire, this one stood just outside the Verdun battlefield and so remained largely intact. Unfortunately, since it had never been burned it was also thick with underbrush. The worst feature, though, was the large number of ravines, generally with creeks at the bottom, that cut through the forest at multiple points. Only one road penetrated the forest, and it cut across rather than followed the American line of advance, roughly from the towns of Binarville on the west to Apremont on the east. Whittlesey and McMurtry would get to know it well.

Two days before the offensive, Alexander sat down to confer at the headquarters of his superior officer, Major General Hunter Liggett, in command of I Corps. A sixty-one-year-old West Point graduate from Reading, Pennsylvania, Liggett was a burly, soft-spoken, and cerebral commander. He was noted for his patience and ability to calm blustery subordinates like Alexander, who bullied subordinates and despised most of his fellow division commanders but treated superiors with obsequious respect.

The 77th Division, Liggett explained, would not be expected to advance rapidly into the forest, but must nevertheless exert maximum pressure on the Germans. The main action would take place to the east, where the 28th Division would push up the Aire River valley to Apremont; and to the west, where French troops, communicating with the 77th Division by means of a liaison regiment of troops from the African American 92nd Division, pushed forward in the Champagne region. Pershing assumed that these attacks on the flanks of the Argonne would force the Germans to withdraw, leaving the Metropolitans with little more to do than follow them out of the woods.[16]

Whittlesey and the other battalion commanders—Major Budd had returned to the 2nd Battalion, sending McMurtry back to Company E—explored the front sector just days before the attack. Like Alexander they wore French uniforms; in Whittlesey's case, one far too small for his lanky frame, making nearby poilus laugh. But they saw little of value except a town that Whittlesey thought looked as if it had been in ruins since medieval times, and a network of mossy, semicollapsed trenches that the French had held since the beginning of the war. Without glimpsing the woods ahead, they returned to their billets where Whittlesey grappled with a sudden influx of green replacements from the mountain west.

During the summer the division had suffered nearly forty-eight hundred casualties, losing many of the Camp Upton men who had shared jokes and suffered trials together. In their place, the army replenished the division with a new infusion of untrained draftees just as it prepared to launch a major offensive into unfamiliar terrain. These were four thousand men of the 40th "Sunshine" Division (the tragic irony of the name would become evident in time), almost all of them from Rocky Mountain western states such as Montana and Washington. Twelve hundred fifty of these greenhorns were shoehorned into the 308th Regiment.[17]

On the afternoon of September 25, Alexander assembled his officers at division headquarters. Clutching a sheaf of orders, he stood up and gave them a pep talk about the task ahead. The whole Allied front was advancing from Switzerland to the North Sea, he said, and the Metropolitans were "only a small cog in a big machine." Success or failure would depend on the leadership of the officers, given the unquestioned valor of the men. Events would show that the message of responsibility got through to the field officers, but ironically failed to impress itself upon Alexander or his staff.

In the last hours before the offensive, Whittlesey pondered a "morbidly meticulous" and utterly useless memorandum titled "Questions for a Battalion Commander To Ask Himself Prior To Taking Over And While Occupying A Portion Of The Front Line." At dark, he helped coordinate the headquarters company in managing last-moment preparations. McMurtry called the officers, noncoms, and men of Company E to order and marched them toward the front past ammunition wagons where the soldiers collected bullets and grenades. Then they slopped across sodden fields and through muddy copses toward the front. Flickers of light and sound announced the arrival of occasional enemy shells. The supreme test was about to begin.[18]

(CHAPTER SIX)

THROUGH THE FOREST GATE

After long hours spent slogging along dripping, tree-lined roads smelling of wet earth, the soldiers emerged into open, shell-pitted country. Noncoms whispered commands as they slithered into ancient mud-choked trenches. In the darkness ahead lay the Argonne. A flickering halo lit the skyline at two thirty in the morning, accompanied by crackling like thunder, and for the first time the trees became visible. The tumult of splintering timber told the watching soldiers that the Allied artillery barrage had hit its mark, and the ground shook with concussions. As they watched the flames rising through clouds of red-tinged smoke enfolding a slivered moon, men wondered how anyone could survive the inferno. For a few moments, they felt sorry for the Germans.

After three hours the bombardment intensified, and a whorl of explosions hammered the forward tree line where the enemy barbed wire and trenches were thought to rest. At five minutes before six the men left their stinking trenches and advanced behind a barrage moving slowly forward into the trees. Whittlesey, whose battalion formed the first wave on the Metropolitan Division's left, was suffering from a sore throat and a touch of dysentery, either from a cold or a whiff of gas. He rasped, "Let's go" and shoved his diminutive companion, Lieutenant Edward N. Lewis, an assistant city editor with the *New York Tribune,* out of the trench. Lewis pulled the major out in turn. Whittlesey looked around, but he could see nothing. A clammy mist had descended during the barrage, merging with drifting smoke to reduce visibility to zero. He found himself in what another officer called a "blind world of whiteness and noise, groping over something like the surface of the moon."

Whittlesey's men advanced in open order. He heard them yelling and firing off shots as the rumbling barrage crept forward. Twisted, rusty wire and collapsed trenches announced the enemy front line. Whittlesey reached for his pistol but there was nothing to fire at. Soldiers exclaimed as they discovered the bodies of what they took to be dead Germans, only to turn away in disgust from the rotted skeletons of long-deceased Frenchmen. Soldiers slid over blasted trees and scampered across craters and small ravines. Occasionally Whittlesey saw a racing shadow and called out; but no one could recognize officers amid the cacophony of voices.[1]

Whittlesey walked alongside his adjutant, Lieutenant Arthur McKeogh, a slight-framed twenty-nine-year-old Manhattan newspaper editor. A few dozen runners and signalmen followed behind, uncoiling telephone wire and struggling to keep their commanding officer in view. The major kept a mean pace, his tall frame slightly stooped and hands clasped behind his back. This would soon earn him the nickname "Galloping Charlie." For most of the men, though, it was slow going. Engineers clipped at barbed wire that the artillery had not already cut, or laid out planks and logs to form temporary footbridges over bogs and shell holes. Explosions and machine guns boomed and rattled in the distance. Here and there a man cried out. For the most part, it was the unseen, the unanticipated, that was most frightening.[2]

Captain McMurtry, leading Company E in the second or support wave, moved forward as Whittlesey's battalion dispersed into the Argonne. He and his officers still had not mastered the tactical innovations that came as second nature to their French and British allies, and they had no experience on this kind of terrain. Some of Major Budd's 2nd Battalion company commanders became confused by the mist and one ordered his men to stop and wait for the fog to clear. German artillery began inflicting casualties. McMurtry maneuvered his company efficiently through into the woods, only to end the day stuck in the mud of an abandoned German trench.

At seven o'clock in the morning, Whittlesey reported that his battalion was "progressing favorably with little opposition" but confessed that he did not know how much ground he had covered. As the mist cleared and the sun rose at midmorning the men saw him at work with a massive pair of wire cutters. The sunshine also revealed small clumps of men milling about, struggling to read maps and fiddling with compasses. Whittlesey found a dugout in an abandoned German trench and tried to get situated as he heard the first sounds ahead of a firefight. A private walked by holding a flare pistol that he trained on a middle-aged, sobbing German prisoner. "Where did you get this old fellow?" the major asked with a smile, and sent them to the rear.

Whittlesey studied his map and discovered that he had advanced about one and a quarter miles, just a few hundred yards short of the objective line, which division planners had

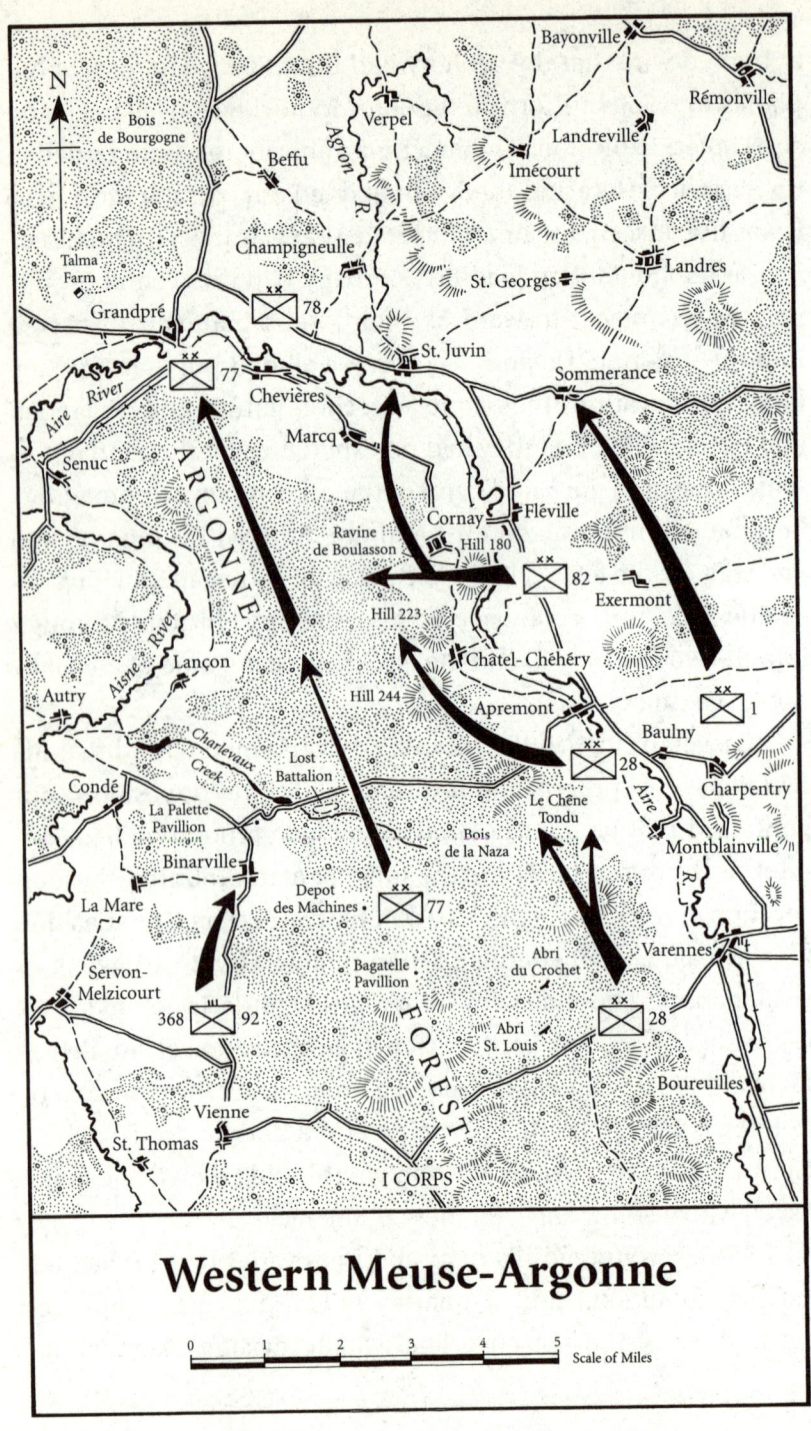

Western Meuse-Argonne

thoughtfully placed squarely in the middle of a swamp. Whittlesey halted the advance on the spot. At midday a runner arrived with orders to continue forward behind a renewed artillery barrage. The major obeyed, but the terrain was so jumbled and formations so confused that the regiment had little hope of accomplishing anything. German rearguard machine gunners opened fire and pinned down the doughboys. By midafternoon they were back where they started.

As evening descended a cold rain began to fall. Whittlesey sensibly moved his headquarters into a nearby collection of abandoned German concrete huts replete with cots, chairs, and tables. Somebody scrounged several bottles of mineral water left behind by the enemy. Runners flew about as the major attempted to locate his companies and those of adjacent units. The left flank was worryingly bare. Otherwise the line was intact even if units had intermingled. The rain intensified as the men, stuck in old trenches and hastily dug funk holes, shivered without the slickers and overcoats that they had been ordered to leave behind. Although Whittlesey established contact with regimental headquarters by phone, no one had any food.[3]

The Metropolitans woke up on the morning of September 27 in an unfamiliar and intimidating environment, feeling as if the outside world had disappeared. Whittlesey never went to sleep. All night long he struggled to maintain communications with his companies and adjacent troops. The rain that poured all night made poison gas attacks impossible. Enemy artillery fire, however, cut the telephone cables, interrupting contact with regimental headquarters.

General Alexander sent orders before dawn insisting that his officers push ahead energetically behind a morning barrage, without regard to their flanks. He wanted immediate pressure on the enemy. Thanks to a staff mix-up, however, the orders went unconfirmed. Whittlesey watched helplessly as the barrage rolled off without any movement by his men. Over the next several hours the major perused reports from his company commanders, who told him that his troops were not cooperating effectively. New Yorkers and western replacements tended to stay in groups to themselves. As a result, the replacements frequently got lost and took unnecessary casualties.

The rain, which had tapered off during the morning, resumed just as confirmation orders arrived and the attack resumed early in the afternoon. German machine gun nests hidden in the underbrush opened fire and dropped several Americans as they crept forward through swamp grass, stumps, and bogs. Junior officers tried to lead their men in taking out these nests by sneaking up under cover and using grenades. In places mortars were brought into action, and the troops employed some unreliable French light machine guns prone to jamming.

Beyond the enemy machine gun outposts, the Metropolitans encountered a strongly held German trench system that they lacked the organization or firepower to storm. Whittlesey called forward his support troops, including McMurtry's E Company, but they succeeded only in crowding and confusing the front line without inconveniencing the enemy. By late afternoon the attack had broken down after advancing barely over two hundred yards.[4]

Unbeknownst to Whittlesey, the situation at division headquarters had become explosive. Pershing was unsatisfied with the 77th Division's rate of advance, and he passed on his displeasure to Liggett, who passed it on to Alexander. He, in keeping with his preferred leadership style, decided that the best way to get results was to hector his brigade commanders into moving faster. When Johnson told him about the 308th Regiment's failure to attack that morning, Alexander ordered him to instantly relieve Colonel Prescott for dereliction of duty.

Whittlesey first learned of the leadership change during the predawn hours of September 28 when he, Major Budd, and Lieutenant McKeogh reported to regimental headquarters to meet Prescott's replacement, Colonel Cromwell Stacey. Nobody had liked Prescott, and they had high hopes for his successor. Stacey, a forty-two-year-old Nevadan who had been in the army since age sixteen, had seen combat in several American conflicts. In the summer of 1918 he had commanded a regiment in severe fighting along the Marne.

Stacey was the type of commander who didn't know how to give anything less than his best. He led from the front, and had been cited multiple times for gallantry. But his nerves were fraying. He found regimental headquarters in disarray in the wake of Prescott's departure, and Alexander and Johnson lectured him about how he must set things straight. This left him grumpy and disenchanted on his first day on the job. After shouting at Whittlesey and Budd for a few minutes, he gruffly handed them orders to launch their two mixed battalions in an all-out attack at six in the morning. They were to break free of the swamp, capture the German trench system, and climb Dead Man's Hill.[5]

Captain McMurtry's company received its first ration detail at four o'clock on the morning of September 28 in the form of bread, beef, and cabbage—all cold. Other companies received odd combinations of butter, bacon, bread, and cans of golden syrup. They were the lucky ones. Many received nothing at all. Those who had food refused to share with those who didn't, even with men in the same platoon, unless they came from the same part of the country. Soldiers hunched in groups in the rain according to their background. The best disposed teased their counterparts as city or country boys. Others stared in suspicion or blank incomprehension.[6]

Artillery fire crashed into the woods just before dawn. Whittlesey, Budd, and their dwindling complement of officers spurred the men forward at six o'clock that morning. The usual fog choked the woods, and as soon as the assault squads disappeared in the murk the officers lost command control. Noncoms took charge as the doughboys approached the German trenches, expecting a fight. Incredibly, they discovered that the enemy had withdrawn. Without a pause, the men pushed forward into bracken thicker than anything they had seen before.

Two hours passed. As the fog lifted, soldiers of Company B broke through the tree line into a small, partially open ravine framing a narrow-gauge railway. Their relief dissipated quickly. Well-sited enemy machine guns allowed the Americans to venture out of cover and then open fire, inflicting casualties and driving the survivors to ground.

Soldiers looked to their noncoms for guidance. First Sergeant John T. E. Monahan was an Irishman from Queens who had already been cited for conspicuous gallantry and won the trust of his men. Without waiting for someone else to do the job, he crept forward to locate a German machine gun and direct his platoon to take it out. His doughboys silenced the enemy gun, but not before a bullet pierced Monahan's head. He died in a hospital a month after the war ended.[7]

Whittlesey established his command post at the lower edge of the ravine. His men had captured little more ground than the Germans willingly gave them, about half a mile. Now they had stopped again. He remembered the blustery orders that Alexander had issued to his officers that morning, declaring, "WE ARE NOT GOING BACK BUT FORWARD!" The general had also illegally directed his officers to execute any man who suggested retirement. Now, though, Alexander ordered him to pull back a few hundred yards so that artillery could pound the new enemy positions. The men withdrew, and found a ration detail waiting for them.

The barrage seemed to do the trick. Whittlesey's contingent, which included Major Budd and some of his 2nd Battalion troops, resumed the advance that afternoon, successfully crossing the ravine, clearing an old German war cemetery, and approaching their objective at the crest of Dead Man's Hill. But all was not as it seemed. Captain McMurtry, advancing with Company E to Whittlesey's right, had to pause when German troops infiltrated *his* right flank. This left a gap between Whittlesey and McMurtry, and the Germans pushed in there too. With enemy troops driving in both of his flanks, McMurtry had to do what Alexander had warned his officers against, on penalty of death—pull back.

Whittlesey and Budd were unaware of McMurtry's withdrawal. Instead of pulling back they established their command post in an old German bunker and assembled their remaining officers and acting company commanders, telling them to hold positions for the night on the ravine's northern slope. They had about four hundred men, who dug funk holes in about a three-hundred-yard, well-outposted perimeter. He dispatched a runner to brigade asking for ammunition, food, and especially drinking water, and then settled to await developments.[8]

The Germans did not wait. As darkness fell, they probed soft parts of the American lines. Platoons of German soldiers festooned with grenades and carrying machine guns infiltrated the gaps. Gusts of wind and pouring rain masked the sounds of their movements as they advanced in short rushes and placed machine guns. The doughboys, who had received no fresh drinking water, turned their helmets upside down to collect the rain, but did not notice the enemy troops who cut them off. American runner posts intended to keep contact with the rear were located by the Germans and silenced. By morning, Whittlesey's command was surrounded.

Whittlesey and Budd were Harvard men who had attended Plattsburg in 1916 and 1917. Budd, a thirty-eight-year-old Manhattan native and dry goods merchant with iron-gray hair, was like his counterpart a tall, thin, almost ascetic-looking officer who tended to intellectualize command decisions. As dawn arrived on September 29, they took stock of the evidence—loss of contact with regimental and brigade headquarters, and with gaps on their right and left—and agreed that the Germans had cut them off.

Officers and men did not panic. Budd outranked Whittlesey but worked with him as a colleague. The two officers conferred over their maps and agreed to dispatch Lieutenant McKeogh with eight runners and fifteen men to recapture the old cemetery behind them. Within minutes after starting, however, the detachment came under heavy enemy fire from all sides. Hours passed. Nightfall found McKeogh crawling through underbrush, hearing the voices of enemy soldiers, and thinking weirdly of his German barber on 42nd Street. Looking at the stars above, he thought of the evening crowds on Broadway and wondered if the revelers could see them through the glare of the city lights.

Back in the pocket Whittlesey and Budd urgently tried to reestablish communications with the outside world. A runner turned over some maps found in a dead German officer's tunic, but they proved little help. Scouts found Germans in every direction. Whittlesey and Budd dispatched carrier pigeons to inform divisional headquarters of their plight. Refusing to stay in their bunker, the two officers walked and crawled from one post to another, visiting the men in slimy funk holes half filled with rainwater. They also agreed not to tell the men they had been cut off. It was a mistake—the men knew anyway, and wondered who the officers thought they were kidding.

Colonel Stacey learned about the situation from McMurtry, who had made his way back to regimental headquarters the previous night. Luckily for him, the colonel did not tell Alexander that McMurtry had withdrawn. Even so the general was furious. He vented his rage on Johnson, who in turn castigated Stacey. Stacey kept his calm, and sent Lieutenant Colonel Fred E. Smith of North Dakota—a good friend of Whittlesey's and beloved by everyone in the regiment—forward with a squad to try and reestablish contact. While making his way through the woods on the morning of September 29, Smith was shot and killed by a German machine gun.

As evening fell, tension built among the surrounded troops. German mortars began to shell them. Ammunition was low and there was no way to care for the wounded. Food had run out. There was nothing to drink but muddy rainwater. With night the terrors increased, thanks to the jarring sounds of gunfire, groans, enemy taunts, and even the howls of a dying German courier dog. Officers and noncoms warned the soldiers to keep watch for possible enemy attack. Men instinctively looked to each other for support, whispering encouragement, sharing supplies, lending watches.

Colonel Stacey had just sat down to breakfast on the morning of September 30 when a mud-caked soldier, one arm hanging limply and dripping blood, entered his dugout, saluted with his good arm, and introduced himself as Lieutenant McKeogh. Just after sunrise the lieutenant had escaped the ravine and made contact with American patrols who directed him to the rear. The colonel whipped out his map. McKeogh ran his dirty fingers over it to indicate the position of Whittlesey's command. Stacey immediately dispatched runners to report the situation to brigade while McKeogh stuffed himself with hotcakes. Between bites he tried to tell the colonel everything he had seen, but Stacey told him to shut up. "You eat and say nothing!" he shouted. "I'm going to send you on a detail as soon as you're through."

In the pocket, nobody knew that McKeogh had broken through or whether any relief efforts were under way. They could only sit and hold. Whittlesey made the rounds again and again, striding in his usual pose with head cocked forward and his hands behind his back, assuring the men that relief was on its way. They didn't know whether to believe him but they respected his concern for their welfare. As the day progressed, though, the cracking sounds of gunfire to the south crept closer. Men wondered if their officers would order a breakout. Instead they were told to stay ready and keep their heads down.

The sounds of firing tapered off just before dusk. As the air grew quiet, the doughboys noticed that hours had passed since a German mortar shell had exploded among them. Then figures emerged through the gloom to the south and identified themselves as a relief party. Early that morning Alexander had ordered vigorous attacks all along the line. They finally paid off as the Germans withdrew under pressure from elements of Johnson's brigade.

Captain McMurtry accompanied the relief party. Seeming equal parts grave and ebullient, he handed Major Budd a paper with orders to report to division headquarters for transfer to staff officers' school. McMurtry would take command of the battalion in his place. As Budd celebrated, McMurtry turned to Whittlesey and told him that his friend Fred Smith had taken a bullet to the head while leading the relief.

McMurtry left Whittlesey and emerged from the command bunker. If he had any feelings of guilt or regret about pulling back E Company two days earlier, he didn't show them. Instead he turned to the muddy, hungry men and asked with a broad smile as a large ration detail arrived, "How would you like to have a good thick rare steak smothered in onions and some French-fried potatoes?" McMurtry had his priorities straight. "Practically O.K.!" he laughed as the men received and wolfed down their food.

Even Whittlesey smiled as he made his way to the rear past soldiers too busy eating to salute. But his thoughts were on Smith. It was the blackest night Whittlesey had ever seen, made worse by his near-sightedness. Guides reinforced his sense of helplessness, holding his hand to pass him from one reserve post to another. He stepped into Stacey's dugout, made his report, and was rewarded with hot cocoa and cigars. Then it was back out into the blackness, passed hand to hand back to the front. Orders were to attack at dawn, but for now he left arrangements under McMurtry's efficient and energetic management. Whittlesey first had to discharge what he considered a personal responsibility: write to Smith's widow informing her of his death.[9]

The Meuse-Argonne offensive ground to a halt on September 30. Judged by its progress so far, it was a failure. To the east the Americans had occupied useless ground along the Meuse River without attempting to take the high ground infested by German artillery. These guns fired accurately into the American flank, slowing the advance. In the center, attacking divisions lost a golden opportunity to cut off and capture the German strongpoint at Montfaucon, allowing the enemy to withdraw at leisure. On the left, the 28th Division made only slow progress along the Aire River valley. Likewise, on the far left at the juncture between the US First Army and the French in the Champagne, the 368th Regiment had essentially dissolved. Casualties were horrendous all along the line.

In the Argonne Forest, this failure had several results. Because the Germans suffered no pressure from their flanks, they easily held the line against the 77th Division. General Alexander, on the other hand, had to monitor both his flanks. His left, at the edge of the Argonne adjacent to the 308th Regiment, was open. There was no one there. On the right, the 28th Division had stalled at Apremont, and German artillery in the upper Argonne fired into First Army's center with impunity. With reorganization imperative, Pershing temporarily halted the offensive. But not the 77th Division. Since his plan to pinch out the forest had failed, Pershing ordered the Metropolitans to take it themselves, in head-on attack.

At the beginning of the war, the War Department had insisted on creating oversized, "blockbuster" divisions of nearly forty thousand men, more than twice the size of an average European division. The idea was that these divisions could absorb a lot of punishment and keep pushing ahead without relief. The oversized divisions tended to crowd the line, however, leading to increased casualties. They overwhelmed the supply network, causing massive traffic jams behind the lines and ensuring that the troops never got enough of what they needed. Most important, the blockbuster concept took no account of combat fatigue.

Trench warfare was an exhausting experience. The European powers didn't realize this at first, but as the conflict degenerated into a war of attrition they discovered that men could only endure limited time at the front before wearing down. How quickly this happened depended on whether troops were engaged in active combat, in reserve, or occupying a quiet sector. As a result, the British and French established systems of rotation intended to provide their soldiers with adequate rest.

The Americans took no notice of this or many other lessons of warfare that their compatriots had learned. For Pershing and his officers, success boiled down to aggressiveness and numbers of men available. Units like the marine brigade during the protracted fighting for Belleau Wood in June fought in the lines until they practically ceased to exist. Afterward, generals perused strength reports and wondered where their troops had gone.

By the beginning of October, the Metropolitans had stayed in combat for six straight weeks. They entered the lines on the Vesle on the night of August 11–12 and remained there until September 14. Twelve days later, after little rest and plenty of marching, they plunged into the Argonne. In five days they suffered roughly fifteen hundred casualties, for a grand total of about sixty-three hundred since mid-August. Headquarters hurried to make up for these losses by injecting thousands of untrained men from depot divisions; promoting noncoms and junior officers; and replacing them with ninety-day wonders. Meanwhile, exhausted or incompetent staff officers were removed, reassigned, and replaced every day.

But numbers told only a small part of the story. Officers and men who had not been injured simply stayed in the lines. Others suffering from relatively minor injuries or the aftereffects of poison gas took brief visits to aid stations and then returned to the front. Some, like Whittlesey, were gassed but never reported themselves as casualties, and so never left the front. Nobody received leave to Paris, let alone the United States.

Military authorities knew that prolonged exposure to combat produced symptoms including sleeplessness, homesickness, depression, and anxiety. But these were considered transient problems easily solved by rest, pep talks from upbeat officers, or, where necessary, bullying. Those who resisted such treatment were shirkers or malingerers—not the type for whom a man like Teddy Roosevelt, unofficial mascot of the 77th Division, would show any sympathy. A good American man was self-reliant and resilient.

Shell shock, a term invented in World War I, was different. As the name indicated, it was thought to result from one overwhelming experience (such as being buried alive by an enemy shell) rather than the cumulative effects of sleeplessness, wearing gas masks for days, taking cover from enemy machine guns, dodging shellfire, or seeing buddies wounded or killed—all the constant stress of battle. Such things, staff officers believed, might tire a man but could not by themselves make him unfit for combat. It was all in the head. Trembling hands and blank stares were merely the temporary results of exhaustion. Only toward the war's end did European psychologists diagnose "war neuroses" as serious and sometimes permanent conditions.

Charles Whittlesey and many of his men were by September 30 displaying all the symptoms of combat fatigue. They were listless, distant, their reflexes fading. Their bodies trembled and some approached emotional collapse. Enlisted men grumbled to each other, and bonded on deeper emotional levels, but were not encouraged to express their feelings to noncoms and officers. Officers, for their part, had no outlet. McMurtry set the ideal standard of gritty determination and gruff humor, holding his suffering deep inside where it remained until it reemerged after the war. Whittlesey endured quietly beneath an increasingly brittle and artificial surface of unruffled calm.

General Alexander believed that anyone who hesitated should just be pushed harder, relieved, or even shot. He had already let his officers know that their soldiers' appetite for war should not be questioned. The blame for every failure, he declared, fell squarely on field officers. Alexander also had little respect for professional military men and their textbook concepts of the possible. When First Army collapsed in exhaustion on September 30, he endorsed Pershing's decision that the Metropolitan Division would not rest but press ahead. It had not met its objectives. That was unacceptable. Failure did not demand reassessment, let alone finesse; it just meant pushing harder at the forest gate until it opened. If his officers—men like Johnson, Stacey, and Whittlesey—did not comply, he would relieve them.

No division commander pushed his officers harder. No officers gave of themselves more freely. And none suffered more.

Whittlesey assembled his company commanders just before dawn on October 1. The weather was cold but clear. He handed them their orders for the day and briskly said, "Leaders, get your men up!" When the troops assembled he cried, "Everybody ready. Let's go! Forward!" and they moved out. Until noon the doughboys had easy going as they pushed up to and over the crest of Dead Man's Hill. From here the 308th Regiment continued along the swampy north-south Argonne Ravine, which the enemy had plugged with immense coils of barbed wire. Bracken and rough terrain slowed the advance, but there was no resistance until midmorning. Then the enemy machine guns opened fire.

The major heard the shooting and ordered his two lead companies to deploy and outflank the enemy guns. Mortars were useless, and full cover impossible. Enemy observers directed fire on them. One man fell after another, beginning with junior officers and noncoms. Whittlesey reported the resistance to Stacey, who ordered him to push forward. The major obeyed, telling his officers to continue the attack. McMurtry's troops supported the attack, but to no avail. Dozens more men fell, wounded or dead. The attack had stalled.

Couriers scurried, pigeons flapped, and telephone lines buzzed as the firing subsided, carrying news from companies to battalions to regiments to brigades to division to corps to army and back again. Each command post was a small hive of activity with captains, majors, colonels, and generals at the center and adjutants and chiefs of staff as the gatekeepers. Officers and staffers were often strangers to each other, thanks to frequent reliefs and reassignments. Many spent all day and night in stinking dugouts, surrounded by activity, with little time to eat, and no time or space to sleep. Everyone felt overwhelmed and overworked.

Generals like Pershing, Liggett, Alexander, and Johnson were far from complacent. Each felt the burden of command and knew that his decisions condemned men to injury and death. But knowledge was one thing, experience another. Media and official reports declared that Germany approached collapse. The British and French were making good progress. Why, then, had the American attacks bogged down? Working on the assumptions that the doughboys were superior and the Germans tired, few in number, and short on supplies, they concluded that inexperienced American officers were making excuses about lack of support, losses, disorganization, and open flanks. They must be told to stop worrying and push ahead at all costs. Eventually they would break through.

Alexander felt personally responsible for the Metropolitan Division's success. Disgusted at his officers' lack of "push," he called corps headquarters and got Liggett's chief of staff, who told him that Pershing deplored the 77th Division's slow progress. The Metropolitans must push and push some more; its flanks, the chief of staff told Alexander, "will be taken care of by our own people." Alexander called Johnson to pass on the news. Johnson demurred; what about the flanks? Forget them, Alexander said; orders were orders. Johnson called Stacey and said that the regiment must attack again and win at all costs.

The colonel could hardly believe his ears. Was the 308th Regiment carrying the entire weight of the First Army and the Meuse-Argonne offensive on its own shoulders? Whatever gains the regiment made would be untenable, he told Johnson. "Are you questioning my orders?" the general snapped back. "No, sir," Stacey said. "But if you send them up there you will have to give me the orders in writing, and I will also write a statement to the effect that if you order me to send the men up there I will do so, but I will not be responsible." He got his written orders. And Whittlesey in turn received orders, at dusk, to attack up the ravine and advance "at all costs."

Whittlesey knew his men were tired, exhausted. He had seen the ravine, and the results of the previous day's attacks. Many men had died on his orders. He felt responsible for each one of them, and he felt responsible now, maybe too much so. That evening he made his way back in the blackness to regimental headquarters, again being passed from one clammy hand to another, but this time with McMurtry holding on to his coat.

Whittlesey questioned Stacey as the colonel had questioned Johnson. True to his calling as a professional soldier, Stacey refused to pass the buck. Blasting Whittlesey's objections about flanks, fatigue, and enemy resistance as "nonsense," he restated the orders as given. The major asked again, and Stacey yelled that he would do as ordered, attacking straight ahead without regard to flanks or cost. It may as well have been General Pershing shouting in the major's ears. His was not to reason why.[10]

(CHAPTER SEVEN)

INTO THE POCKET

None of Whittlesey's officers or men remembered seeing him sleep for long. From mid-August to October, evidence suggests that he rarely indulged in more than the occasional nap. October 1–2 was a typical night. He and McMurtry returned from regimental headquarters well after midnight. Whittlesey then studied battalion returns and field messages before sending a situation report to Stacey. Two hours later he was still awake, poring over maps and assigning personnel for the morning attack. When noncoms roused their men just before five in the morning to a chilly dawn, the major walked about and inspected dispositions. It had been this way for weeks, but he never questioned the grueling routine.

The supporting barrage landed on enemy lines as Whittlesey and McMurtry briefed their officers at half past six. Their commands were terse. A Company, shattered in the previous day's attacks, was to man runner posts. Two companies would maintain pressure on the left side of the ravine, drawing enemy fire and preventing counterattacks. The remainder of 1st battalion, with machine gun sections and McMurtry's 2nd battalion in close support, would press forward along the bottom of the ravine and toward their objective, just about a half-mile ahead, the east-west Binarville-Apremont Road. The majors didn't waste words: every man knew he would do his best.

One test of command is whether men come together or break apart under stress. On that basis alone the 1st and 2nd battalions were exceptionally well led. The several hundred officers and soldiers included men who had been total strangers just weeks earlier. As they moved out at seven o'clock that morning on October 2, however, no hints of disunity emerged.

In delegating assignments, Whittlesey and McMurtry demanded nothing but ability. Lieutenants and noncoms passed on orders, which men obeyed without complaint. Sunshine Division newcomers didn't ask for handholding—in a few days they had learned basics that it had taken months to impart in camp. As the soldiers gathered iron rations from a small mound, filled canteens, and replenished cartridges to 220 rounds per rifle, they didn't talk about their farms, and the old hands didn't reminisce about New York. Instead they griped about things they could share in common. Officers. The enemy. Rain. Cold. Rations of hardtack and corned willy. Muddy water. The present was the only thing that mattered. There were leaders and naysayers. Without realizing it, men were becoming comrades.

No one remembered how it started. Whittlesey probably said, "Let's go!" McMurtry may have grumbled, "O.K." Then the men stood up in their mud-stained uniforms, beneath dripping helmets, some erect and others crouched, slipping around trees or hopping from bush to bush along the sides of the ravine or squelching along its marshy floor. The enemy was strangely silent. Machine gun nests that had resisted them before were empty today, the gun pits smashed and scattered by the supporting artillery.

Whittlesey and McMurtry advanced just behind point. As they had been ordered, no one looked to the right or left. Eyes looked north toward the enemy, or south toward the lines of communication. Whittlesey operated by the book, leaving behind runner or "Cossack" posts of two or three men every two hundred yards. Here and there shabby field-gray figures emerged from the bracken, with hands up—old men the enemy had left behind to offer temporary resistance, or just get them out of the way. Within an hour the doughboys picked up thirty of the seniors and gestured them to the rear. The Americans also "captured" three rickety, mud-caked machine guns. Some of the green troops grew hopeful that the enemy had fled, but officers and experienced men just held their breath. Hardened German troops, they expected, had evaded the artillery bombardment by withdrawing overnight to stronger positions. They soon learned they were right.[1]

Bullets pinged the ground. Men fell. Mortar rounds exploded, and more soldiers toppled. Enemy machine guns opened fire. The holding companies to the left took most of the heat at first, but then the Germans on the ridges above fired into the bottom of the ravine and at the assault parties that Whittlesey had deployed to the east. The farther ahead the Americans pushed the worse it got. The generals had told them to ignore their flanks, but the German bullets commanded attention.

The enemy guns were well sited and unpressured from either direction. At points, small parties of Germans attacked, inflicted losses, and quickly withdrew. If he pushed ahead without regard to flanks or losses, Whittlesey knew, every man in his command would die. Just before ten o'clock he sent a courier with a note for Stacey: "Advance held up by machine-gun fire ... progress impossible without aid from both flanks."

The colonel, practically trembling with stress and fatigue, read Whittlesey's report and fumed, knowing how it would be received further up the line. He phoned the major's report to General Johnson, who listened in silence and hung up. Johnson phoned divisional headquarters. Alexander was away for the moment, but staffers shook their heads disgustedly. When a few German machine guns opened fire, it seemed, American officers just ordered their men under cover, refusing to move until help arrived. Everyone knew how Alexander would respond when he returned.

"Where is General Johnson?" Alexander shouted into the phone at a hapless liaison officer who had been unlucky enough to pick up the receiver. Told that the general was moving his post nearer the front, Alexander exploded. "You tell General Johnson that the 154th Brigade [307th and 308th Regiments] is holding back the French on the left and holding back everything on the right," he lied, "and that the 154th Brigade must push forward to their objective today! By 'must' I mean 'must' and by 'today' I mean 'today' and not next week. You report heavy machine gun fire, but your casualties do not substantiate this. Remember that when you are making these reports." Topping off this piece of bluster, Alexander undercut his argument by huffing that he had not received any casualty reports from the front since yesterday.

A short time later, Alexander got Johnson on the line. "General, that will not do," he yelled. "If that line does not move, I will have to get somebody up there to command it! That line has got to move." Johnson demurred, and Alexander insisted again that the troops on the left and right had moved far ahead. They both knew he was lying, but Johnson agreed to push the brigade forward. Alexander had no idea what was actually happening at the front, let alone a sense of how to solve the problems that the troops faced there. Perhaps if he yelled loudly enough, the echo would pass on down the line to men like Whittlesey. AEF doctrine stated that the will to win was sufficient to victory.[2]

Whittlesey was talking to some of his men in hastily dug funk holes when Second Lieutenant Sherman W. Eager of Bloomington, Indiana, found him and handed over a message from Colonel Stacey. "The commanding general is dissatisfied with your rate of progress" the note said. The attack must resume immediately. Whittlesey's features hardened but he remained calm, asking Eager to accompany him back up the ravine to the battalion command post. There they found McMurtry, who had already seen the orders. He exchanged a look of concern with Whittlesey but said nothing.

Whittlesey phoned Stacey. The exchange was brief. The colonel said the orders could not be changed. "It will only lead to the same thing again—" the major exclaimed, remembering his recent ordeal. "We'll be cut off!" Stacey, who was far nearer collapse than the major, interrupted. "You're just getting panicky," he said. "Proceed with the attack as ordered, Major!" "Alright, I'll attack," Whittlesey said; "but whether you'll hear from me again I don't know." McMurtry, standing grimly alongside, took the silent handset as Whittlesey left the post.[3]

A light mist settled as the troops stood up to move forward. It was just after noon. The American artillery fired a few shells into the forest ahead. This was the "barrage" that the troops must follow. Again the doughboys trudged forward up the ravine. German bullets whipped through the underbrush, dropping men, but Whittlesey and McMurtry hardly noticed. There was no firm line of enemy defense, and they couldn't see any machine gun nests.

It was as if the Germans were luring them in. But orders said to push ahead regardless of losses, and the Americans pushed. Imperceptibly, the enemy flanking fire increased in volume and so did the casualties. But nobody looked at the flanks. Instead they counted steps forward. By one thirty they had advanced three hundred yards along the meandering ravine. The general demanded progress, and that was what he got.

Whittlesey and McMurtry walked side by side as their battalions merged. Shifting back and forth to either side of the ravine, they detailed ad hoc platoons to cover the flanks. Whittlesey thought constantly of his lines of communication, and established regular runner posts. Now and then he stopped to scribble a brief message to Stacey. The men appreciated their officers' dedication, and fought for them. A few isolated German machine gun posts emerged ahead, but instead of halting in despair and exhaustion as their bodies told them to do, the men slowly but determinedly eliminated the enemy posts.

Three hours after the attack had begun, forward parties approached the north end of the ravine. Only then did Whittlesey and McMurtry appreciate the scale of their casualties. Although only eight men had been killed, ten times that number were wounded; most lying in the bracken but a few still stumbling forward. Whittlesey gave no thought to stopping or even slowing down, however; the general said push; he must push. Casualties and flanks meant nothing.

Then the incredible happened.

Topping a rise alongside the ravine's north edge, the two majors discovered a deep, formidable German trench system. It was empty, with not a German soldier in sight. Ahead lay a wooded east-west valley, also apparently uninhabited. They had broken through![4]

General Alexander had been wrong about the flanks. The French on the left and the 307th Regiment on the right were well behind the 308th. But they had been attacking hard, making slow but steady progress and chewing up the enemy defenses. The commander of the opposing German division decided that he had stopped Whittlesey's advance and need not worry about it again for some time. He thinned his line in that sector to no more than a few machine guns, and transferred his reserves to hold off the menaces to the east and west. Whittlesey's aggressive advance caught the Germans by surprise, as the 308th Regiment destroyed the machine gun nests protecting the ravine and broke into the open ground beyond.[5]

The Americans faced a rare opportunity. If reserves had been made available, Alexander might have driven a wedge into the gap and rolled up either of the enemy flanks, rupturing the German defenses in the southern Argonne. But Alexander's instructions had been simple to the point of childishness. He knew no direction but forward, no tactics beyond frontal assault, and no method but to bludgeon the enemy into submission. As a result, in his frustration and impatience he forgot that the enemy would not submit until he had first been defeated, and neglected to give his troops the tools that they needed to win.

Neither Whittlesey nor McMurtry knew that they were advancing into a gap. The way ahead was clear, and if the flanks seemed dicey they must count on their neighbors to clean them up—that was all. Whittlesey ordered a brief pause at the trench to consolidate, and to give the company commanders time to sort out their commands. At three thirty he sent a runner to Stacey with news of his position, but received no instructions in return. This had been the case all day. What was there to say, anyway? Orders had been clear: push forward until the 308th Regiment reached the objective assigned by Alexander. That lay on the opposite side of the east-west valley, labeled on Whittlesey's map as the Charlevaux Ravine. To stop at the lip of the ravine with the objective in sight and no enemy present, because of worries about the flanks, would be to invite instant dismissal as soon as word reached divisional headquarters.

After a brief consultation, Whittlesey sent McMurtry forward with some scouts into the valley to test enemy resistance and get the lie of the land on the opposite side. McMurtry stolidly obeyed. About two hundred yards ahead across the woods he could just see the rise of the ravine's north edge. Along this ran the Binarville-Apremont Road that constituted the regiment's objective. In between lay a swampy lowland that the Germans were unlikely to attempt to defend. Four hundred yards to the west, indistinguishable among the trees, stood an abandoned mill. Otherwise the valley seemed devoid of Germans, or for that matter of French or Americans. McMurtry plunged into the woods and returned after half an hour with confirmation: they were empty and so, apparently, was the slope on the opposite side.

The major and captain conferred again. The men were tired. The sun slid on its downward arc. The way ahead lay open, but so did the flanks. The Germans continued to fire into their right and left rear from along the edges of the Argonne Ravine. As Whittlesey stood contemplating, two German soldiers appeared in the distance to his left, watching him dispassionately with hands in their greatcoat pockets. He pointed them out to a nearby soldier, a diminutive cowboy named Carl Rainwater from the little town of Cut Bank near Glacier, Montana. Rainwater took two shots and spat in disgust. "Missed," he grumbled, adding in a voice loud enough for the major to hear: "I'd do better if I had some chow." The Germans disappeared.[6]

Communications with regimental headquarters so far remained intact. To stop here remained unthinkable, and the marsh ahead offered no kind of shelter. The only option was to push their main force ahead to the north slope of the Charlevaux Ravine and dig in there for the night while trying to detail enough troops to keep open communications to the rear. Not permitted to consider the safety of their flanks, they could only hope that the French and the 307th Regiment would break through on either side, not realizing that the Germans had concentrated the bulk of their forces in either direction.

The light dimmed as the Americans filed down into the Charlevaux Ravine and entered the woods with McMurtry at their head. Whittlesey watched them go. A few minutes later, after fussing over dispositions to his rear, he joined them. Stalking ahead quickly as was his wont, the major followed a path that meandered through the woods between dense clumps of underbrush, beneath trees whose leaves were just beginning to change color. Halfway across he traversed a small footbridge across a little brook. The path continued on the other side and Whittlesey, pausing occasionally to establish runner posts, forged ahead until the path ended at a disused wagon road. Nearby he noticed a little spring and his mind unconsciously registered "water source." His eyes, though, were fixed overhead—steep overhead, where a rock-studded slope ascended over three hundred feet to the road. He could hear and just see his men moving about up there, McMurtry growling orders as they prepared their positions. Whittlesey climbed the slope.[7]

A phone rang in Alexander's headquarters just as Whittlesey arrived at the south end of the Charlevaux Ravine. It was Johnson with a report from the front. Alexander's chief of staff, Colonel John Hannay, held the receiver and looked inquiringly at the general. Alexander shook his head, so Hannay returned to the phone and asked for the report. Johnson told him about the 308th Regiment's advance to the end of the Argonne Ravine, as indicated in reports received from the front, but refused to leave it at that. Still smarting from Alexander's words that morning, he pointed out that, contrary to what the division commander had repeatedly said, the French on the left and the Americans on his right remained well in the rear. "I want him to understand absolutely these conditions," Johnson concluded in a huff. "I know what I'm talking about. I have been ahead from the beginning, I am ahead, and I don't think I deserve the criticism you gave."

Alexander's response, relayed through Hannay, was a sarcastic "Congratulations." Whipped now into a fury, Johnson growled, "No, I do not consider it a matter for congratulation, but I wished to put him absolutely in possession of the facts." "Just do your best," Hannay responded placatingly. "I am, have been, and will continue to do my duty to the best of my ability," Johnson snapped. "And anytime he feels that I am not doing this, he is perfectly free to say so and relieve me." The phone clicked dead. Over the course of the conversation, neither general had wasted a moment discussing how to exploit the evident breakthrough.[8]

As night fell, Whittlesey and McMurtry arrayed their forces into an oblong perimeter about four hundred yards long and eighty yards deep from the base of the hill to just below the road. Above the road, which in some places had been cut out of the hillside, the slope became steeper, even vertical at points. The

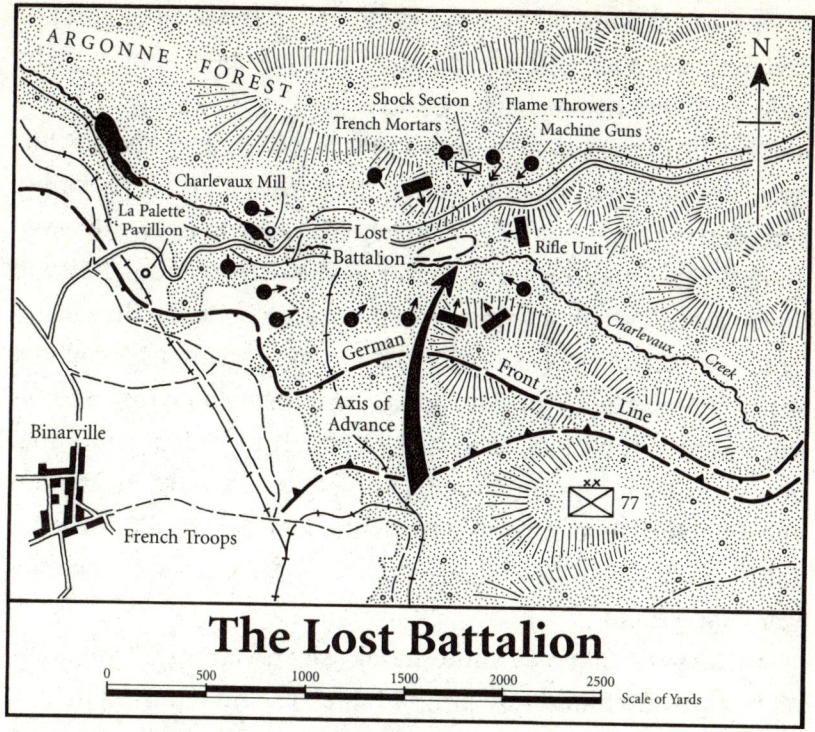

The Lost Battalion

enemy waited above that in unknown numbers, but the two senior American officers believed that by occupying a reverse slope they would at least be secure from enemy artillery.

Whittlesey had little confidence that the forces on his flanks would come up anytime soon, and he especially distrusted the French on his left. He therefore placed his strongest force on that flank, Company H under Lieutenant William J. Cullen—a New York lawyer with a sandpaper personality—along with elements of Companies B and C, and six heavy machine guns from the 306th Machine Gun Battalion. The remnants of A Company guarded the rear downhill toward the ravine. The rest of the troops, Companies E and G, he deployed in freshly dug gun pits and funk holes along the north and east perimeter, supported by more light and heavy machine guns.

The funk holes were in some cases just a few feet apart. Whittlesey insisted particularly on that. Even though their proximity provided the Germans with relatively easy targets, it gave the men a sense of mutual support that they needed. As the men finished digging and settled in with one to three men per hole, they heard ragged firing and occasional shouts around them, especially to their right and left rear. Here and there a thrifty man dug into his iron rations, if he had been lucky enough to collect some that morning. But most went hungry. As night fell, so did a murky and portentous silence, broken only by the whispers and occasional grunts of "Shut up" from sleepy noncoms. McMurtry was characteristically silent.

No one saw Charles Whittlesey fall asleep. Halfway through the night a private found him groggy but alert, and reported that he had heard German voices in the woods "back the way we came." Whittlesey told him that he was probably just having nightmares, and should go back to sleep.[9]

(CHAPTER EIGHT)

SURROUNDED

The Argonne Forest played host to a bevy of unlikely characters at the beginning of October 1918. Manhattan gamblers and gangsters, ballplayers and street hawkers, cowboys and farm hands, delicatessen owners and brokers huddled in the pocket with Major Whittlesey and Captain McMurtry. Journalist Damon Runyon, at home in the Polo Grounds or Madison Square Garden, had just stepped off a boat from America and caught his first sight of the Argonne around October 3. Tennessee mountaineer Alvin York, his training finally complete, marched toward the forest with his comrades of the All-American Division.

No man seemed more out of place in the Argonne Forest on the morning of October 3, however, than Captain Nelson Holderman. Yet none was more purely a soldier. Born in the flatlands of Trumbull, Nebraska, in 1885, Holderman spent his first eight years on the prairie. In 1893 his parents moved him and his five siblings to Tustin, California. Today among the southeastern suburbs of Los Angeles, Tustin was then a sleepy rural backwater where the family grew walnuts, oranges, and apricots on a dusty thirty-acre farm.

Nelson, called "Neb" by family and friends, was a short but handsome and easygoing young man, and he had no trouble with ladies. In 1910 he married an eighteen-year-old girl named Margarite Talbott, and the two soon had a son named Charles. But not much happened in Southern California in those days, and sticking around home was not for Neb. He enjoyed adventure, and the company of other adventurers.

In 1916, apparently with Margarite's blessing, Neb joined the army as a private, telling the army that he was twenty-nine rather than his actual thirty-one years, and served under Pershing's bandit-chasing army along the Mexican border. He loved the military life—surviving photos of Neb in uniform show him happy and at ease—and earned the trust of his fellows for his courage and devotion to duty. By the time the United States entered World War I he had already been promoted to captain.

Neb's journey to frontline service was long and convoluted. After repeated reassignments he ended up in the 40th Sunshine Division. Had it not been for all of the casualties suffered by the 77th Division in the late summer of 1918, Holderman might never have seen the front lines. On September 14, however, he was assigned to the 307th Regiment and ten days later he was placed in command of the regiment's Company K, 3rd Battalion. Two days later he and his men attacked into the Argonne.[1]

Late on the evening of October 2, General Johnson phoned General Alexander. This time the division commander came to the telephone. For once the 154th Brigade had some happy news. Although the 307th Regiment had not made much progress in the day's attacks, the 308th Regiment had burst through the enemy lines and actually achieved its objectives. Neither Alexander or Johnson used the word "breakthrough" and they still did not worry overmuch about Whittlesey's security. In time the

307th Regiment and the 153rd Brigade to the east should be able to reach the same point by pounding through the enemy lines. In the meantime, Alexander told Johnson to send reserve troops of the 307th and 308th Regiments to pry open the gap in the enemy lines and reinforce Whittlesey's command. Alexander also reminded Johnson to try and get rations up to the men.

The reinforcements began moving forward at midnight on October 2–3. Four companies of the 307th Regiment took the lead, headed by Holderman's Company K. He placed First Lieutenant Thomas G. Pool, a husky, fair-haired cotton worker from Port Arthur, Texas, who had transferred with him from the Sunshine Division, in charge of the company advance with Lieutenant Joseph Heuer of Illinois and a few guides. Holderman followed up at the rear. Pool, like Holderman a dedicated soldier, led the company slowly but unerringly up the Argonne Ravine, stepping over bushes, sleeping men, and corpses, and picking his way around strands of barbed wire.

Occasional flare shells lit up the scene, forcing the men to stand still. At one point, Pool heard what he thought were German voices. "No talking, boys," he hissed to his men, who were proceeding in single file with their hands hooked into each other's belts. "Keep quiet and follow the lead man." Not realizing that the leader of the company immediately behind them had stopped to rest and lost contact, or that all of the other reinforcing companies had veered off track, the ninety-eight men of K Company kept doggedly on.

The advance platoon made contact with one of Whittlesey's runner posts at three thirty that morning. Half an hour later they crawled over the shoulders of Argonne Ravine and tumbled into the Charlevaux Ravine. Holderman, who had made his way up and down the line constantly through the night, thus covering twice the amount of ground as his men, sent Pool into the ravine to reconnoiter; but the lieutenant returned to say he could not find Whittlesey's command. Realizing that he had lost touch with the rest of the battalion and unwilling to plunge his men into the woods without knowing their proper location, Holderman ordered his company to dig in.[2]

Daylight found Whittlesey wide awake and conferring in a funk hole with McMurtry, whom he placed in overall charge of the perimeter. Someone produced a precious carton of Salisbury cigarettes, and the men of the headquarters detachment lit up. Elsewhere around the perimeter men used the growing daylight to put the finishing touches to their funk holes, checked ammunition and lines of sight, chatted quietly with each other, or slept. They wondered when the rations would arrive.

Whittlesey sent his sergeant major, grocery store clerk Ben Gaedeke of Yonkers, son of German immigrants, to check on how many men he had lost the previous day, and how many were left. The answers: about one hundred casualties, and about five hundred fit for duty. The major had just finished a futile interrogation of a teenage German soldier who had wandered into the lines, when word arrived that Holderman's Company K had arrived on the other side of the Charlevaux Ravine. But the ravine itself was no longer empty.

Half an hour later Holderman appeared in person, shook hands with Whittlesey and McMurtry, and delivered his report. His company had pushed through overnight to reinforce the major's command. Although he had lost touch with the rest of the battalion he expected they would appear soon. Holderman's calm

Alvin C. York
(*Library of Congress*)

Alvin C. York, formal portrait with
medals (*Library of Congress*)

Young Damon Runyon
(© *Getty Images*)

Troops of the 308th Regiment, 77th Division, pose with pet lambs in between drills at Camp Upton, Long Island, New York, in 1917. (*Library of Congress*)

The 308th Regiment marches down New York City's Fifth Avenue and off to war, February 1918. (*National Archives*)

Major Charles Whittlesey in France, 1918 (*National Archives*)

Major George McMurtry returns home from France, 1919. (*National Archives*)

Major General Robert Alexander, commanding the 77th Division, parades in New York City with his staff, 1919. (*National Archives*)

The battle-tested 77th Division on parade in New York City, April 1919. (*National Archives*)

exterior didn't betray his nerves. He had lost contact with the trailing companies early in the evening; they could be anywhere. The trek across the ravine that morning had been perilous, and signs indicated that German troops were entering it in force.

As he scanned the perimeter, Holderman's trained eye found much to criticize. The position seemed subject to enemy observation and vulnerable to attack. Whittlesey's lines of communication, resupply, and retreat were uncertain. But he said nothing about this, perhaps recognizing that criticism wouldn't do any good. Instead, Holderman projected a can-do demeanor that reassured well-intentioned amateurs. Even Whittlesey relaxed for a time. "Oh, then we're alright," said McMurtry, and meant it. "Where do you want me?" asked Holderman, and Whittlesey ordered him to reinforce the right flank.

Whittlesey's confidence dissipated as Holderman departed to assemble his command. The first glints of sun crept through the foliage, and enemy rifle fire increased in intensity. Shells crashed behind the perimeter: ranging fire—the enemy was trying to find them. Fortunately, as Whittlesey had hoped their position on the declivity kept the Americans safe from long-distance artillery. A little later, the doughboys caught brief glimpses of German troops rushing in small parties around the flanks—not north, away from the fighting, but south into the ravine. During the encirclement a few days earlier, the enemy had seemed content to wait it out. But not this time. One thought occupied every soldier's mind: will they come?[3]

Whittlesey's senses were acute to the danger. He could not afford to await developments. Given time to assemble, the enemy could attack the American perimeter in overwhelming force, or at least cut communications with the rest of the division. The major's first instinct was to detach his strongest company, H, along with Company E in an attempt to punch a hole through to the left rear and form a chain for bringing up reinforcements and supplies.

When the major mentioned his plan, the usually silent McMurtry spoke up. Detaching two companies, he warned, would seriously weaken the perimeter. Better just to send the best company, E: the one he had drilled himself, the one that had shown its stuff at the Hippodrome. Efficiency counted over numbers. Whittlesey had a level of comfort too; he knew and liked E company's interim commander, Lieutenant Karl Wilhelm. Nodding his agreement to McMurtry, Whittlesey said to get Wilhelm over to his hole.

A tall, balding, athletic patent lawyer and former Cornell University student from Buffalo, New York, Lieutenant Wilhelm had been one of the original Plattsburg volunteers. He and Whittlesey understood each other: they came from similar backgrounds and had imbibed the same ethos of responsible leadership at Plattsburg. In a hurried conversation, Whittlesey told the lieutenant to assemble his company, make to the left rear, reestablish contact with the runner posts, and for God's sake hurry up reinforcements, food, and plenty of ammunition. How Wilhelm made it happen was up to him—just see to it. Wilhelm saluted and departed. A few minutes later, Holderman's doughboys slipped into their funk holes and gun pits.

Wilhelm was a good officer, and his men moved efficiently. But they were tired, and when a man is tired he doesn't think straight. The soldiers slipped down the slope and walked cautiously through the ravine, sensitive to the presence of enemy soldiers on every side. They had just reached the south rim and begun climbing through the woods up the other side when a gruff voice suddenly called out:

"Americans?"

They fell quiet for a moment before Alfio Iraci, a plump little Sicilian immigrant who made his living as a pants maker on the Lower East Side, couldn't stand the silence anymore.

"Yeah."

"What Company?"

"E," called a few men.

More silence. Then the voice whispered urgently to another, and another, and the doughboys could hear bodies moving hurriedly on either side. Private Louis Probst, a German-speaking Brooklyn dockyard worker, turned to Wilhelm and exclaimed, "He's giving them our range!"

A shower of potato masher grenades flew down the hill and landed among them, followed by a string of explosions and agonized screams. Machine guns and rifles opened fire from above, right, left... and behind. Giving or following orders was out of the question. Many fell. Some fired back, and collapsed; charged at the unseen enemy, and tumbled to the ground; or just ran. Many of the runners fell too, but five men including Wilhelm, who was shot in the hand, managed to find their way, after dodging and crawling all day and the following night, back to the pocket. All the remaining men of Company E, McMurtry's personal command and the finest in the regiment, were killed or captured.[4]

Whittlesey didn't realize that he had sent Company E to destruction, gravely weakening his own position. The crackle of rifle fire and explosion of grenades would have been audible to him, but probably just blended into the other battle noises in the background. His mind wandered elsewhere. Just at sunrise he received a message from Stacey, written twelve hours earlier, commending his progress and promising supplies, but showing no awareness of his predicament. Still, it was news from the outside world.

Strangely refusing to engage with the reality of his command's predicament, Whittlesey commenced scribbling messages and dispatching runners to follow Company E to the rear. McMurtry, who had decided with Holderman's arrival that everything was "O.K." and refused to change his mind, remained sympathetic as always to his men's needs and dispatched a fifteen-man ration party. All of them disappeared, but their loss didn't register with either officer until much later.

A whistle, a whump, and crash of branches and debris stunned the men in Whittlesey's command hole. Another explosion followed, and another. For a few minutes, everyone wondered if the enemy artillery had somehow managed to find them on the reverse slope. Then it began to register that these shells were coming from one weapon—not ahead, but behind. A few more minutes passed before Whittlesey, scanning the ravine with his binoculars, spotted the gun from its smoke. It was a trench mortar, one of the only effective heavy infantry weapons in this terrain.

One shell followed another. Most missed, but one eviscerated two men in a funk hole. Shrapnel cut chunks out of anyone foolish enough to stand. Just as Whittlesey ordered a detachment to go take out the mortar, more worrisome news arrived: all morning, scouts on the perimeter's southern edge had been trying to reconnect with the runner posts left in the ravine. Only now did they decide conclusively that all the runner posts had fallen victim to the enemy.

Communications obstacles plagued soldiers in the First World War. Wireless technology remained in its infancy. Telephones were in widespread use, but shellfire easily cut the lines. Semaphores were hard to use in low visibility. Horses could not easily navigate the cratered front lines, and men were slow, vulnerable, and easily confused. The Germans had some success with messenger dogs, usually (appropriately enough) German shepherds. The Allies preferred pigeons, although the Germans used them too.

Homing pigeons have been used in warfare since ancient times. Trained to roost at headquarters, they could be released miles away and return unerringly. Carrying messages attached to their legs, they could flap over battlefields almost invisibly, taking minutes to cover ground that it would take men, horses, or dogs hours to traverse. But it was dangerous work. Poison gas, shrapnel, and bullets easily killed the birds, and soldiers on both sides trained raptors to pounce on airborne messengers. Thousands and possibly millions of birds died in the line of duty. Some, such as a pigeon known only as "2709" who carried a critical message for British forces fighting in Flanders in 1917 despite mortal wounds, received medals for gallantry.

Every dead or injured bird brought tragedy to the men detailed as pigeon handlers, and to those detailed to carry the pigeons to the front in wicker baskets and care for them under often unspeakable conditions. Their only consolation was that when they released a bird they had no choice but to forget and move on. The pigeons could only fly from the front to headquarters, and not vice versa.[5]

Charles Whittlesey cherished the small contingent of pigeons under his command. So did his handlers. They were a precious commodity that had proved invaluable during his previous encirclement. Nobody knew this better than pigeon handler Private Omer Richards, who carried a wicker coop containing eight birds during the advance to Charlevaux Ravine. A native French Canadian who had arrived in the United States in 1910 at age sixteen and worked as a lumberman in Ogdensburg, New York, Richards cared tenderly for the pigeons. He named each one of them and spoke to them in his native French. Each of the pigeons that Whittlesey ordered him to dispatch disappeared forever, and so Richards saved his favorite for last—a two-year-old black and gray English racing pigeon named Cher Ami.[6]

Richards found himself returning to the coop again and again on October 3. Realizing with a shock that his runners were not getting through and frantic that Stacey, Johnson, and Alexander should receive word of his predicament, Whittlesey turned to Richards and ordered him to prepare his pigeons. The first pigeon departed at 8:50 A.M. with a message giving his coordinates—accurately—and asking for artillery support. Another went out at 10:45 A.M., reporting his coordinates again, noting German infantry movements and the troublesome mortar, and strongly suggesting that the command was about to be surrounded. Knowing how headquarters frowned on any suspicion of unsteadiness, the major tried to convey urgency without panic.

He would hold, but he needed help as soon as possible.[7]

Holderman meanwhile worked his way back slowly through the ravine with a detachment from Company K, trying to find and take out the German mortar. They were able to cross the footbridge and move up the ravine's southern slope. Then they too heard German voices on the ridge above them. Unlike the well-drilled but naïve men of Company E, Holderman's soldiers kept quiet, cutting through a strand of German wire and ascending the ridge.

But the attempt was futile. The Germans sensed that something was under way and their machine guns opened fire, although they were unable to locate the Americans well enough to deploy the devastating grenades. Holderman tried to press the attack until he realized that the Germans were working around his own flanks to cut him off. Then he extricated his men in sections like a pro, while Pool, fighting hard and cussing savagely, carried out a deft rearguard action that saved the lot. By early afternoon Holderman had returned to the pocket with a few men killed and several wounded, but his command largely intact.[8]

As Holderman's command limped back into the pocket, grim but determined under a field commander they clearly admired, Whittlesey took stock. Holderman and Pool delivered their report. The enemy had infiltrated into their rear in large numbers and probably sealed the pocket. Company E had disappeared, and there was no guarantee—in fact it looked increasingly unlikely—that Lieutenant Wilhelm's men had made it through. Company K was mauled but intact. The runner posts had all been wiped out. Wounded men piled up as enemy fire increased. Driving home the lesson, the mortar ticked up its shellfire.

It was a quiet, tense discussion. The troops might try to pull out, but if so they would fight a hidden enemy on his own ground. And, as Whittlesey pointed out, it would mean leaving the wounded behind. The major felt certain in his own mind that he had no choice but to order the men to hold their ground until relieved; but he did not yet have the confidence in his authority, especially around Holderman, whose ease of command threatened to cast Whittlesey into shadow, to argue the case on his own account. Instead, the major took pains to consult his officers while pointing out that pulling back now would violate standing orders to keep moving forward or where necessary hold, but never turn back.[9]

To ensure everyone knew the stakes, Whittlesey passed this message on to all of his company commanders: "Our mission is to hold this position at all costs. No falling back. Have this understood by every man in your command."[10]

The devastating truth behind that favorite military cliché, "at all costs," soon became apparent.

※

At around three o'clock, the American outposts just below the road heard sounds of movement atop the ridge. After a few minutes of silence, grenades tumbled though the foliage and a series of explosions drove the Metropolitans deeper into their funk holes. They waited, but nothing happened at first. A few minutes later, more rustling in the underbrush, this time intermixed with German voices, became apparent to the right and left as well as above. Not realizing how many of their own former countrymen now wore American uniforms, the Germans carelessly called out commands that doughboys translated and whispered along the lines. Machine guns were primed and sited along probable axes of attack. Former grocers, laundrymen, cowboys, clerks, and college athletes settled deeper into their holes, held their rifles, kept their eyes open, and waited. When the assault came they were ready.

German rifles and machine guns opened fire all along the perimeter, including some recently emplaced in the valley behind. The trench mortar stepped up its volley too. Grenades tumbled in again from above, left, and right. But the Germans were firing blind. In a few places they scored lucky hits, but for the most part the bullets and shells were absorbed by the underbrush and the trees. If a man kept his head down, he was probably okay. Only just below the road did the doughboys present easy targets. Several of them scrambled down the hill to take cover in the underbrush farther downslope.

But this was just a preliminary. Off to the left, a German non-com or officer began calling roll, to be answered by voices at various points along the perimeter. The call went on for so long that it became ridiculous, and the Americans wondered if the Germans were trying to put one over on them by making their force seem bigger than it really was. One irrepressible Metropolitan interrupted one name to yell, "He fucked off!" and nearby Americans erupted in laughter. Moments later the German soldiers attacked, moving in short rushes from cover to cover.

The enemy's goal at this point was not to storm the position—they had no desire to take useless casualties—but to panic the Americans into opening fire and revealing their positions. The tactic worked. Rifles opened fire all along the line, but the Germans didn't worry about those. It was the machine guns that counted. The six tripod-mounted heavy guns that Whittlesey had posted on the left perimeter and the two on the right all opened fire, usually at targets they could not see and without regard to ammunition. "Take it easy, take it easy," Whittlesey shouted. "Don't get excited. Hold for clear fields of fire; make it count." But to no avail. The results were disastrous.

As soon as the American machine gun positions became apparent, German machine guns targeted them with counterfire. The enemy mortarmen watched carefully too, and not many minutes passed before well-directed shellfire peppered the pocket, silencing one machine gun after another. German infantry followed this up by rushing the suppressed guns. In a few cases the American crews abandoned their weapons. At other points, they stuck to the guns doggedly, but at severe cost.

One who paid the price was Lieutenant Maurice Revnes, a stage manager with Fulton Theatre on Broadway and one of

Plattsburg's tired businessmen. A short, dark, and slender man who came from a privileged family in Queens and had celebrated his twenty-eighth birthday in the forest just five days earlier, Revnes had little practical experience with machine guns but a deep reservoir of personal bravery. Rushing to the left perimeter and discovering the machine gun outposts crumbling, he calmly directed the removal of casualties and assigned men to take up guns that their comrades had abandoned. Revnes then sat down to take personal charge of a machine gun—all under heavy enemy fire.

The lieutenant held off the Germans until a red-hot sledgehammer hit his leg twice. Revnes looked down to find his calf exploded into a lump of hamburger and his foot nearly torn off at the ankle. As doughboys dragged their lieutenant back inside the pocket, McMurtry arrived with fifteen men and took the machine gun posts under his control just as the enemy fire began slackening off. After half an hour, the attack ended.[11]

Dazed, Whittlesey ordered Private Richards to prepare another pigeon for a message to the rear. In it the major detailed the exact quantities of ammunition he needed—as if he had any chance of getting it short of a full-scale relief operation—and listed his casualties. Strangely, he said he only had one killed, although there had been many more than that, and that he had 245 effectives when he actually had over twice that number. Just after the bird fluttered skyward the Germans renewed their attack.

It was five o'clock. At about this time in New York City or the mountain west, the men would have been returning from work and washing up for dinner. Instead, on empty stomachs, they again raised their weapons. Once again the cocky German troops were unsubtle in their preparations, calling to each other boisterously and laughing. Then, with a sudden barrage of grenades hurled from the trees from every direction, they rushed through the trees like human torpedoes. Grim faced in field gray and coal-scuttle helmets, the Germans probed for weak points, pausing to fire at Americans foolish enough to reveal themselves in profile against the trees.

Grenades exploded with pounding echoes as gunfire erupted and wounded and frightened men cried out. In such moments, each man only had time to take in his immediate neighbors, who formed indistinct shapes glimpsed from the corners of his eyes. Sensations crowded one upon another: heart pounding, firing at dashing figures, hoping that each one is not launching himself directly at you. The enemy bayonets formed a tangible presence even when unseen, as if a man could feel one thrust into his gut. For the unlucky, a moment revealed a German form at close range, followed by split-second horror as he tried to fend off bayonets and fight with any available weapon.

Machine gunners were the only doughboys with a strong sense of placement and geography. The Germans concentrated their efforts on the left, hoping that most of the American guns had been wiped out or abandoned. They were wrong. McMurtry, quietly insistent, and Cullen, barking savage commands, complemented each other as they whipped the gunners into total efficiency.

Each gun crew member had to be aware of a dozen things at once: of his field of fire and the approach of the enemy; of the riflemen in support, ahead and on the flanks; of the yank and kick of the gun. Has it jammed? Is it overheating? Is it out of ammunition? Has the enemy spotted my position? The gunners' mouths felt as if they were full of grit and oil, but only afterward did they become aware of their raging thirst. More than anything, the machine gunners knew that they were the enemy's primary targets. With this came a strange mixture of power, and of fear and vulnerability. All of these senses and emotions passed through McMurtry's mind before he took a bullet in the leg below his kneecap. Hardly anyone knew it had happened except him, and it was not his habit to complain.

Whittlesey and the men at his command hole felt sensations of a different sort. Practically speaking, there was little they could do. They received reports of guns knocked out and of points under pressure, but they had no reserves to allocate. Their ears more than their eyes monitored the steadily shrinking pocket, and the lapping waves of enemy pressure. They heard and felt the concussion of explosions from grenades and trench mortars. But most of the time they could only sit, staring grimly about, subconsciously registering their surroundings, maybe in their hearts wondering if the time would come soon when they would have to direct the last stand.

As darkness fell, the enemy gunfire petered out and the doughboys wilted in exhaustion. Wounded men lay everywhere: Germans along the perimeter, and Americans in the pocket. Their cries filled the air. Soldiers—there were no doctors and just three designated amateur "first aid men"—tended to their comrades, adding bonds of nurse and patient to those they already shared. Soldiers crawled from hole to hole. There was no total relaxation, for German snipers stayed behind to administer the ultimate price to any doughboy lazy enough to forget the danger.

McMurtry, who had bandaged his own knee, hobbled over to Whittlesey's command hole where the two men engaged in a quiet conference that Holderman and some of the lieutenants soon joined. Nobody wasted any words on criticism or praise, or spoke of the possibility of having to hold out for days. Whittlesey ordered a patrol to test the enemy lines, though he knew it was hopeless, and urged the officers to tell their men to search German corpses for spare provisions.[12]

At night, only two types of soldiers were quiet: the unwounded, who could only look about and pant with exhaustion—and the dead. The wounded called out involuntarily as the numbness faded from the first shock of their injuries. Whittlesey, after his officers departed on their errands, slipped out of his hole to visit and where possible help care for the men. On each of these rounds, which he continued regularly through another unsleeping night, his mind took in each dead body, each suffering man, and branded each sensation permanently within his memory. Somewhere deep down the thought registered, inarticulately: "This man is going through this because of me." Me—unwounded, unmindful of his own sufferings and so imagining that he does not suffer even as he feels the pressure of the predicament, of leadership and responsibility, weighing down upon him.

McMurtry, like everyone in the pocket, came face to face with himself. But on the surface, at least, he was untroubled. Like Holderman, but in a different way, he demonstrated an elemental confidence in himself and what he was doing, and transmitted this reassurance to his men. To the commanding officer he increasingly became a bedrock presence. Holderman was an effective and respectful subordinate, but he was also a newcomer from another regiment, who gave first attention to his own men. McMurtry had lost his company. But more than that, in the several weeks they had spent together he had become Whittlesey's friend—and more than that, his comrade.

September had been cold and wet. The ground was still spongy. Now, though, the men remembered that summer had passed just two weeks earlier. It had not rained for a few days, and three hours of intermittent combat had badly dehydrated them. Instinctively the doughboys began to look about, swirling the little water maybe left in their canteens. Some shared with the wounded, whether still alert or dying, and wondered if they should have kept what little remained for themselves. Imagination became their worst enemy, as they felt growing thirst and contemplated staying here for hours, all night—maybe days! Word passed around. Are there any springs? Maybe we could dig one. No, we're too far up on the hill, there's nothing here. Any dead Germans with canteens? We're sure we killed dozens, but now for some reason we can't see any though the major told us to search their bodies for food. Their friends must have dragged them off.

Finally, someone—maybe several at around the same time—remembered the spring they had passed on the previous day alongside the wagon road at the bottom of the slope. There's fresh water back there. German snipers are about, but surely if a man keeps his head down? Some asked their officers or noncoms for permission to go for the spring. No, not safe, the Plattsburgers said; stick it out. Other doughboys knew better than to ask. An officer can't watch everything. After a whisper to a neighbor, or a promise to a wounded man begging for water, individual soldiers began slipping off.

The Germans did not at first recognize what was happening. Some doughboys reached the spring, drank and filled their canteens, and crawled back up the hill. As their numbers increased, though, one of the Germans caught on. A rifle report cracked through the forest, and an American at the spring slumped over dead. Other doughboys making their way down stopped and carefully retraced their routes. They weren't yet that desperate. But then they had to return and tell wounded buddies that they couldn't bring the water they had promised, and watch them quickly turn their heads to conceal the despair on their faces.

Night settled in over a pocket filling with an increasing sense of dread. Although the men were exhausted and desperate for rest, now that silence had come the hours seemed to drag. These were the moments that they experienced most intensely. They were also the most powerfully shared. In the years to come, veterans of the Argonne pocket especially would remember the nights. They lived stories that could never be told, except to other men who had been there, and that was a solace. For those who could not or did not allow themselves to share, however, men like Major Charles Whittlesey, these hours would in time coalesce into a dark presence that beckoned just for them.

(CHAPTER NINE)

FRIENDLY FIRE

Dawn's feeble glow revealed shadowy figures crawling from hole to hole, and in some places prone shapes that had still been moving at nightfall. A little rain had fallen overnight, not enough to fill canteens, but some filtered through the forest canopy to dampen parched lips. The last of the food had disappeared the previous day. Cries of the wounded had continued through much of the night but faded toward dawn, to be replaced by low groans, whispered conversations, complaints, and reassurances.

The few fresh bandages that the first-aid men had carried into battle two days earlier were now all in use. Men unraveled their puttees—strips of protective cloth wrapped around their legs from ankles to knees—and used them to bind wounds, or tore off shreds of uniforms. The dead could not be buried properly, but were shifted as gently as possible toward the pocket's center, close to Major Whittlesey's command post, and pushed into shallow graves or covered with leaves, the telltale mounds constantly visible.

Each man bore a burden of personal responsibility to help his fellows. No one could shirk and not be noticed—and no one wanted to. But the officers bore the heaviest burden. Many of them were wounded, but injured or not, the men looked to them for leadership. Lieutenant Revnes's leg throbbed white-hot with pain. McMurtry, less badly wounded, was in agony too but refused to display any discomfort. His gruff certainty emanated from inside himself. Holderman carried the burden naturally. He was in his element, devoted to his company and willing to play his part for the whole. Lieutenant Cullen didn't give a damn if his men hated him so long as they did as they were told, and in his own way he got the best out of them.

Whittlesey was different, and not just because he bore the greatest burden of responsibility. A natural loner, he had constantly to play a role. But this was no collegiate club or legal boardroom. It was a cruel, dank pocket of the forest where half a thousand men, surrounded by enemies, depended upon him for their existence. The intensity of the major's battles to fend off negativity betrayed the power of the emotions he felt inside.

Alone among the men in the pocket, Whittlesey shaved every day and tried to keep his uniform spotless, feeling that this was expected of a commander. He must have dozed off from time to time, but took care that his men found him instantly alert and available if they needed anything. Endlessly giving of himself, he refused to let one negative word pass his lips. This was not the expression of a trained professional soldier who had dedicated himself to the service, but of a civilian turned amateur soldier who believed that a privileged individual was duty bound to his country and the welfare of his fellow men. The sacrifice did not come easy.

In maintaining this façade, Whittlesey became wrapped in a web of self-delusion. Action, he knew, was essential. A man who sat in a hole all day lost his edge and became prone to depression. At Plattsburg, the army had told officer trainees to maintain the psychological upper hand by patrolling constantly. That was part of the reason why Whittlesey ordered early morning patrols to test the enemy positions around the pocket. He also embraced any hope that the Germans might have left a gap in the perimeter or, better yet, had withdrawn. The men who carried out these patrols, however, had trouble venturing outside the illusory safety of the pocket and became increasingly gun shy. Time and again they crawled off into the woods, looked around for a little while, and returned to tell the major they hadn't seen anything.

It took a while before Whittlesey realized what was happening. When his first morning patrols returned at about seven o'clock and reported that the forest was quiet, the major leapt to the conclusion that the enemy might have withdrawn. At seven twenty-five, then, he sent off another pigeon reporting to division: "Our patrols indicate Germans withdrew during this night. Sending further patrols now to verify this."[1]

Actually the situation had not improved. The remainder of the two battalions that Holderman had left behind on the first night had made no progress whatsoever. And though Alexander had received Whittlesey's pigeon messages and ordered the division to advance to the major's relief with all of his usual bluster, his force was utterly exhausted. Ordered to attack and relieve their comrades, soldiers stood up, moved forward, came under fire, and lay down again. Despite their good intentions they could do no more. Bullying no longer availed with officers who were mentally deflated and so lacked drive.

Elsewhere, the remainder of First Army spent the first few days of October resting, but not the Metropolitans, and now they had simply reached their physical limits. Only the much despised French, well-trained in the art of conserving energy and resources, refused to give up. To Whittlesey's left rear the French launched persistent attacks that failed to break the German lines but applied so much pressure that the enemy had to divert reserves in that direction and so postpone active operations against the pocket.[2]

None of the men in the pocket knew about the methodical French and stalled American attempts to relieve them. The sound of distant shellfire was more or less constant, and often drowned out by shelling closer at hand. The Germans had pulled back a little distance and didn't seem ready to attack again just yet, but the Chinese water torture of intermittent shelling never let up. Two more trench mortars transformed what had been a solo act into a trio, but fortunately their accuracy was poor and many of the shells plunked into the mud and stayed there without exploding—duds. Men hunkered down, waited, rested, and hoped somebody would get them out, but this of course left them vulnerable not just to creeping demoralization but to surprise attack. Whittlesey kept dispatching patrols, and by midmorning they discovered conclusively that the Germans had pulled back but not departed. Otherwise, the patrols incurred casualties without result and so increased the number of wounded who had to be cared for.

While the constant activity may have kept the men out of the doldrums, they became increasingly cynical. Attitude was natural to the New Yorkers, many of them the same guys who had interrupted the bandmaster's impromptu concert at the Polo Grounds by chanting for soda pop and then catcalled Boyce's Tigers. German soldiers who tried to unsettle the surrounded Metropolitans by shouting orders or insults were paid back tenfold, often in their own language and always in a uniquely Metropolitan style. At one point, a German yelled in typical B-movie fashion for the Americans to order their coffins. Private George F. Speich, a construction foreman of mixed French-German parentage from Company K, responded with a snarling stream of German invective and concluded by reflecting on the enemy's propensity for uncontrolled flatulence. Other doughboys picked up on these phrases and repeated them gleefully, punctuated with well-placed rifle shots.[3]

It was this shared sense of attitude, more than shellfire or Whittlesey's patrols, that established and maintained the Metropolitans' psychological dominance over the enemy. It was as if they claimed the Argonne as their own domain, like a run-down neighborhood on the Lower East Side. They hated it, but they were damned if anyone could make them leave until they felt good and ready. This cynical bravado became the glue binding the men together. And as this corner of the Argonne became a microcosm of the big city, it absorbed the westerners and country boys into the same sassy outlook. Soon they all reacted, talked, and thought the same way—all Metropolitans, all Americans. They were not Whittlesey's textbook soldiers, but it hardly mattered. He never became one of them, but they looked up to him all the same. Slowly, without being aware, they built invincible mutual respect.

Thinking up creative curses to hurl at the enemy provided no outlet for Whittlesey, who sat and pondered alone. By midmorning his spirits had tumbled again, partly as a by-product of fatigue and lack of sleep. The need to reach out, even to a listener who could not reply, was compelling. He turned to Private Richards, told him to prepare another bird, and penned a message redolent with solitary thoughts and hints of creeping despair. Correcting his earlier message, he said that the "Germans are still around us, though in smaller numbers." But the overall situation was awful. "Cover bad if we advance up the hill and very difficult to move the wounded if we change position. Situation is cutting into our strength rapidly. Men are suffering from hunger and exposure and the wounded are in very bad condition. Cannot support be sent at once?" And off the bird flew at ten thirty-five. As it departed Richardson looked into his coop: only two birds remained.[4]

Noon passed. Food was a memory. Soldiers scraped invisible remnants from ration tins they had scraped several times before, and searched pockets and haversacks they had already turned inside out. The sky, incredibly, was blue; but though they scanned frequently no one saw an airplane. The doughboys looked through the trees for approaching enemy, or for the patrols heralding the dreamed-for relief. They saw nothing but kept looking. Men watched in shifts while their buddies tried to sleep, and the wounded struggled to rest. The Germans seemed quiet too. It was a waiting game.

Shellfire became audible at about two thirty in the afternoon, landing on the hills well south across the ravine. It had happened before; the Germans back there were getting pasted again. Sleeping soldiers settled deeper into their funk holes with satisfied grunts, while those on watch or stretching their tired muscles in the open turned onto their backs to watch the smoke rise. Presently the volume increased as a tendril of shellfire crept forward from the ridge and peppered the Charlevaux Ravine. This was good—must be the artillery was cutting a corridor straight through to the trapped men so that relief could force its way in or Whittlesey could order them out. As the explosions crept ever closer, however, soldiers shifted nervously, looking to their noncoms and to their officers. The horror that the men saw in their officers' faces sent their own stomachs plummeting.

The first shell hit the perimeter not far from Whittlesey's hole, exploding with a horrifying crack that raised a collective howl of terror and sent soldiers scrambling for the closest cover available. A few more shells hit nearby, then dozens, then too many to count. Trees shattered, scattering lethal wooden splinters in all directions along with shrapnel and fiery blossoms of high explosive. Concussions slammed like repeated blows to the head from a two-by-four. Many funk holes filled to overflowing with men; but they had not been dug to keep out heavy artillery fire, which compared to trench mortars like lead weights to whiffle balls.

Soldiers were blasted to pieces outright, or horribly torn. Even those who escaped the splinters felt their bodies dissolving to jelly as they lost control of their senses, their muscles, and their digestive tracts. The Germans had been through this kind of thing before, and on a huge scale. That was why they dug trenches and deep, impervious dugouts. Pershing's soldiers, though, had been raised on the cult of the offensive. Any earthworks they built were merely temporary, to shelter men in the short pauses between endless attacks. In theory, the best way out of a bombardment was to move forward and take on the enemy in his own trench. No one had taught the officers what to do when they were being shelled by their own guns.

Again the men looked to their officers, who never showed greater courage or inspired such strength. Not one of them panicked. Instead of looking to their own safety, the officers sought out their men and dragged the wounded and terror stricken into cover. Mostly all they could do was keep straight-faced and yell words of encouragement. It would end soon, they said; the men would be safe if they kept under cover. Just wait it out.

George McMurtry found his moment. Without flinching, fully embracing the role of command, he clumped with his bandaged knee from hole to hole across the pocket. Hurried but incapable of moving fast—injured or not, nobody ever saw Captain McMurtry run—he simply ignored the explosions, moving doggedly back and forth as if there were a small fire somewhere that he wanted to put out. His pug-ugly, begrimed face with upraised eyebrows would have been enough to make anyone laugh under better circumstances. At one point, he spied a terrified soldier whimpering in his funk hole, paused, and reached down to shove his mug in the soldier's face. When the soldier opened his eyes McMurtry gave him a slow, wry Irish wink. "Just like the 4th of July, isn't it soldier?" he shouted above the din, and then got up and hobbled on. "After that," the man later remembered, "I wasn't so much afraid."[5]

Major Whittlesey stayed where he needed to be—at his command hole. Hopes that the shellfire would just move on faded fast. Soon the German trench mortars joined in. With all of his willpower the major shut out the surrounding chaos and forced himself to concentrate. Pulling a message book out of his tunic, he slowly began writing, crafting each word carefully, forcing clarity to his prose. There was no room for panic, less for uncertainty. It was up to him to make the terror stop.

Private James F. Larney, an engineer from Watertown, New York, who had made it into the army despite having lost part of his foot in a prewar train accident and now served as a signalman with battalion headquarters, watched Whittlesey write. As he did so he noticed a small stream of blood oozing down the side of the major's nose. "Major, are you alright?" he yelled. Whittlesey ignored him. Larney yelled again with the same result. On the third try, which the private shouted directly into his ear over the crash of the bombardment, Whittlesey reacted. Touching a finger to his nose, he stared at the dab of blood and after a brief shake of his head he returned to his writing.

"Our own artillery is dropping a barrage directly on us," the message read, repeating the pocket's coordinates. "For Heaven's sake, stop it."

Tearing out the message, Whittlesey turned and handed it to Richards. "Get it out right away!" he rapped. With trembling hands, and the major and surrounding men staring at his every move, the pigeon handler rolled the paper and slipped it into an aluminum tube for fastening to the bird's leg. Just as he reached into the coop and seized one of the two remaining birds, however, a shell exploded nearby, hurling debris. Stunned, Richards opened his hands and in an instant the bird flew beyond the reach of his desperate lunge.

Whittlesey could hardly believe his eyes and barely maintained control. He glared at Richards, at the disappearing bird. "Fuck!" he spat.

"I'm sorry, sir!" Richards nearly sobbed, and turned back to the coop for the last bird, his darling Cher Ami. Straining to hold the pigeon tight but not too tight, he fastened the tube to its leg, checked to make certain it was secure, and then released the bird to the sky.

Cher Ami flapped frantically, circled twice, flew a short distance down the hill, and perched in a tree.

Whittlesey and Richards stared at the bird and at each other. So did a dozen pairs of nearby eyes. "What the hell!" Richards exclaimed. "Can't you do something?" the major yelped.

"Hey! Hey! Go on there!" Richards shouted in his French accent. Picking up a stick, he hurled it at the bird, but Cher Ami just fluttered to a higher branch and sat there staring at them, obviously in panicked paralysis. The major, the men, threw more sticks and rocks—not too large—as explosions continued to land nearby.

Finally, shouting curses that merged into the surrounding chorus of desperately swearing men, Richards ran down the hill and hurled himself into the tree. In a moment he arrived just below Cher Ami's branch, shaking it savagely and shrieking at the top of his lungs.

"Come on you goddamn bird! *Fly!*"

And Cher Ami flew.

As the pigeon flapped over the battlefield it seemed to every watching soldier as if artillery, mortars, machine guns, and rifles all zeroed in on it at that moment. Air eddies from exploding shells hurled the bird this way and that. Just as Cher Ami began crossing over Charlevaux Ravine a huge shell exploded beneath it, simultaneously snuffing out the lives of five doughboys and sending the bird—minus one eye and one leg, and with a piece of shrapnel in its breast—plummeting crazily toward the treeline, where it disappeared.[6]

The shelling continued and more men died. Ben Gaedeke, Whittlesey's trusted sergeant major, was blown to tiny pieces. Wounded men crawled in from the outer perimeter toward what passed for an aid station below the command hole, where they joined an ever-widening circle of suffering. As German infantry in the surrounding woods gleefully contributed their own rifle and machine gun fire to the barrage, someone among the wounded constructed a shelter out of corpses. Others joined in and the macabre wall rose steadily higher. McMurtry, recognizing that the sense of panic here was greatest, ceased pacing around the pocket and settled with the wounded to try and keep them calm.

Above the din the men heard the noise of an airplane engine overhead and strained to see if it was Allied or German. It might have been either. Whittlesey nevertheless turned to Private Larney and told him to lay out white-cloth signal panels that were standard issue for any headquarters detachment. Larney quickly obeyed. Others heard the plane too, and tried to signal it by frantically waving bloody bandages and filthy rags. But the plane just buzzed off.

McMurtry hauled himself up the hill to what remained of Whittlesey's command post. What, he asked, if they tried to move the men down along the ridge away from the worst of the shellfire? Some of the men were already trying to do so of their own volition. Whittlesey, hitherto uptight and speaking only in clipped tones, unwound a little in the captain's presence. After thinking it over, he responded: "No, that would be out of the frying pan into the fire. At least the German artillery can't get at us here, nor their trench mortars very much, and our own guns can't keep this up forever."

It was wise counsel. Anywhere the men shifted would take them into the open away from their funk holes, and into the sights of an alert enemy. When the shelling finally ceased it would be a slow and difficult process to get back under cover. They would have to abandon their machine guns. Worse, as Whittlesey had been insisting all along, it would be practically impossible to move the wounded—they would have to be left where they were, desperately hugging a wall made out of the tattered, bloody corpses of their friends while the others fled. The likely result would be disorder, demoralization, maybe even panic. No, there was nothing to do but stay put.

Whittlesey had no sooner made this decision than the shelling stopped. The enemy guns fell silent too.

The sudden absence of sound was disorienting. Men stared about them in stunned disbelief. Some wounded men whimpered, but nobody said anything. What could they say? It was four in the afternoon.

Ten minutes later the German machine guns opened fire in a rising crescendo that enveloped the pocket from all directions. Rifles spat, and the mortars resumed their torment. There were not many more casualties, but the surviving Metropolitans kept their heads down. You'll have no chance to rest, said the enemy guns. You can't lift your head even for a moment. There's no safety anywhere. The whole world is against you. The doughboys heard the message loud and clear.

The mortar fire stopped, then the machine guns. After a pause, as if on cadence, dozens of grenades rained down. Some were tied together in bunches. Explosions erupted in staccato rhythm along the perimeter, and then running German boots thumped the tortured earth among the trees. The enemy came from every direction.

The hill's base was strewn with a small landslide of corpses. Among them lay some live men, maybe two dozen, too stunned to react to the onslaught. Rough German hands grabbed them by the collar and hauled them off through the ravine. A few Americans had the presence of mind to hide by burrowing beneath dead bodies, but one lieutenant, his nerves shot, could not stop twitching. The Germans found him and dragged him away. They moved on, climbing up the slope toward the center of the pocket, certain it was theirs.

Similar episodes took place elsewhere. At first the Germans met only scattered resistance and captured small clumps of shell-shocked prisoners. But the enemy's humanity proved his undoing. Twenty-five years later during World War II, German soldiers in a similar situation would have ruthlessly shot or bayoneted the wounded and dazed Americans, pushing forward rapidly to destroy the pocket. Only then, maybe, would they have sorted out the survivors and dispatched them rearward. This time, though, the surviving core of three hundred or so Americans had the opportunity to shake their heads clear, pick up their guns, and fight back. One man opened fire, then another and another until resistance became infectious.

Second Lieutenant Gordon L. Schenck, a handsome twenty-five-year-old former student of Adelphi Academy in Brooklyn and clerk with the Munson Steamship Line, orchestrated the defense at the pocket's critical northern tip. No officer in the pocket was more beloved by his men. Back in June, while training his troops in France, he had written a letter home that the local newspapers picked up: "The only thought in all minds is to 'get' the Germans. Every day is filled with hard work . . . The boys are convinced that America is the finest country in the world."

Now at the head of Company C, with a badly wounded foot that he had refused to report, Schenck directed his men to pull back a short distance and then "get" the Germans as they rushed downhill and attempted to push through gaps in the shattered foliage. Even as he did so, moving about in a tattered uniform, Schenck took personal charge of caring for his sergeant, Lionel Bendheim, a shoe salesman from the Upper East Side whose legs had been shattered by enemy bullets. Bendheim would survive the war. Schenck wouldn't.[7]

The attack continued for over almost two hours. The Germans probed one spot and another, and when they thought they detected weakness they charged. They drew fire from the heavy machine gun crews, and then once again sat back to let their own mortars and machine guns take the guns out. Lieutenant Cullen's men fought fiercely, replacements steadily taking the places of men who fell. Only two of the guns remained in operation along with a handful of the light machine guns. And they were running dangerously low on ammunition. Pros like Holderman counseled their men to fire only when it counted, but men thought only of surviving the moment.

The German attacks ceased precisely at six o'clock, as if on cue. The light was fading. When it became apparent the enemy wouldn't assault again, at least for a time, Whittlesey huddled with McMurtry. Again the captain spoke of shifting positions. This time the major agreed, but only to the extent of pulling in his perimeter from the left to further concentrate his dwindling force. He had no idea how many men he had left—perhaps half of the five hundred or so who had entered the pocket? What he did know was that he had well over a hundred wounded who could not be cared for; few machine guns; little ammunition; no grenades or support weaponry; no food; little water; and no communication with the rear. The only thing he possessed in abundance was dead men. They too were countless, but in his heart, he charged every single one of them to his personal account.[8]

Lieutenant General Richard Wellmann was an old-school Prussian army officer. He had spent over forty of his fifty-nine years in the army, beginning in 1877 as a second lieutenant and working his way up by merit (for he lacked aristocratic blood). He commanded an infantry brigade during the invasion of France in the summer of 1914, and subsequently led troops during nonstop service on both the Western and Eastern Fronts. Wellmann witnessed it all, from the infernos of the Somme and Passchendaele in 1916–1917 to the icy steppes of Russia and the Baltics. His dedication was total, along with his willingness to sacrifice: two of his three sons were killed in combat, but he never questioned the cause for which they fought. His assignment to command the 1st Reserve Corps in the Argonne Forest in August 1918, soon to face the attack of the 77th Division, presented another challenge, that was all.

By October Wellmann, his officers, and men knew they had lost the war. The German spring and summer offensives had definitely failed. Germany's allies Austria-Hungary and the Ottoman Empire verged on disintegration, and former ally Bulgaria had already dropped out of the war. Their instability and Russia's fall to the Bolsheviks fed the flames of revolution through central and eastern Europe and the Middle East. The German people, meanwhile, faced starvation thanks to the British naval blockade. What if they too rose up in rebellion?

The German army had lost about two million dead and twice that number wounded. The surviving troops were exhausted from years of combat almost without letup, and in the summer they had begun suffering from the ravages of the growing influenza epidemic. And now here came the Americans, by the millions—untrained, to be sure, but quick learners, aggressive, brave, and healthy to boot.

Why continue to fight? Many German soldiers chose not to. By the autumn of 1918, German military authorities tried to make up for their horrendous losses by packing the army with elderly reservists and teenagers barely past puberty. These were just fillers. Field officers assumed that they would surrender quickly, and they did, creating a false impression that the German army was disintegrating. Contrary to the picture of wholesale demoralization and despair later portrayed in Erich Maria Remarque's novel *All Quiet on the Western Front*, a hard veteran core remained determined to fight on to the end.

Some of it was pride—in their nation, in their army, in their units, in themselves. Germans also had no way of knowing, despite President Wilson's much ballyhooed Fourteen Points, what sort of peace terms the Allies would seek to impose. Perhaps they would be draconian; perhaps (as many British, French, and even Americans in fact advocated) they would try to dismantle and occupy all of Germany. The best way to prevent that from happening, to the ruin of their families and themselves, was to fight on until they could struggle no more, inflicting such casualties on their enemies that they would think twice before trying to impose a humiliating peace.

That was what Wellmann and many of his officers and men believed, and so the isolation of Whittlesey's force presented the Germans with a vital opportunity. None of them underestimated the Americans. Experience had shown their fierceness in combat; in the summer, small groups of isolated doughboys had fought to the death rather than surrender. German intelligence had also, however, reported on the disproportionate role that the media, in particular newspapers, played in forming American public opinion.

From the beginning of their appearance on the Western Front, the Americans had at times launched operations solely to impress the media. An attack by the US 1st Division to capture the tactically meaningless village of Cantigny in late May was a case in point. Much ballyhooed by the American military authorities and media, it actually accomplished nothing of practical military value. Noting this, the Germans at times fought fiercely for relatively unimportant terrain features, such as Belleau Wood in June, in order to try and convince the American press that the United States would take terrible casualties if the war continued for much longer.[9]

Destroying the Argonne pocket would drive home that lesson with special force. The story would be compelling—one, perhaps two thousand doughboys left isolated because of the incompetence of their commanders, and wiped out to a man while their comrades fought uselessly to relieve them. In the short run, such a disaster would probably lead the Americans to remove the 77th Division from combat (as had been done in recent days with other underperforming outfits) and buy the Germans time. But that was less important than the propaganda coup. Though subject to censorship, the long American tradition of freedom of the press made it a potentially fickle friend, maybe even an enemy, of the US war effort. News of a military disaster would get through, and reporters like Damon Runyon would not hide it.

The American junior officers and doughboys captured during the afternoon action of October 4 did their best to mislead their German interrogators. They exaggerated the number of troops in the pocket from one to two full-strength battalions, so hoping to convince the enemy to call off his attacks. The German officers on the scene took the bait, and were temporarily intimidated into cancelling close-quarters attacks with the limited troops—no more than one tired regiment—at their disposal. Wellmann, however, smelled opportunity. The troops on hand, he conceded, might not suffice to crush the "American nest." Elite storm troops were another matter. Picking up his headquarters phone, he called his army group to ask for reinforcements. With them, he felt certain he could wipe out the Americans.[10]

General John J. Pershing prided himself on his iron self-control. Ever since his wife and daughters had been killed in a horrific fire at the Presidio in 1915 he had maintained a rigid, erect posture akin to a cast-iron shell. He had occasional affairs with women, including Lieutenant Colonel George S. Patton's younger sister Nita, to whom he was briefly engaged in 1917. But most people found intimacy with Pershing impossible. His devotion to the AEF was total. He lived on willpower. Only he understood the brittleness of the veneer he presented to the world.

Pershing worked under immense pressure. He bore it willingly, even welcomed it, but by October 4 he had passed far beyond the limits of exhaustion. Since the war began, he had insisted on the creation of an entirely American force, and after its creation in August the entire burden for First Army's success or failure rested upon him.

Pershing's roles were both military and political. He had not only to craft First Army's operations and oversee their implementation, but to serve as President Wilson's primary liaison with both Allied military and political leaders. Wilson and his secretary of war, Newton D. Baker, made certain that Pershing understood his responsibility not just for winning on the battlefield, but for ensuring that the United States sat as an equal partner, if not the dominant power, at the postwar peace table. To accomplish that he had not only to succeed in the Meuse-Argonne, but win resoundingly.

So far, Pershing was failing. Since September 26, First Army had suffered over twenty thousand casualties while making hardly a dent in the German positions. The Americans had not come close to breaking through. European leaders noted the suffering First

Army had endured, and shook their heads—if Pershing had placed his troops under European command, they muttered, this never would have happened. French premier Georges Clemenceau, a fiery, white-whiskered little bowling ball of a man known as the "Tiger," took a tour behind the American lines on September 29 and got caught in a titanic traffic jam. New Yorkers would have wryly endured the backup, but he found it intolerable. After finally extricating his staff car, the Tiger let everyone know what he thought of this incompetent American army and its arrogant general. Wilson and Baker could not help but take notice.

Pershing had probably learned about Whittlesey's plight by the evening of October 4. The news was doubly unwelcome. First Army had resumed the offensive that morning after three days of rest, and promptly bogged down again. Part of the problem was the German artillery in the upper Argonne, which fired into the flanks of the 28th and 1st Divisions attempting to move forward just to the east. Now it appeared that the 77th Division, which General Alexander had insisted needed no rest, had gotten itself into an embarrassing, and dangerous, predicament.

Pershing cared about his men, but the fate of the five hundred or so Americans in the pocket worried him less than the potential political consequences if they were wiped out. That would not just affect the personal reputations of Pershing and his officers, but create a public relations explosion with shock waves that could have geopolitical implications. Whittlesey and his missing command had to be rescued.

The timing could not have been worse, for Pershing hovered on the edge of a nervous breakdown. Overwhelmed with his responsibilities, he seemed incapable of doing more than urge his commanders to attack, and attack again. That was what he told General Liggett, commanding I Corps. Liggett in turn passed it on to General Alexander, who furiously browbeat his own officers. Attack, he told General Johnson, and rescue Whittlesey—or I will get someone who can.

Johnson then turned on his regimental commanders, including Colonel Stacey, whose 308th Regiment had degenerated into a disordered mess. Attack, he demanded, and rescue Whittlesey. The regiments attacked, and attacked again, but got nowhere. They were too exhausted, and the German defenses too strong. The Metropolitans could only be hurled frontally at the Argonne so many more times. Everyone, from Pershing on down to the lowliest 77th Division private, had reached the end of their tethers—with one exception.

Hunter Liggett was not a brilliant man, or a tactical wizard. But he had been in the military since he was a teenager, and he understood his craft. Most important, he kept his head in a crisis. Where other men, including good soldiers, degenerated into living wrecks under the constant pressures of command, Liggett sailed calmly forward. He kept regular schedules and slept well as opportunity permitted. When problems seemed insoluble, he sat down to play solitaire. It helped him think. Every time he rose from the card table, he did so in a more peaceful and fertile frame of mind.

As reports came in from the front on the evening of October 4, Liggett carefully scanned his maps, stopped to play solitaire, and then returned to study his maps again. His corps included three divisions, from left to right: the 77th, the 28th, and the 1st. The 77th was bogged down. The 28th "Bloody Bucket" Division, Pennsylvania National Guard, was fighting hard to push north along the valley of the Aire; but although it was a veteran, high-quality formation the men were tired and unable to make much progress. The 1st Division, which had justified its superb reputation many times over, was making significant progress toward Exermont but taking severe casualties from German guns in the Argonne.

Two days earlier, Liggett had received welcome reinforcements. The 82nd Division, barely blooded but finally trained and eager to fight, was released from army reserve and placed at his disposal. With the 28th Division wearing down, it made sense to designate the All-Americans as an eventual replacement. At some point Liggett's thoughts clicked into place. Bending over the map, breathing quietly, he laid his chubby finger on the symbol for the 82nd Division. Slowly pushing his finger forward, he dragged the symbol toward the Argonne.[11]

Alvin C. York was not yet aware of the descending finger from above, and the pressure that would be placed on him. But he knew something was up. In late September he and his men had boarded huge, ancient white French omnibuses. The drivers came from the French colony of Indochina, and they drove like maniacs. York's rusty-red hair stood on end as the buses jounced over the narrow, rutted roads and swerved wildly on corners, hurling bewildered doughboys to either side and sometimes overboard. After hours of this punishment they debarked in the rolling farmland below the Argonne and encamped in friendly, unspoiled copses amid rustic farms. Not far away, the men could hear the guns' rumble.

With each following day York and his fellow All-Americans moved closer to the front. As the miles passed the signs of war grew starker: columns of trucks, supply wagons, and artillery navigating traffic-choked roads; fresh troops moving forward; battered, filthy, hollow-eyed soldiers walking toward the rear; ambulances full of wounded doughboys. The terrain became shell pocked and trench scarred from the ravages of the 1916 Battle of Verdun. The gunfire grew louder and then the men saw the guns: batteries of American and French artillery firing salvo after salvo at the Argonne, one of them unwittingly pummeling Whittlesey's men.

York's 328th Regiment assembled on October 3 near the village of Varennes, recently captured by the 28th Division. Word came down that the All-Americans would not stay in reserve for long. In true AEF fashion, Pershing decided that now, just as the 82nd Division prepared to enter major combat for the first time, was the right time to effect a change in command. General William Burnham, who had commanded the division since its formation and knew its officers and men intimately, as they knew him, did not seem sufficiently aggressive in Pershing's eyes. And General George B. Duncan, still seething from his enforced departure from the Metropolitan Division, was available. On October 4 Burnham was relieved, and Duncan rushed over from Paris to take control of a division about which he knew nothing, not even its location.

Officers and noncoms roused their men early that morning, assembled them into columns, and turned them northwestward toward the central Argonne. The forest ahead buzzed like a furious nest of hornets. Airplanes droned overhead as observers studied the woods for signs of enemy activity and signaled their discoveries to the artillery. German planes were visible too, usually reconnaissance aircraft seeking out American troop concentrations and artillery.

Occasional bursts of German shellfire exploded in the vicinity—not within hitting distance of York's column but close enough to make the doughboys think. Dead horses lay strewn about, their rotting bodies enveloped in nauseating pockets of stench. Groups of dead German and American soldiers were visible too, carefully blanketed and arrayed in rows to await the burial details that would deposit them in temporary field cemeteries. As York took in these sights and gazed on the woods ahead, he felt as if he approached the climax of his being, and his newly won faith. Turning his head to the sky, he murmured: "Through Shells or Death with all their agitation Thou wilt protect me if I will only trust in thy Grace bless thy holy name."[12]

The Argonne Forest had become a magnet commanding attention and deciding the fates of thousands of lives. Among those falling under its influence in the autumn of 1918 was a reporter with the *New York American*. Damon Runyon had spent the spring and summer stewing, his eyes on boxing, baseball, and women, but his mind obviously elsewhere. In between sports stories he published verse about soldiers at the front with an undercurrent of yearning that must have been increasingly obvious to his readers.

Hearing of the exploits of General Omar Bundy's 2nd Division in the early summer, Runyon fantasized about his victorious doughboys, who seemed representative of all Americans. The many pieces of patriotic verse that he penned for the *American*—some okay and others excruciating, for poetry was not his forte—included one of a soldier returning home on leave (actually a near impossibility) lecturing civilians about the difference between "over there" and "over here":

> "If you're all right, over here," he said
> "And leaving no job undone
> They'll be all right, over there, all right
> Till they've ended the thing, and won.

> If you've done your share the best you can
> And your conscience is sound and clear
> They'll be all right, over there, all right
> And you all right, over here."

But Runyon was not all right, over here, and his conscience was not clear. His bit was over there.[13]

Runyon's boss, William Randolph Hearst, could tell like everyone else that his star reporter was unhappy. He also felt pressure to make up for his own past isolationism by adopting a more strenuous patriotism than any of his competitors. Whether for those reasons, or just to dissuade Runyon from composing more reams of corny verse, Hearst invited the reporter to meet him at his opulent apartment complex, the Clarendon, at 86th Street and Riverside Drive. Runyon, who had just taken an apartment up at Riverside and 116th Street, awaited the newspaper mogul in an antique wood-paneled parlor studded with medieval and Renaissance art masterpieces.

After a long wait, Hearst, who had constructed a secret walkway from the Clarendon to an adjoining apartment to avoid process servers on investigations into his alleged pre-1917 involvement with German agents, strode bombastically into the room shouting, "You can be of immeasurable assistance to America!" Without waiting for Runyon's response he declared that the reporter could contribute directly to Allied victory by going to France and writing stories from the front that would inspire popular patriotism and determination to finish Germany. When Runyon mumbled something about the coming World Series, Hearst cut him off. "You name your replacement," he thundered. There would be no debate (Runyon didn't want to argue anyway). As the reporter took his hat and walked toward the door Hearst shouted, "Don't forget Pershing! Let's enshrine him."

The announcement didn't go over well at home. Damon's wife, Ellen, had just had a baby boy whom they named after his father. She also knew about her husband's affairs with girls he met during his frequent all-nighters on Broadway. Going to France right now might get him away from the flappers, but it also left Ellen to take care of the children, and took them both further from the house along Fifth Avenue he had promised to buy her someday.

Damon brushed her objections aside. He took the train to Washington, DC, to apply for a passport and credentials as a war correspondent attached to the Universal Press Service, and then shopped New York clothiers for natty military uniforms. It took three weeks for the official papers to clear, just in time for Runyon to board the liner *Chicago* in New York Harbor on August 21 and commence his journey to France.[14]

Runyon began seeking out soldiers just as soon as he arrived in Europe. His first instinct was to follow the men he had known back home, from athletes, especially baseball players, to Broadway high rollers. Fortunately, most of them had ended up with three divisions—the 42nd, including the Fighting 69th Regiment of the New York National Guard; the 77th Metropolitan Division; and the 82nd All-American Division. All were in the Meuse-Argonne region; but the 77th, which Runyon had covered at Camp Upton, was actually in the forest. He fixed on that as his first destination.

Runyon's credentials as a war correspondent arrived at the beginning of October. Thankfully Palmer, who had known him from the Mexican border, raised no objections. When the welcome news arrived, Runyon set off for the Argonne, his mind fixed on finding and interviewing men like former Giants ballplayer Eddie Grant. As he departed, gossip spread among pressmen about something big happening in the Argonne, and more than just hard fighting. Word got around that a battalion of men, maybe more, had been cut off and lost, and was about to be wiped out.

As the Germans had predicted, the story had no chance of remaining buried for long, even in an atmosphere awash with censorship. Lieutenant Kidder Mead, a press officer with Liggett's headquarters who had previously reported for the *New York World*, got news out to the general press corps stationed at Bar-le-Duc that a battalion had become isolated in the Argonne. From then on the sensation was unstoppable.

Fred S. Ferguson, a diminutive, baby-faced United Press reporter from Indiana who had never ventured outside the United States before he began covering the fighting in April, cabled word back to his stateside editor, Harold Jacobs. Jacobs was thrilled and begged Ferguson to "send more on lost battalion." The name stuck, and the story spread beyond any hopes that Pershing or Palmer might have had to control it. They loved their country, but they were still reporters, and news was news. The first confused reference to the "Lost Battalion" appeared in the *New York Herald* on October 3.

The possibility of witnessing the war's biggest American disaster electrified every American reporter in France. Most of them plied their way to Pershing's headquarters at Chaumont in order to seek his take and glean staff gossip. Reporters were typically not allowed in the combat zone, and the best information emanated from the top. Knowing that, Palmer hovered about to watch and make sure their reports did not get out of hand by violating military secrets or conveying undue pessimism. The reporters' presence nevertheless implicitly threatened what would happen if the Lost Battalion stayed lost.

For Runyon, though, the personal angle was paramount. Many of the surrounded men were New Yorkers—he was sure he must know some of them personally, and many by sight even if he could not identify them by name. The city would want to know about them, each one, and what they experienced. More than that, Runyon had to know for his own reasons. Already in the woods, he had to get as close as possible to Charlevaux Ravine—not for the spectacle, but to encounter the men. Gaining a pass from the always media-conscious General Alexander, Runyon spent the night of October 4 with the soldiers of the 307th Regiment, talking with them and getting as close to the front as officers would let him.

The biggest American story of the war was about to break.[15]

(CHAPTER TEN)

THE TEST

By the morning of Saturday, October 5, the men of the Lost Battalion had gone without food for about three days. During that time, they experienced periods of extremely intense, high-stress physical activity interspersed with long hours of waiting. Without fuel, their bodies were consuming the last reserves of energy they had accumulated over the past month of on and off combat, and had entered the initial stages of consuming themselves. These were healthy young men for the most part, and although definitely fatigued they had days to go before their bodies began to break down. Mentally, though, they had already passed the threshold beyond which it became difficult for a man to think rationally.

Starvation's early symptoms, besides the obvious fatigue, include obsessive thoughts about food, restlessness, impulsivity, and irritability. Add to this the fact that most of the men suffered from sleep deprivation—especially those, like Whittlesey, with command responsibility—and the side effects of combat fatigue, then known as shell shock. Each man felt the effects differently. It was the supreme test of character.

The wounded had it much worse. The physical effects of their wounds intensified every moment. Sedatives were unavailable, not even alcohol. Cigarettes had run out too. Injuries throbbed with insistence that could not be denied or ignored. Forced to lie prone for hours on end, the suffering had little to do but think. Men were aware of their wounds every moment—staring at them, contemplating their dimensions, worrying about signs of infection, whether they would get out in time for treatment, if they would be crippled for life, if limbs would be amputated, if they would die. One glance would reassure a man for a moment that he was not becoming infected; another would convince him that he was. Wounded men and their friends sniffed suspiciously for gangrene, and if they smelled something they wondered if it came from them or a neighbor. The only small blessing accompanying these worries and their physical side effects was that they expunged thoughts of food; instead, casualties thought obsessively of water. Occasionally a man was able to slip down and bring up something from the brook; but most of what the wounded got came from the sky.[1]

Second Lieutenant Maurice S. Revnes was a sensitive, thoughtful man. He believed in the cause for which he fought, cared about his men, and did his best as an officer. But he was, like thousands of other American junior officers in this war, an amateur. Revnes had attended camp in Plattsburg before the war and trained there in 1917, and imbibed its ethos of optimism, courage, and loyalty. No one, though, had provided guidance on how to spend days sitting without food or water in a cold, damp funk hole with your foot half blown off, wrapped in filthy bandages, under fire from your own artillery, surrounded by the enemy, and not knowing when or if you would ever escape.

THE TEST

A thoughtful, rational man would have to wonder. Every officer accepts that in certain circumstances, granting an honorable enemy who accepts prisoners and treats them well, there is a threshold when further resistance becomes futile and surrender a matter of humanity. Contemplating the possibility did not make a man a coward; it was a simple matter of calculation. Did there remain hope of rescue? What purpose did continued resistance serve? If they continued to hold out, what would happen to the wounded? How much more could they endure? Every single man in the pocket asked himself the same questions, but no one could answer them alone. Turning to the only ones who could understand—each other—they began to talk.

Revnes shared a funk hole with Sergeant Herman G. Anderson and Private Sidney Foss. Anderson, a big, working-class man from Brooklyn, had distinguished himself under fire and tending to the wounded, but had been shot in the face. Foss, a blond, blue-eyed youngster with an English accent from Holderman's Company K, was one of the western replacements: he had been born in Cornwall and settled in 1910 with his parents and many siblings on a farm in the high Rockies of western Montana. He had not been wounded, though he would be later, but tended to the other two badly injured men. As he did so, the three men discussed their situation.

The conversation began with a survey of their surroundings. Sounds of battle in the hills to the south, heralding vigorous relief attempts, had grown faint. The only thing they could see or hear down in the ravine was enemy soldiers. There seemed to be more of them every hour. The pocket, meanwhile, steadily contracted. Revnes knew better than anyone about the machine gunners' plight. Almost all of the heavy machine guns had been knocked out, their crews killed or wounded. And they, like the light machine guns, were almost out of ammunition. Caked with mud and filth, the guns jammed every few shots. Rifles were all the men had left. The trapped men could not cut their way out; they could only defend.

The main thing was the wounded. Many were beginning to fall unconscious and some had died. Among them was Second Lieutenant Marshall G. Peabody, a handsome, fair-haired scion of a prominent Wall Street banking family. Beloved by his soldiers and his fellow officers, including Revnes, he had already received a Silver Star for gallantry in fighting during early September. Wounded by an enemy bullet on October 3 and unable to move from his funk hole, he called out regularly to encourage his men. At night, though, his friends could hear him groaning. Only when Whittlesey crawled over to his hole did Peabody admit his agony and beg for water. But the major could give him nothing. On the evening of October 5 Peabody's men found him dead.

Once Revnes, Anderson, and Foss began talking about the wounded they could not stop. The lieutenant and sergeant themselves suffered badly and wondered if they would be permanently disabled or disfigured, or if they would die. And what about the rest? How many of them would die because of Whittlesey's stubbornness? They briefly wondered if the Germans would let them evacuate the wounded, but quickly dismissed it as folly. Finally, Revnes asked the most important question: "Would it be dishonorable to surrender if we weren't relieved at a certain time?"[2]

George McMurtry refused to consider that the men might break. He never questioned or admonished, but simply let them know through words and actions that he expected them to endure just as he did. Holderman, fitting easily into the role of military leadership that he had embraced for life, maintained an easy confidence and businesslike manner. Both officers kept a sense of humor. Even the crotchety Lieutenant Cullen cracked a few jokes. Later, all three men denied that any man in the pocket lost heart, even for a moment. Their refusal to entertain the possibility of demoralization transmitted itself to many of the men, who kept their spirits up simply because there was nothing else to do. Eventually, though, they would reach a point where denial of the obvious became impossible.

Charles Whittlesey did not lose heart. But he was not like McMurtry. Deeply conscious of the sufferings of his men, whether wounded or not, he took upon his own shoulders the responsibility to engage with each and every one of them and do what he could to help. When not assessing the tactical situation, assigning patrols and other duties, or carrying them out himself, he crawled from hole to hole to talk with the men. Downtime, opportunities for rest and sleep, did not exist for him. Whittlesey provided first aid when he could, and shared anything he had with a man who needed it, keeping nothing for himself.

Like the intellectual he was, Whittlesey substituted words when action seemed impossible, which was almost always the case. For every man who seemed to be losing hope, the major wracked his brains for some kind of argument to maintain optimism, to hold on, to fight. Encountering individuals or groups who begged permission to break out, which would have been sheer suicide, the major did not pull rank to order them to stay, but engaged in extended debating-room arguments to talk them out of it.

Simple assurances that help was on the way had become stale, so he tried to bolster them with historical arguments, telling the men about sieges through history that had lasted much longer and still ended in victory. "We have been here only four days," he concluded, "so we can stick it out a long while yet." At times, he spoke like a sleepwalker, which was close to the truth. But the men realized that he knew how they felt, and that he cared, and that meant the world to them. The only thing that Charles Whittlesey denied was his own suffering.[3]

Revnes was right: the Germans were increasing in numbers and preparing to attack. But they were not ready yet. When it came, the final assault would have to be well organized, concentric, and delivered in overwhelming force. In the meantime, they did what they could to whittle away at the Americans' strength and deny them any opportunity to rest. Throughout the day the woods erupted in sudden rifle and machine gun bursts, mortar shells, or bundles of exploding grenades. It was impossible to keep always on guard.

Whittlesey and McMurtry shifted their positions constantly. The friendly fire barrage had wrecked their first command hole, so they dug a new one farther upslope. An alert German sniper noticed the change, however, and took them under fire, forcing the two officers to roll and slither away to the first available shelter they could find, a little hillock that McMurtry thought was only about six inches high. A German machine gun followed them there. Bullets churned up the ground inches from their faces as they tried to claw their way into the unyielding earth. The barrage lasted twenty minutes—it seemed like twenty hours. Neither wasted any words, but Whittlesey later remembered it as "most unpleasant."[4]

Then a new barrage began. Artillery. "Friendly." Across the ravine, approaching the pocket.

Nerves already taut, men jumped and fled for cover, or cowered more deeply into their holes. Some prayed, or cursed, or both. Others cried. Most silently endured. As the explosions crept closer, wounded men lay helplessly in expectation of further torment, maybe hoping for quick death. McMurtry stood, yelling for the men to stay calm. Whittlesey, tense faced, stood too, shouted for the men to hold on, and walked around the pocket at a half crouch. Typically, he thought not of himself but of how the men were taking it, and felt responsible to buck up each one individually.

A shell landed with a vast explosion of dirt and splintered wood just below the pocket.

Then silence.

A few moments later, another shell landed—on the ridge line *above* the pocket—and then two, a dozen more. The sounds of German screams pierced the woods, followed by a growing crescendo of lusty American cheers. Somehow, word had gotten through. Division knew their location, the artillery was again their friend. Private Richardson thought of Cher Ami, and wondered.[5]

Each chill, foggy dawn in the Meuse-Argonne reverberated with the sound of airplane engines revving at fields near the front. As light permitted, air crews and fliers inspected their French- and British-manufactured machines. From a distance the planes seemed delicate, gossamer contraptions. Flight was not yet twenty years old in 1918. Technology was simple. Though made largely of wood, stretched wire, and canvas, however, the craft were remarkably durable. They could take plenty of punishment in the air and still make it home. If not, many fliers landed safely in meadows or even on battlefields and walked or hitched rides back to base. If worse came to worst, however—such as catching fire in midair—pilots died terrible deaths. They wore no parachutes.

Colonel William "Billy" Mitchell, chief officer of American aerial forces in the Meuse-Argonne, deployed over eight hundred aircraft for the battle. But doughboys rarely saw them. An early advocate of strategic bombing, Mitchell ordered most of his fliers to bomb targets such as railway stations well behind the German lines. This left the enemy with near total command of the air over the battlefield. Their reconnaissance aircraft flew unmolested, observing American military dispositions and reporting them to German artillery, which pounded them with spot-on accuracy. German fighters, meanwhile, strafed and bombed American infantry with impunity, or sought out and shot down slow, poorly armed American reconnaissance aircraft.

The Meuse-Argonne was the only major battle during the age of flight in which the United States voluntarily ceded control of the air over the battlefield to the enemy. The doughboys paid the price. So did American observer airmen, who could only hope the enemy didn't find them. Their average life spans were brutally short.

Two-seater reconnaissance aircraft flew over the Charlevaux Ravine every day, observers craning their necks to look for signs of Whittlesey's command while pilots scanned the skies for German hunters. After their daily flights lasting up to a few hours, the fliers could return to their air bases and have good food, sleep in beds, and never have to worry about artillery or gas. Yet none cut short their time in the air in order to hurry home. Although the airmen couldn't smell the odor of gangrene wafting up from the pocket, or feel the pinch of hunger from their seats in the sky, they all felt deep sympathy for the infantrymen on the ground, along with a strong sense of responsibility and a desire to help.

But their job was almost impossible. From the air, the Argonne looked just as impenetrable as from the ground. It remained so even on a good day with clear visibility. There were no obvious trench lines or landmarks. Nor did the infantry have effective means of signaling them. On the whole they were not well trained on how to communicate with friendly aircraft, and the means, such as cloth boards or panels, were flimsy at best and easily imitated by the enemy. In the pocket, Whittlesey and his men usually had to keep down for fear that signaling the aircraft would draw enemy fire. Climbing trees was out of the question. Anyway, fog settled into low spots such as the Charlevaux Ravine for much of the time, blocking observation.

The crew of one American aircraft thought they found Whittlesey on October 5. A pigeon, half dead and carrying a message capsule that dangled from the stump of a severed leg, had brought news of Whittlesey's precise coordinates. These allowed American artillerymen to target their fire effectively, as they had done that afternoon. Identifying ground coordinates from the air was much more difficult, but from watching the pattern of shellfire and other hints the observer thought he had figured it out.

Dodging enemy (or was it friendly?) antiaircraft fire and struggling to navigate between the forest canopy and low-hanging clouds, the aircraft dropped a message packet that floated, dangling from a parachute, slowly to the ground. Inside was an urgent communiqué to Whittlesey from division headquarters:

> *The Brigade Commander is now attacking the German trenches in the ravine southeast of the Moulin [ravine] de Charlevaux. The Division Commander directs that you retire and fight your way through, attacking the Germans from the rear while our troops engage them in front.*

It was an insane order, tantamount to homicide. And it hit the ground three miles from Whittlesey's pocket.⁶

General Alexander was in a foul mood. That morning he had received a message direct from Pershing:

> *Direct that a vigorous effort be made this afternoon to relieve the companies on the left of the 77th Div. that are cut off. Suggest that they be notified by airplane of the attack so that the action of the people cut off will be co-ordinated.*

General Liggett waded into the roiling chaos of division headquarters to confront Alexander and drive home the message in person: what people were now calling the "Lost Battalion" must be found, and relieved.

This time, Alexander at least had something positive to tell him. The previous afternoon a battered pigeon named Cher Ami had flapped feebly into the divisional coop and collapsed, barely alive. But it bore a message giving Whittlesey's precise coordinates. There had been a brief, regrettable friendly fire incident but it had ended. The important thing was that the surrounded companies still held on. Alexander had already ordered the artillery to adjust their fire and deliver support; he would also tell his tired battalions to resume their attacks toward the Charlevaux Ravine, and send a message to Whittlesey to cut his way out.

Alexander really knew nothing of conditions at the front, let alone in the pocket. Whatever the obstacles, however, he felt certain that they could be overcome with the proper application of willpower. The men, he believed, remained capable of anything;

but he thought less of their officers. Barely concealing his contempt for a man he assumed to be an overtrained and thus too deliberate professional soldier, Alexander turned savagely on General Johnson and demanded that he push harder. If he failed, Alexander refused to accept an iota of blame—the responsibility, he insisted, would all rest on Johnson's shoulders.

Johnson too refused to accept blame. When Alexander cut off his attempts to explain the situation at the front, Johnson, only slightly less ignorant of conditions there, turned on Colonel Stacey. He must attack, instantly and with every man at hand, and relieve Whittlesey. Johnson was not interested in excuses or tactical details. If Whittlesey's command disappeared, he declared, the entire blame would fall squarely on Stacey.

Stacey also denied responsibility for the plight of his men. They had attacked over and over again during the previous few days, to no effect, and with terrible casualties. Battalions and companies had almost completely run out of officers; the men could barely stand. And Stacey himself was breaking down. He could not sleep, trembled noticeably, lashed out at his staff, and could not remember orders he had given moments before. The constant hectoring and yelling from Alexander and Johnson finally took Stacey beyond his limit. Receiving orders for a renewal of the attack on the morning of October 5, he not only refused to accept responsibility to carry out further offensive action but asked to be reposted to the supply train.

Johnson relayed Stacey's refusal to Alexander, who immediately obliged. Dubbing the colonel a "weak" man "whose will power and nerve had completely forsaken him," he ordered Johnson to send Stacey to a hospital and find a replacement. Who commanded the 308th Regiment was "immaterial," he growled, "so long as the officer at its head could and would fight." Johnson went to the cupboard, but there was only one man there, next in seniority: Captain Lucien S. Breckinridge, a thirty-nine-year-old Manhattan lawyer, owner of a Silver Star dating from the August fighting—and an officer ready to fight.[7]

Generals argued over responsibility that field officers embraced—officers like Captain Edward Grant, former third baseman with the New York Giants. A Harvard graduate originally from Franklin, Massachusetts, Grant had retired from baseball in 1915 and prepared for a career in law. America's entry into the war, however, inspired in Grant a sense of duty that he carried to Plattsburg, where he and fellow trainees learned what it meant to be a good officer who took responsibility for the lives of his men.

When word arrived on October 5 that he had been appointed to command the 308th Regiment's second battalion, Grant was already so exhausted from days of fighting that he could barely lift a cup of coffee to his lips. Nevertheless, he walked forward along the Argonne Ravine to assemble what remained of two companies to launch another attack. As he did so a well-placed German shell landed nearby and killed two men as well as injuring Grant's adjutant. More shells whistled in the distance, coming closer. "Flop, everybody!" the captain yelled. They flopped but he didn't. Instead he stood by his adjutant and called for a stretcher-bearer. Another shell hit Grant in the side. He died instantaneously.[8]

A short time later the battalion, now commanded by a lieutenant, moved forward. The attack failed.

While Grant lay dying General Alexander complained to General Liggett about all of the trouble his field officers were causing him. None of them were worth a damn. Alexander had yelled until he was hoarse. He had bullied, pushed, and prodded. None of it did any good. The division was fine, he said. The men were not particularly tired and they had not taken serious casualties. But when the odd German machine gun fired off a few bullets the men stopped and took cover, showing no initiative. The officers were to blame—all except for "Old Wit," who was doing his best. After listening to the rant, Liggett's aide dryly remarked in his diary: "One gets the impression that [Alexander] stands quite alone in the whole show."9

Liggett had no interest in or time for complaining. When Alexander, still fuming, departed, he returned to his map. The ideas he had mulled since yesterday looked clearer now. East of the Argonne the 28th Division still fought hard, but only made incremental progress. To its right, however, the sturdy 1st Division seemed poised to break through. Attacking boldly despite the artillery fire into its flank, the unit had pushed as far as Exermont, and German forces to its front seemed to be weakening.

AEF doctrine—the same that had led Whittlesey into his pocket—said to keep pushing forward, ignoring the flanks. Glancing again at the symbol for the 82nd Division, however, Liggett's thoughts crystallized. First he called in his I Corps chief of staff, then the First Army chief of staff, Brigadier General Hugh A. Drum, to study the map with him and talk it over. What if the 1st Division continued to push forward, not too aggressively, but enough to keep the Germans' attention? At the same time the 28th Division, tired but still full of fight, would halt its northward advance and push westward, directly into the Argonne. The new element would be the 82nd Division, thrust into line at Apremont between the 28th and 1st Divisions and also attacking west into the Argonne. Everything depended on the fresh but green All-Americans. If they could make a quick thrust into the woods and seize the high ground north of the 77th Division, the Germans might be forced to pull back and abandon their efforts to annihilate the Lost Battalion.

The maneuver was hardly complex, but it demonstrated a tactical finesse practically unthinkable in the AEF at the time. And it broke all of Pershing's rules. For the first time, the AEF would slow its northward attack against crumbling German defenses and turn horizontally to aid struggling friendly forces on its flank. Liggett and Drum had reason to doubt that Pershing would approve. To their astonishment, though, he did, and promptly too. This reflected Pershing's deep concern about Whittlesey as press publicity about the Lost Battalion escalated—and also, ironically, his increasing fatigue and flagging ability to manage the battlefield.

Recognizing the situation's urgency, Liggett allowed little time for preparation. Some delay, however, was unavoidable. The attack would go forward on the morning of October 7. Until then, Whittlesey would just have to hold on.

Alvin York spent October 5 near the partially ruined little town of Varennes. Hitherto it had been known to history as the place where French revolutionaries captured King Louis XVI and Queen Marie Antoinette in 1791 after their flight from Paris. York didn't know much about history, but as he paused to clean his already spotless rifle, he could not but have noticed the large German war cemetery beside which the doughboys encamped. The Argonne woods rose just beyond.[10]

Damon Runyon left the front on the morning of October 5 to return to Bar-le-Duc and catch up on the latest reports. Most reporters spent just about all of their time there, and he found the place a hive of activity as word passed back and forth about American and German dispositions, artillery, aircraft, and so on. Of personal details, though, there was nothing.

That afternoon, Runyon rushed back to the front. He was looking for Eddie Grant, and for news of the Lost Battalion. Hardly anyone he met knew anything, but there were plenty of stories. It took a while for doughboys to recognize that the guy in glasses with a wry grin cared and understood how they felt. Maybe he told them a little about his time in the Spanish-American War—not bragging about battles, but sharing jokes, songs, and gossip about officers, booze, and whores. Maybe he told them about boxers and ballplayers. Or maybe his carefree cynicism got to them. Whatever the cause, they opened up. With each soldier who talked, Runyon got closer to the front.

The enemy attacked one more time before dusk. Machine guns and mortars opened fire on the pocket from all directions. German soldiers threw what seemed like hundreds of grenades, in singles and bundles. Most of the pressure fell on Company K, where Holderman, bleeding from several wounds including a shattered wrist, kept the defense firm and well organized. Lieutenant Schenck stood there too, rallying the men with his presence. Lieutenant Revnes crawled out of his hole and fired his .45. So did Lieutenant Pool, who kept firing until a bullet pierced his torso.

As Pool writhed in agony the perimeter around him began to crumble, and a few men began falling back. McMurtry arrived on the scene just in time, hauling the weary men back in line, firing his pistol into the woods and calling for aid for the lieutenant.

Private Irving Sirota, a Russian Jewish jeweler from Brooklyn who had been naturalized just before the division left New York, grabbed Lieutenant Pool under fire and dragged him to safety in a funk hole.

As darkness fell and the attack faded, McMurtry crawled back to the funk hole he shared with Whittlesey. He seemed to understand that the major had come to depend on having him nearby. McMurtry was not much with words, but his steady good humor sufficed to keep Whittlesey from descending too deeply into gloom. As he settled down this time, Whittlesey noticed a strange protrusion from the captain's back.

"What have you got there?" he said. "Turn around."

As he did so Whittlesey saw a piece of wood, which he instinctively grabbed, yanked, and pulled free. McMurtry howled like a demon and turned on the major.

"Murder! If you do that again I'll wring your neck!"

Whittlesey laughed, maybe for the first time in weeks. Together the officers looked at the piece of wood, which turned out to be the handle of a German grenade. "Go get it dressed," Whittlesey said, tossing the bloodstained wood aside. "I won't do it again; there was only the one. Didn't you know that you were wounded?" In the dusk, they both chuckled quietly. For a few precious moments, their tension evaporated.[11]

General Wellmann spent much of the day on the phone. He was an experienced soldier and no fool. Although he had held the main body of the 77th Division at bay with ease, army reports warned him of the American 1st Division's progress off to the east. Whatever the Americans did, withdrawal would only be a matter of time. If the enemy recognized his opportunity and assaulted west into the Argonne, however, the end might come sooner than anticipated. Wellmann pressed this danger on army group headquarters again and again—he must have storm troopers, and now, if there were to be any opportunity of crushing the pocket in time. Finally, on the evening of October 5, he received the news he had been waiting for: army group headquarters was sending a whole battalion of storm troopers, and they would be ready by morning to deliver the assault, fully equipped with flamethrowers.[12]

(CHAPTER ELEVEN)

THE QUALITY OF COURAGE

October 6 was a Sunday. Alvin York, recently promoted to corporal in recognition of his steady service, hardly noticed. The days had become a blur to him, and as he later admitted the Germans did not take off the Sabbath so neither could the Americans. Lately he had just gone to religious services when he could, whether Protestant, Catholic, YMCA, or Salvation Army. Today he went to a service led by the battalion chaplain Daniel S. Smart—a Presbyterian minister and part-time small-town newspaperman from upstate New York who would be killed in action a week later. Knowing that many of the several dozen doughboys in attendance would shortly enter the sinister Argonne, Smart read from 2 Timothy:

> For I am now ready to be offered, and the time of my departure is at hand. I have fought a good fight, I have finished my course, I have kept the faith: Henceforth there is laid up for me a crown of righteousness . . .

The rest of the day was spent waiting, cleaning rifles, checking gear, talking quietly, and eating as much as possible.

Not until dusk did orders arrive from Liggett's headquarters, outlining the attack and designating the objectives for the next day. After hearing them, some officers left to reconnoiter the line of advance and path of assault, without benefit of sunlight. Others stayed with the noncoms to prepare the men. York hitched up his pack and rifle at eight o'clock, fell into line, and moved off. There would be no sleep tonight. The attack would begin at dawn.[1]

Damon Runyon woke up among the funk holes in the woods south of the Charlevaux Ravine. By now he had learned of Eddie Grant's death, but few could tell him the circumstances. That would come later. For now, he watched the remnants of the 308th and 307th regiments assemble wearily and prepare to enter combat one more time in the same place and against the same machine guns. And return with the same results—more men dead, no gain.

Pershing didn't have to worry about Runyon, who dropped by only occasionally at Bar-le-Duc and did not join the reporters hounding AEF headquarters at Chaumont for information. Everyone talked about the Lost Battalion. Palmer kept them reasonably in line for now. Pershing and privileged generals and staff looked to the east, where Liggett had prepared his master stroke. Only Alexander, who learned about the pending rescue operation that morning, continued to hope that his tattered rag of a division could batter its way through the German brick wall. While determined to evade responsibility if the pocket collapsed, he intended to claim responsibility for any rescue. If the Germans withdrew, the Metropolitans had to reach Whittlesey first.

At about two thirty that afternoon, two fliers climbed into a reconnaissance aircraft at an airfield near the hamlet of Vienne-le-Château. Pilots had attempted since the previous day to drop small packages of supplies to the Lost Battalion, and some thought they had managed to hit within the perimeter (actually not a single package reached Whittlesey's men). Enemy ground fire steadily increased all day, but incredibly no German fighters showed up, possibly because they saw no purpose in preventing the Americans from pouring resources into an obviously hopeless job. Nevertheless, Lieutenant Erwin Bleckley, a bank teller from Wichita, Kansas, and Lieutenant Harold Goettler, a former University of Chicago student athlete turned real estate broker, determined to give it a try.

Ground mist was especially trying. It arose before dawn, burned away by midmorning, but then often returned after noon. Such was the case this day, and Goettler piloted his plane just over the treetops while Bleckley, facing to the rear behind the plane's machine gun, searched for signs of the Lost Battalion. The airmen took their time, circling slowly back and forth over the woods and taking increasingly intense fire from Germans and trigger-happy French and American ground troops. The airmen willingly ran the risk to increase their chances of dropping their small packets of food and ammunition on target.

No one ever determined who fired the explosive bullet that hit Goettler in the head, killing him instantly. And Bleckley could never share his thoughts as the plane slowly banked and then plummeted to earth. The Americans who rushed to the plane found Goettler unrecognizable, tangled in the wreckage. Bleckley lay some distance away, breathing feebly but mashed practically to a pulp. He died before reaching an aid station. Both men received posthumous Medals of Honor.

Ernie Pyle, the famous World War II correspondent, supposedly invented the saying that "there are no atheists in foxholes." The phrase had more meaning in 1918 than it did twenty-five years later. Religious observance was high among the doughboys, especially those who had, or whose parents had, been born in the old country. AEF chaplains such as Father Duffy kept busy, living daily with the men, tolerating if not actually smiling at their bawdy songs and rough language, and tending to them with compassion through the rigors of combat. Like the Reverend Smart, they carried on their work at the front and many paid the price with their lives.

Some quarter of a million Jews wore American uniforms during the war. That accounted for about six percent of the total number of men in service, or about twice the percentage of Jews in the total American population. The 77th Division, though, was about one-quarter Jewish by some accounts, thanks in part to the large number of draftees coming from Manhattan's Lower East Side. Almost all of them, like Private Sirota who saved Lieutenant Pool's life, were enlisted men. Whittlesey remembered one of them, Private Jack Herschkowitz, a Romanian Jew from Brooklyn. He was "thick-set, stupid-looking, extremely foreign, thoroughly East Side"; and yet at one point early in the battle when the major needed a runner for dangerous duty Herschkowitz was the only man who volunteered, and he did so four times in one day. All of which proved to Whittlesey that East Siders were "equal to anything."

Although Jews faced persecution and prejudice in other AEF outfits, that did not apply in the incredibly diverse 77th or 82nd Divisions. But there were not enough clergy to attend them. The

77th Division's senior chaplain was Rabbi Elkan C. Voorsanger of St. Louis, who fell wounded in action. Rabbi Benjamin Friedman of Niagara Falls also served as a chaplain with the division, and worked with Jewish soldiers directly. Together those two men tended to the several thousand Jews in the division; during Passover 1919 they managed to get a ton of matzos delivered to the men.[2]

There were no chaplains or rabbis in the pocket with the Lost Battalion, but the men didn't need help to pray. Christian soldiers, churchgoing or not, all knew that October 6 was a Sunday—and the weather was beautiful too. Some could not have helped thinking about their families going to church back home, and drawn solace from the knowledge that their families prayed for them.

Lieutenant Schenck, a Christian Scientist, spent part of the morning reading a volume titled *Science and Health* by Mary Baker Eddy. Sergeant Martin F. Tuite, a son of Irish immigrants who worked for the Edison Company in Manhattan, asked Schenck about it. "This is like food and drink to me," he said. "A wonderful comfort." Tuite showed the rosary he had been praying. "This is my comfort," he replied, and both men smiled. But Christians also listened respectfully when Jews prayed on Saturdays and other days, and vice versa.[3]

George McMurtry, a Catholic, was not an overtly religious man. People said that he simply denied, or ignored, the existence of evil. He expected the best out of everyone he met, and expressed compassion without sentimentality. Thanks in part to these qualities, the men in the pocket, Christian, Jewish, or unbelieving, anointed him a kind of priest. Men with family problems ran them by McMurtry; semiliterate soldiers asked him to help write their letters home, some believing those letters would be their last. Though his own wounds were infected, the captain sat that morning with a young soldier dying of a stomach wound, soothing him until the boy slowly slipped away.

Whittlesey, not religious at all, lacked the same gift of connectivity. Even in praising men like Private Herschkowitz, he acknowledged their difference. By the time the sun rose on October 6, however, Galloping Charlie had earned his men's complete trust. They knew his flaws and forgave them, as he did theirs; all were doing their best. Through that morning and afternoon, he continued his usual rounds. Many of the men slept from fatigue or tried to forget their obsessive hunger; Whittlesey worked to ensure sentries stayed alert. But he could no longer do so himself.

The major presented a figure that might have seemed ridiculous to some, but struck his soldiers with awe. His cheeks were stubbled and streaked with mud, a large scab on the side of his nose where shrapnel had struck him during the friendly bombardment. He wore an oversized private's overcoat above his own filthy uniform. An old winter cap, picked up somewhere in the woods, perched atop his head. His eyes, though, shone bright with determination and love for his men.[4]

During his regular tour of the perimeter the previous evening, Whittlesey had encountered a young, badly wounded private shivering alone in his funk hole. The major slipped in to keep the soldier company and ward off the autumn chill. While sitting there Whittlesey dozed off, perhaps for the first time in days. Each time he did so, a surging sense of responsibility jolted him awake, and he turned to check the boy's condition, mumble a few words of encouragement, and adjust his bandages.

Finally, though, Whittlesey fell completely asleep.

He awoke in the middle of the night to find himself in the young soldier's embrace. Their cheeks were touching. The boy's skin was ice cold.

Officers and men shared all of the most fundamental elements of living and dying—and the kind of half death of their current existence. All divisions of religion, ethnicity, and background had long ago been forgotten. But the results were not all positive. By now the soldiers in the pocket were supersensitive to each other. They had sheltered close together for so long that each emotion instantly spread everywhere. Officers and men shared the same feelings as they watched aircraft sputter by and drop packages that fell far out of reach. They all felt the same rise and fall of emotions as firing to the south surged and faded. Everyone tried to help tend the wounded, and anguished at their helplessness. Whittlesey no longer tried to prevent men from risking their lives to bring water.

No one in the pocket knew about the pending flank attack into the Argonne, but everyone recognized and anticipated the Germans' intention to wipe them out. Each man imagined dying on the hillside. By afternoon, a sense of futility and hopelessness crept through every officer and man. Every few minutes, it seemed, officers had to turn down the requests of individuals and small groups to attempt escape. Discipline started to crumble.

The Germans chose this moment to launch what they hoped would be their final attack.[5]

McMurtry was with Holderman's company when the attack started with the usual machine gun and mortar barrage, followed by an avalanche of grenades. "Take your time," he hissed, "they don't know where they're throwing those things. They can't hit anybody." But they did, and could. One grenade landed smack dab in the middle of one of three remaining American machine gun pits, blowing the contents into a mélange of scrap metal and flesh.

The next moment a wave of heat and smoke swept over the center of the pocket. A man ran screaming to Whittlesey's hole. "Liquid fire!" he bellowed. "Liquid hell!" the major snarled. "Get back there where you belong!" The man obeyed.

The flame throwers initially generated shock and awe, just as the Germans intended. Over on the right where the assault fell heaviest, soldiers whimpered in terror, and a few shifted back or ran. But these were Holderman's men, and their commander stayed with them. So did McMurtry. Holderman could no longer stand, but propped himself in a funk hole on two broken rifles. McMurtry's leg had swollen to twice its normal size. But the two captains held steady as rocks.

Desperate American counterfire calmed, grew steady and precisely targeted. "Let's get up there and kill some of the bastards!" someone yelled. Driving home the point, a Chauchat-wielding doughboy opened fire with a stream of bullets that caught one flamethrower man square in the forehead. Other storm troopers bayoneted some weakened doughboys and pushed back the perimeter only to be driven to ground in turn by persistently even and well-aimed fire.

Another surge of storm troopers followed grenades and flamethrowers toward the center of the pocket. The steep downslope at first aided the defenders. Germans bearing the unwieldy flamethrowers stood at the road's edge and flamed the upper pocket but could not negotiate easily downhill. Nor could the regular storm troopers charge blindly; after hurling grenades they had to move carefully step by step to maintain balance on the steep grade. Still, they pushed onward, leaving scattered corpses in their wake. Again, a few doughboys fled and the pocket collapsed inward toward the center and Major Whittlesey.

The major stood quiet, still, lifted his revolver, and fired at the advancing enemy. Some of them tumbled to the ground.

The Metropolitans had been pushed too far. Something snapped. But the reaction was not what the Germans expected.

First one, then another, then several, then every man in the pocket who could stand did so. Filthy, smelling of dirt, sweat, feces, and gangrene, begrimed, swathed in bandages; they screamed as one, opened fire, grappled the Germans face to face, traded bayonet lunges. Men from the tenements and the boonies let loose with knife strokes learned in mean streets and back country bars. Simple farmers fought as if this was all they had ever known. In their rage they poured forth every ounce of bitterness they had ever felt at life's injustice. They also fought for pride: in their country, whether adopted or native born; in their city or town. They fought for their families. They fought for their officers: Whittlesey, McMurtry, Holderman, Cullen, Schenck. Most of all, they fought for each other.

The Germans hesitated; turned; and fled. And the doughboys gave chase.

Germans who stumbled took bayonets in the back. Flamethrower men who had tried lumbering downhill were targeted and killed without mercy. As their flames guttered out, so did the attack. Even the most battle-crazed Americans found themselves unable to pursue the retreating soldiers very far. Within moments they collapsed. Their exhaustion was total. Inevitably, reaction set in. No one exulted. Some sobbed uncontrollably. Most stared silently into the distance, expressions slack, minds blank.[6]

In the attack's aftermath, with the sun setting and another long night on the way, Whittlesey sat in his hole beside McMurtry and watched his men rouse themselves from their torpor to gather weapons, ammunition, and maybe a few scraps of food from dead Germans. A sergeant dropped by to give an after-action report.

Then Private Foss appeared with a message from Lieutenant Revnes.

Whittlesey opened the message and read silently:

Major W.

If our people do not get here by noon [tomorrow], it is useless for us to keep up against these great odds. It's a horrible thing to think of, but I can see nothing else for us to do but give up—The men are starving—the wounded, like myself, have not only had no nourishment but a great loss of blood. If the same thought may be in your mind perhaps the enemy may permit the wounded to return to their own lines. I only say this because I, for one, can not hold out longer, when cornered as we are it strikes me that it is not a dishonorable deed to give up.

Whittlesey handed the note to McMurtry, and as the captain read it he turned to Foss and said quietly that Revnes seemed "a little scared." McMurtry silently returned the note to Whittlesey, who asked Foss where the lieutenant "hung out." Foss told him, and the major said, "I'll go down there." Leaving a brooding McMurtry, the major proceeded down the hill.

Whittlesey and the lieutenant talked for a long time, with Sergeant Anderson listening silently. The major was firm. "There is going to be no surrender," he said. Whittlesey followed up this blunt statement with his standard assurances that help was on the way, and that other men had had it worse in ages past. But he also listened. Other men would later call Revnes a coward, but Whittlesey saw a brave man who was exhausted, hungry, terribly wounded, and scared. As the lieutenant poured out his worries, Whittlesey absorbed them all into himself and imbued in return his own sense of courage and resolve.

Revnes had taken responsibility for transmitting thoughts held by many of the men, but he refused to weasel out by appealing for their support. Whittlesey knew and respected that. As he turned away from the hole, however, the major turned to Anderson and said loud enough for everyone to hear:

"If you see any signs of anybody surrendering or see a white flag or anything, you shoot him!"

"Yes, sir," Anderson meekly replied. But he and Revnes held themselves up a little straighter after the exchange.

Whittlesey returned to his command hole and slumped under the burden of his men's fears. McMurtry let him sit in silence for a few moments. He too understood that neither officers nor men could take much more. Instinctively, he turned to action as the best possible solution. Quietly, he asked Whittlesey whether the time had come to attempt a breakout. No, the major replied irritably, it had not. The command had orders to stay put, and stay put it would. He was too tired to repeat explanations. McMurtry lapsed into respectful silence, and watched vigilantly as his friend entered his final night in the Argonne pocket.[7]

(CHAPTER TWELVE)

THE CRISIS

The Lost Battalion's final morning dawned with thick mist and occasional drizzle. The water was welcome, but not the mist because it made airdrops impossible. Overnight there had been a sudden crash of artillery on the ravine and ridge behind them, followed by the crackle of bullets. Then nothing. Two volunteer patrols, one organized by Whittlesey and the other by McMurtry, had gone out and returned after losing more killed and wounded to no purpose. The hottest commodity in the pocket now was not food, cigarettes, or bandages. These had all long gone. Instead the doughboys scrounged for bits of paper and pencil. Writing farewell letters had become epidemic.

Three kinds of distinctions now existed: living and dead; officers and men (though this barrier had weakened); and bitter-enders and breakouts. Although McMurtry had acceded to Whittlesey's refusal to countenance escape, many of the men felt otherwise. Nearly delirious with craving for food, their thoughts grew convoluted. Soldiers convinced themselves that they were not really disobeying orders. In a way, the breakout attempts just happened.

Private Emil H. Peterson, an Iowa farm boy and son of Norwegian immigrants, had just scrounged some water from the creek for an injured comrade when somebody hissed his name. Looking cautiously out of his funk hole, he saw several doughboys scrambling down into the gully. Unthinkingly, he joined them—maybe they sought an airdropped aid package. That was their excuse when he caught up with them. But they had not actually seen a package, and when they reached the brook the men slithered across into the woods and then just kept on going.

The group was diverse even by the standards of the Lost Battalion, but most were young replacements. It included Private Lowell Hollingshead, a nineteen-year-old railroad clerk from Ohio. He had joined the Metropolitans as a replacement and been busted from corporal to private in September for some infraction. Private Cecil L. Duryea was a seventeen-year-old orphan from Rockford, Illinois. Private Henry Chin had been born in Los Angeles in 1889 and moved to New York City's Chinatown just before the war, where he joined the Young China Association. And there was Private Robert Dodd, a full-blood Paiute Indian from the little town of Nixon, Nevada, along Pyramid Lake. The men, perhaps a dozen altogether, assumed that as a Native American Dodd would have a "nose" to lead them through the woods, and so they elected him their leader.

Dodd was careful, but he and his group didn't stand a chance. Halfway across the ravine he heard something and paused, but it was too late. German machine guns opened fire from multiple directions, killing three men including Chin and wounding all the rest. Once they were certain the Americans could no longer fight back, the Germans emerged and gathered up the survivors, including Dodd, Duryea, Peterson, and Hollingshead. One of the enemy soldiers proudly showed off his machine gun mechanism to Hollingshead, even firing a few bursts before they half carried the limping Americans back to the German command post for aid and interrogation.[1]

With men trickling away and danger looming of a total exodus leading to inevitable disaster, Whittlesey elected to channel the process instead of attempting to stop it altogether. First, the major asked Holderman to select three men he thought best for the job. The captain chose three doughboys led by a "small, emaciated young man" with bad posture and "large, limpid blue eyes": Private Abraham Krotoshinsky.

A naturalized Polish Jew who had been born in 1892 in a little town northwest of Warsaw, Krotoshinsky came to America when he was twenty and worked as a barber at Al Steigerwald's on 55 William Street in Lower Manhattan until he was drafted. Nobody confused Krotoshinsky for a born soldier, but Holderman knew he was tough and reliable and that was all that mattered. The young barber didn't see himself as some kind of a hero, either. He was hungry, tired of being sniped at, and expected to die. But he didn't care. He just wanted peace.

Krotoshinsky and his two comrades slipped down into the ravine, worked across the brook and into the woods. German machine guns opened fire. The other two men—Krotoshinsky only remembered them as an "Irish fella" and a "replacement fella"—fled back to the pocket, one of them badly wounded in the shoulder. But Krotoshinksy kept going, running first with the bullets whipping around his head and then dodging and crawling from cover to cover.

Instead of heading straight across the ridge, the private elected to work his way down the middle of the Charlevaux Ravine to the east. The Germans knew he was in there somewhere, and looked for him. While Krotoshinsky sheltered behind a stump he watched a group of them walking past a nearby thicket, stabbing it with their bayonets and swearing angrily. One gigantic German nearly stepped on his hand. But they moved on, and then so did the American, slowly making his way down the ravine. Other men in his position might have prayed earnestly, but Krotoshinsky's mind was blank. He thought of death constantly, but only as a physical sensation. One moment he would be there and the next he would be gone, that was all. Hours passed and he was still going, often in earshot of the enemy.

Whittlesey meanwhile turned to Lieutenant Schenck and told him to select two of his best men for another attempt to break out and make contact with the rest of the division. Minutes later a true odd couple arrived at the command hole: Privates Stanislaw Kozikowski and Clifford R. Brown. "Boys, you know what you are up against," the major told them. "If you get through, just tell them that we have not surrendered, but that we must have help at once." Brown, a pious young farmer from Ashville, New York, said, "We'll get through, because we're trusting God to get us back." Kozikowski, a Brooklyn machinist who had arrived from Poland in 1912 and not yet even been naturalized, handed over his light machine gun to another man and grimly set his face. The day before the Germans had killed his best friend.

Two other doughboys, trying to break out without permission, joined Brown and Kozikowski shortly after they entered the ravine, only to disappear shortly thereafter without exchanging a word. Brown, maybe feeling a little more comfortable in the woods than his city-slicker buddy, led the way as they passed across the brook and directly across the ravine to the lower ridge. They found it heavily defended with wire, trenches, and machine gun nests. At one point, Brown spied a big German—of course, they all looked big—standing above a trench to survey the scene. The Americans hit the ground just in time. Finding a secluded spot in the bushes they burrowed down, signaling each other that they would wait until dark to move again.

Lieutenant Schenck returned to his command responsibilities as the two men moved off into the woods, and entered the hole that he shared with Sergeant Bendheim. He spent as much time there as duty allowed, trying to keep the sergeant, whose wounds were becoming gangrenous, as comfortable as possible. The handsome young lieutenant's presence did not just console Bendheim, but bucked up everyone around him in what remained of Company C.

This time, though, a German mortar shell landed close by just as Schenck worked his way around a rock to enter the hole. Shrapnel shredded his body, and his face. He died instantly.[2]

Lieutenant Heinrich Prinz, a nattily dressed intelligence officer with the Imperial German Army's 76th Reserve Division, had lived and worked in America for several years as the representative of a German tungsten firm in Washington state. He thought he understood Americans, but the Metropolitan Division baffled him. Each doughboy prisoner that arrived, no matter how ragged, starved, or badly wounded, defiantly refused to answer his questions or fired back sarcastic remarks. Private Emil Peterson followed the pattern by boasting that there were ten million American soldiers in France and that the men in the pocket had plenty of food and ammunition. After a few minutes Prinz sent him away.

Private Lowell Hollingshead appeared next. When his blindfold was removed he gawked at Prinz's spacious, spotless, well-equipped dugout. There was magnificent cutlery, plenty of good

French wine, and even a phonograph. Prinz let him look around for a few moments and then asked the private how long it had been since he had eaten. "Five days," Hollingshead admitted in a daze. "Poor devil," Prinz muttered, and as the American reclined on his couch he proffered food—black bread, vegetables, and meat—and cigarettes.

Hollingshead gobbled up the food like a ravenous animal. His relief at being out of the pocket, fed, and destined for what would probably be a short stay in a prisoner of war camp clashed with guilty feelings about the comrades he had left behind. Hollingshead's personal status was ambiguous. He had been wounded and caught trying to break out. Did that make him a deserter? Perhaps he thought for a few moments of Whittlesey and wondered whether the man was stubborn or a hero.

While Hollingshead ate, the German lieutenant held forth about the bravery of the men in the pocket but lamented the sufferings of the wounded, whose cries echoed through the ravine day and night. Prinz seemed genuinely sympathetic. He went through the motions of asking his prisoner about dispositions in the pocket without really expecting an answer, and he got none. Prinz then asked if Hollingshead would carry a message under flag of truce back to his comrades. The private said he would if he could read it first. Prinz handed the already prepared letter to the American, who read it, nodded in acknowledgment, and signed his name.

After a short nap while the Germans made preparations, Hollingshead expressed his readiness to go. Prinz gave him the note and a cane, reaffixed his blindfold, and said farewell. A German soldier led the doughboy into the ravine, untied the blindfold, pointed him to the pocket, and departed.

Stomach full to bursting but legs rubbery with fatigue, Hollingshead tromped from the ravine back up into the pocket, roughly along the same route he had escaped. The experience felt surreal. He was leaving one kind of captivity among enemies, but at least with food and rest, to another, with friends—were they still friends?—with no food and no rest, and the possibility of death back on the near horizon.

For the first time in days, Hollingshead walked erect without fear of enemy fire. The guns were silent. As he passed the first American checkpoint, and saw his comrades lying exhausted in the mud, gazing at him with hollow eyes rimmed with steel, perhaps he gained some perspective on the meaning of courage.

It was about four o'clock in the afternoon. Whittlesey noticed the sudden silence. McMurtry, as always, sat with him in his command post. The major called Holderman over too. They watched Hollingshead silently as he approached and awkwardly drew himself up. "Sir, I am Private Hollingshead of H Company," he stammered. "I have been captured and I was sent in by the Germans with this letter for the commanding officer." McMurtry stood closest, so the private handed the letter to him.

The gruff captain, temperature rising, turned the letter over and over in his hands without reading it and looked up at Hollingshead. "Why did you leave H Company?" he demanded. As the private tumbled out his story of going for an aid package, McMurtry bristled. Whittlesey intervened just in time to prevent an explosion. "George, let's look at the letter," he said. McMurtry speechlessly handed it to him. The major opened the letter and read:

Sir:

The bearer of the present, Lowell R. Hollingshead [the private had penned his name into a blank], has been taken prisoner on October [another blank]. He refused to the German Intelligence Officer every answer to his questions and is quite an honourable fellow, doing honor to his fatherland in the strictest sense of the word.

He has been charged against his will, believing in doing wrong to his country, in carrying forward this present letter to the Officer in charge of the 2nd Batl. J[aeger] R[egiment] 308 of the 77th Div. with the purpose to recommend this Commander to surrender with his forces as it would be quite useless to resist any more in wiew of the present conditions.

The suffering of your wounded man can be heared over here in the German lines and we are appealing to your human sentiments.

A withe Flag shown by one of your man will tell us that you agree with these conditions.

Please treat the Lowell R. Hollingshead as an honourable man. He is quite a soldier we envy you.

The German Commanding Officer

His face a mask, Whittlesey handed the letter to McMurtry, who scanned it and passed it on to Holderman. Several other men besides Hollingshead had gathered around. They watched the captain attentively.

Holderman's hand fell to his bloodstained knee, and he looked up. The three officers gazed quietly at each other.

And smiled.

The effect was instantaneous, as if all the tension of the past five days shattered suddenly into melting shards of candy glass. "We've got 'em licked!" McMurtry shouted loud enough for the whole pocket to hear. "Or they wouldn't have sent this!"

Whittlesey stood up and turned to the astonished Hollingshead. "You had no business to leave your position under any circumstances without orders from your officer," he barked. "Go back where you belong!" Muttering, the private shuffled off to his hole, where he found the sour-faced Lieutenant Cullen waiting for him.

"If you don't shut up about that," Cullen snarled, "I'll bump you off myself right now!" Hollingshead shut up, and quickly fell asleep.

Back at the command post, a private shyly asked Whittlesey if the note had been a call to surrender. The major said yes, and waited for the soldier's reaction. It was all that he, McMurtry, or Holderman could ask.

Pushing back his tin hat, the doughboy remarked: "Why, the sons of bitches!" A chorus of voices emerged, yelling to each other and to the Germans.

"I wonder what they think we are?"

"Just let me get near one of those Dutch bastards!"

"Go to hell!"

"Kiss our American asses!"

"Come and get us, you Dutch sons of bitches!"

There was more—much more—creative cussing straight from the Lower East Side embellished by a year of army life, and jacked up by weeks of combat followed by days of fighting and starving and worrying and suffering. No one could distinguish the voices of Manhattan businessmen, Bronx street peddlers, tenement bullies, Brooklyn factory workers, Montana ranchers, or Nebraska farm boys. They all exuded the same savagery, the same defiance. "You become like an animal," one of them later remembered. "Does one wild animal surrender to another?"

Whittlesey didn't waste time on words, or consider a response to the German summons. He ordered some men to take in the white cloth panels they had been using to try and signal planes, lest the Germans mistake them for surrender flags. McMurtry and Holderman hustled off to get the men in position for the inevitable enemy attack.

This one would be final.[3]

The Germans heard the curses erupting from the pocket. The tartest were delivered in their own language. Just before five o'clock in the afternoon, a German called down the ridge in halting English to ask if the Americans would surrender, as if he expected anything other than the resounding "Hell no!" he received in return. The Germans then provided their own commentary in the form of grenades, machine guns, mortars, and flamethrowers.

The whoosh of heat and liquid fire did not induce terror the way it had the previous day. The doughboys expected it. Nor was there any scatter of demoralized men. As explosions racked the perimeter, followed by the hasty tromp of German boots and men in coal-scuttle helmets dashing among the trees, every doughboy either stood his ground or shifted laterally at the command of his officer. Whittlesey did not have to tell the men to make their bullets count. This time the defenders did not erupt in a berserk frenzy but worked together like a battered and worn but well-oiled machine.

Private Hollingshead started out of his sleep as the guns opened fire and emptied his stomachful of German food all over his funk hole. Stunned, he began to sob. "What are you crying about?" yelled a wounded neighbor between shots from his rifle. "At least you had something to eat. I ain't got nothin' in me to puke." Elsewhere, McMurtry and Holderman rushed around the perimeter, directing fire and shifting men to shore up soft points.

They didn't need to offer any encouragement. Every German soldier who left cover—Weller had only been able to dig up sixteen storm troopers—met bullets and bayonets.

The doughboys had not stopped cursing since they heard of the surrender note, and as the fighting continued so did their gutter-bred wisecracks. This kind of ammunition never ran out. The soldiers shouted like surly spectators at a ball game. The only things missing were ham sandwiches and soda pop.

A flamethrower engulfed one soldier in fire. His buddies, joined by the sole remaining Hotchkiss, concentrated their guns on the flamethrower men until they collapsed and their tanks tumbled to the ground. Doughboys shouted maniacally at each German soldier who went down. Holderman, still hobbling on broken rifles and firing the last rounds from his .45, whooped lustily each time he found a target. McMurtry probably shouted "O.K.!" more times in a few minutes than he had during the entire war. Whittlesey watched men with arms and legs grown stiff from infected wounds pull themselves out of their funk holes, crawl forward, take aim, and fire at the enemy. Those who couldn't fire because of injury or lack of ammunition pointed out targets for those who could.

As the attackers hesitated and gradually pulled back, Americans who could stand rose and charged in pursuit, driving the enemy back in demoralized clumps. Slowpokes took bayonet thrusts to the kidneys, collapsed, were stabbed until dead, and then bayoneted again. The only Germans who survived were those who escaped entirely. No prisoners emerged; the wounded died where they fell.

The attack was over in twenty minutes. The Germans never came close to breaking into the pocket. As the firing died down and the light faded, however, the Americans checked their magazines. Hardly a man had a bullet left. If the Germans came again, nothing could stop them except rocks and bayonets.⁴

※※

That day, Alvin York took his first steps into Armageddon.

General Liggett's flank attack into the Argonne found General Wellmann's Germans surprised but still determined to resist. On the left, the Pennsylvanians assaulted at dawn. German machine gunners sprayed heavy fire, but these doughboys were no neophytes. Dashing forward in mutually supporting teams, they grenaded the enemy gun pits and made steady progress. The little village of Chatel-Chéhéry on the edge of the Argonne fell quickly. By noon the Pennsylvanians had scaled and captured a well-defended eminence known as Hill 244. The speed of their advance shocked the Germans. To the 28th Division's right, however, the enemy held firm on Hill 223. The All-Americans had run into trouble.

No one could find fault with the 82nd Division's aggressiveness. But its doughboys were green like their officers. On the division's right front, the 327th Regiment advanced on schedule, splashed across the Aire, and climbed Hill 180. They had not yet entered the Argonne Forest, however, and enemy machine gunners on their right flank made the Americans pay for their impetuosity. Hill 180 fell at the cost of many casualties.

On the left, York's 328th Regiment no sooner started moving than it fell into confusion. Inexperienced officers struggled to form up their men in pea-soup fog that choked the lowlands along the Aire and reduced visibility to a few paces. York and his comrades walked a few steps, stopped, walked again, then halted seemingly for good. Hill 223 remained in German hands.

Enemy machine gunners and mortar teams emplaced atop the hill inflicted severe casualties on the Pennsylvanians to the south, threatening to drive them back and endanger the entire offensive.

Cursing savagely, All-American officers and noncoms formed their men up again at eight thirty that morning to attack Hill 223. The 1st Battalion was in the attack wave with York's 2nd Battalion in support. Above them they could hear the enemy machine guns hammering furiously—and imagined the toll they inflicted. But it was no good. In one of those mysteries known only to the military, York and his comrades stood waiting for the command to go forward and kept waiting... and waiting. They stood down, stood up again, and stood down. And waited.

About eleven o'clock the enemy guns stopped, and finally the officers said go and meant it. But as the 1st Battalion's doughboys crossed the Aire and climbed the hill, not a single enemy gun opened fire. When they reached the crest, they found it partially occupied by Americans of the 28th Division who had given up on the All-Americans and decided to take the hill themselves, leaving the 82nd Division boys to mop up isolated German detachments and stragglers.

But the All-Americans were not done. In the afternoon, 1st Battalion troops in conjunction with the Pennsylvanians advanced down the hill and pushed cautiously across an open slope into the Argonne, hoping that the Germans might have gone. They hadn't. Like a wounded animal at bay in its forest lair, the German infantry opened fire on the Americans and counterattacked, driving them right back up Hill 223 and almost throwing them off the crest in close-range combat. York listened in frustration at the bottom of the hill as his comrades took the brunt of the fighting. No one ordered his battalion up the hill in support. Fortunately, 1st Battalion held on and the Germans withdrew—but not far.

Darkness fell. Green like the other doughboys despite his upbringing in violence and confidence in his gun, York stood awestruck at what he had witnessed that day, knowing it was only preliminary. Hill 223 and its surroundings presented an "Abomination of Desolation" such as he had never seen before. The forest environs, with its copses, farms, and alternately rolling and craggy hills might have reminded him of his own home except that the terrain looked as if a cyclone had passed through it. Throughout the day the All-Americans had endured constant enemy artillery fire, well directed by enemy planes. York had seen men blown to pieces—in one instance a whole squad was annihilated by a single shell—but kept moving. He passed wounded men writhing and moaning on stretchers, and saw dead men with mouths hanging open and eyes glazed in eternal stares.

York unknowingly hovered at the edge of the defining experience of his life.[5]

Private Krotoshinsky had no way of keeping track of time. He just kept crawling through the woods. Mist and light rain masked his movements. The smell of damp earth assailed his nostrils as wet, half-rotten leaves crumbled under his hands. His uniform was sodden, every single inch of his body caked in mud. Conscious thought beyond the basest animal instincts was impossible.

As the light dimmed Krotoshinsky sensed rather than saw a German machine gun nest ahead. He stopped, striving to alert every sense even as his body commanded sleep. His eyes made out the barrel of a machine gun, quiet but pointing steadily toward Krotoshinsky's left rear where the pocket festered. He could hear low muttering but couldn't make out any words. With tremendous effort, the private forced his body to move, slower this time, inch by inch, working around the nest no faster than a millipede. He passed the nest without even realizing it, and just kept crawling.

Krotoshinsky nearly faded out again when the woods leapt into life. German voices sounded louder now, not muttering but growling urgently. He could hear equipment gathered, tones of command and obedience, and caught glimpses of soldiers rushing purposefully through the woods—from right to left, to the north. In the settling dark one or more Germans might have jumped over the prostrate doughboy like a mud-drenched log. With what shreds of consciousness remained to him, Krotoshinsky wondered if the Germans were marshaling for a final, all-hands attack on the pocket.

Darkness fell, silence returned, and the private resumed crawling. He had edged toward the south end of the ravine, and pulled himself uphill by his elbows, pushing with his knees.

Pitch black loomed before Krotoshinsky's groping hands and he tumbled headlong into an enemy trench.

He thought it was all over.

But the trench was empty.

Climbing out of the trench and wrenching himself upright, Krotoshinsky stumbled on—and into another enemy trench. The signs of recent occupancy were all here: discarded refuse, boot prints, the smell of sweat and excrement. But this trench too was uninhabited.

Again Krotoshinsky hauled himself out of the trench and staggered onward. Shortly he heard voices, barely distinguishable. In his near-delirium he thought these sounded different, softer, less harsh, a little more familiar.

Krotoshinsky had reached his limit. Standing as upright as he could manage, sucking in his breath, eyes rimmed with tears, he yelled:

"Hello! Hello!"

A few hundred yards away at about the same time, Privates Kozikowski and Brown from the second breakout group, also unable to crawl any farther and stomping through the woods upright, stopped in their tracks as a soldier cried, "Halt!" They threw up their hands.[6]

A heavy rain began to fall.

The 77th Division troops south of the Charlevaux Ravine carried on their attacks all day, determined to rescue their comrades but without much hope of breaking through. They pressed forward when enemy resistance weakened in the afternoon, but without any feelings of triumph. The Germans had done this before. Sometimes their short withdrawals just presaged a stronger line of resistance farther north. The doughboys advanced cautiously.

Enemy snipers continued their deadly work. Every few minutes another doughboy fell to the ground with a bullet through his body, forcing the Americans to stop and deploy. When they moved on again the Germans had disappeared, but how far nobody could say. Those walking point courted instant death.

Eventually the Americans entered the Charlevaux Ravine. German snipers and machine guns exacted a steady toll, and maddeningly withdrew to take up new posts. Night approached, presaging another halt, another night of despair. The enemy withdrawal could mean anything, including the possibility that the Germans had wiped out the Lost Battalion. Even if Whittlesey's command still survived, none of the relieving troops had any idea of where to find it. The march north through the ravine was no headlong, victorious advance, but a hesitant, fearful venture into the unknown. Every man conjured horrific visions in his mind of what lay ahead. More German guns? Empty woods? A pile of corpses?

Private Robert E. Pou was a stereotypical lanky westerner—a cowboy. Born in 1895 in the little town of Ballinger southwest of Dallas, Texas, he worked as a teenager for the Texas Oil Company and stayed with it for the rest of his life. Pou was drilling oil wells along the Montana-Wyoming border not far from Yellowstone National Park when America entered the war. He was drafted into the Sunshine Division, sent east for training, shipped to Europe, sent as a replacement to the Metropolitan Division, hurled into the Argonne Forest, and trapped with a bunch of New York wise guys and western farmers in a filthy little pocket on a wooded ridge, attacked on all sides by German soldiers.

In the five days he spent there, Pou came to love his fellow doughboys as no friend, no parent, no sibling, no spouse could ever love another. He would kill, or die, for any of these men.

Pou had somehow made it to this point without injury. Not so his friend, a badly wounded fellow private—origins now unknown—who was fading fast. Pou spent the afternoon with him, checking his bandage, providing sips of precious muddy water he pilfered from the brook, and whispering words of encouragement.

Night had fallen and he expected to spend another sleepless night next to his buddy, hoping that he would make it through until morning. Just as he settled down a dark shape tumbled into the hole, hitting the injured private hard.

The doughboy screamed. Without thinking, Pou lunged at the shape with his bayonet, the blade slashing in front of a man's startled eyes. The man jumped out of the hole like a rocket and rolled away just in time to avoid another thrust that plunged into the soft earth.

"What's the matter with you?" he howled. "I'm looking for Major Whittlesey's command!"

"I don't give a damn who you are and what you want," Pou growled, still brandishing his bayonet. "You step on my buddy again and I'll kill you."

After a pause, the shape revealed himself as an American. "I didn't mean to step on your friend," he gasped. "I just fell in the hole in the dark. Where is Major Whittlesey? I'm Lieutenant Tillman of the 307th. You're relieved and we'll have food up to you right away."

Moments passed, and Pou put his bayonet down. "I'm sorry, sir," he mumbled. "I didn't see. Do you have any tobacco, sir?"

While the lieutenant pulled out a limp cigarette, Pou turned to his friend. "See? We're relieved," he said with the biggest grin he could force. "I told you we would be all right." A trembling smile rewarded him.[7]

Other Americans emerged behind the lieutenant, who stared about uncertainly and thanked God for his narrow escape. Pou pointed them toward his friend and turned, his tall form bent wearily, toward the command hole. He found Whittlesey and McMurtry sitting there, talking in quiet undertones. "Sir?" he interrupted gently, and told the major that an officer had arrived who wanted to see him.

"Alright," Whittlesey said. Turning to McMurtry, who was massaging his wounded leg, he said: "George, you stay here and I'll see what this is all about." He and Pou left as McMurtry dazedly kept rubbing his leg. Minutes passed before the captain realized what he had just heard, climbed out of the hole, and hobbled down the hill. Whittlesey, Tillman, and relief awaited.

Tillman struggled to make out forms in the dark. Lit cigarettes sparkled across the ridge like late-summer fireflies, revealing glimpses of trembling hands and grimy faces. The lieutenant's mind registered set jaws and tortured eyes glinting red from lit cigarette tips. His nostrils screamed in revulsion at the stench emanating from the ridge around him. Every odor imaginable mingled there, dominated by that of rotting flesh. Not until dawn would he see the unburied bodies, pulverized to scrap by bullets, shrapnel, and high explosive.

McMurtry walked right past Tillman, who didn't notice him, to the bottom of the ridge. On the old wagon road, he encountered a group of men standing and silently regarding a figure in their center. The red sparkles reflecting in his spectacles gave him away. It was Major Whittlesey, chewing solemnly, the remains of a steak sandwich in one hand and a canteen in another. "For God's sake!" McMurtry shouted, "Give me a bite of that!" Whittlesey handed over the sandwich and the water too, and grinned as McMurtry tried to get himself outside of both of them in record time.

The Lost Battalion was found.

But its saga had only begun.[8]

(CHAPTER THIRTEEN)

HEROES

The generals' glory dawned golden on the morning of October 8. But their victory was not yet won.

General Johnson, claiming credit to the 154th Brigade for the Lost Battalion's relief, rushed forward the remnants of the 307th and 308th Regiments with food and supplies, although the troops needed no urging. General Alexander, proudly boasting that his division had relieved the Lost Battalion and that the triumph was his responsibility (finally, when he told the officers to push, they had pushed), assembled his entourage with the newsmen at headquarters and hurried toward the front that he had not heretofore visited.

General Liggett, meanwhile, studied his map alongside sheaves of field reports. The 28th Division's aggressive thrust into the Argonne, he saw, had been the immediate cause of the Lost Battalion's relief, outflanking enemy positions east of the Charlevaux Ravine and forcing the enemy to pull back. But the Germans were far from defeated, and might even turn to savage the worn-out 77th Division, which seemed to be taking no precautions against such a possibility. Much work remained to be done.

The Argonne's fall would depend on what the still-inexperienced All-American 82nd Division could accomplish this morning.

Oblivious to the decisive action pending just to the east, Alexander raced toward the pocket in his staff car, leaving the reporters to follow as best they could. Along the way he decided to stop at the magnificently comfortable headquarters bunker complex of the 153rd Brigade, pointedly ignoring Johnson's 154th, picked up that brigade's commander, and continued to a point about a mile from the pocket. Here he got out and walked, ostentatiously ignoring occasional German shells that exploded in the distance.

The first man he encountered was Private Robert Manson, who sat with his back to the general at the edge of a funk hole trying to scoop food out of a can with one filthy hand while his other drooped down in a mass of bandages. A draftee from Brooklyn who had worked before the war as a law office clerk and become Whittlesey's orderly, Manson had just undergone a fit of hysterical laughing and sobbing and could hardly talk. "Where's the major?" Alexander demanded. "Who in hell wants the Major now?" Manson croaked. Then, whirling around and recognizing his mistake, he dropped his food in the mud, got up and saluted, and pointed to a group of standing men. The general continued.[1]

Alexander approached a small group of men reclining around McMurtry, whose wounds had swollen from infection to the point he could barely move. The men started to stand but the general motioned them to sit down and stood looking around him, dapper walking stick in one hand and a cigarette in the other. After a few moments taking in the scene of misery and desolation, Alexander decided the men had earned a little gentle chastening. "Well, you men have sat heavy on my chest for a week," he said. "I guess we lost more men trying to get you out than you had in here, but never mind that. Where's Major Whittlesey?" They pointed, and sat staring at each other as the general bustled off.[2]

Whittlesey had been up since daylight. He spoke with Private Krotoshinsky, who told him how the voices he had called out to in the forest the previous evening turned out to be soldiers of the 307th Regiment. They had picked their way forward toward the pocket and eventually found the area abandoned by the Germans. Whittlesey also listened to Privates Kozikowski and Brown, who explained how they had been challenged by an American sentry. Fortunately the sentry was not trigger happy, and he led them to safety. All three privates had helped to guide the relieving troops to the pocket.

Most of the time, though, Whittlesey spent tending to the men. He took on the military duties of McMurtry and Holderman, who both endured painful wounds. The major stalked the perimeter of the pocket several times, making sure that medical men tended to the most grievously wounded. He also personally distributed food to the hungry while admonishing them not to eat too fast. Now and then he snatched a bite to eat for himself.

Alexander found the major handing out cans of hash to a group of privates. When Whittlesey turned around the general grabbed his hand before he had a chance to salute and shook it warmly. "How do you do?" Alexander said, smirking over the cigarette sticking from his mouth. "From now on you are Lieutenant-Colonel Whittlesey." He stood smiling at Whittlesey for a moment as if expecting the erstwhile major to let out a whoop and jump for joy. Instead Whittlesey glanced aside and mumbled something indistinct, and then turned back to the general and just silently stared at him. After a few uncomfortable moments the general dropped his eyes first, and then looked up at the trees to avoid Whittlesey's steady gaze. "Well, I can see why the airplanes couldn't find this place," he said.

Private Phil "Zip" Cepaglia, a blond little Italian kid from the Bronx, where he would later make a living as an elevator operator, had been sitting there watching the exchange, his gorge rising. And he could no longer keep quiet. "General, the artillery certainly found it!" he bitterly remarked.

Alexander whirled on the private. "Oh no," he corrected Cepaglia. "That was French artillery." The private said nothing—and what could he say? The general departed the silent group. After walking around the pocket for a while and gathering scraps of information, Alexander issued orders for a formal aid station to be set up to tend to the wounded before trucks evacuated them. On the way out, he barred the waiting reporters from entering the noisome pocket—they would have to wait back in the ravine. Alexander had other plans for Whittlesey and the two hundred or so men who could still walk.[3]

The first stretcher-bearers arrived just after the general left. Moving around the pocket accompanied by aid men, they gingerly lifted injured doughboys onto the stretchers and carried them off under the anxious eyes of their comrades. Other men assigned to burial detail set to the grimmer task of placing the dead, and pieces of the dead, in shallow temporary graves. Where possible, they marked each grave with broken rifles or sticks draped with the aluminum dog tags of the deceased. Whittlesey watched the gravediggers too.

Whittlesey would not even consider leaving until every single wounded man had been cared for and evacuated. Nor would any of his unwounded officers, or Holderman, who observed the process attentively despite his own suffering, or McMurtry. Forcing himself to move despite the agony in his knee and his back, the former stockbroker bustled about the hillside all morning, talking with the men and letting the stretcher-bearers know that they better not stumble or they would have to deal with him.

When Whittlesey tried to shoo him off to the aid station, McMurtry just paused and said, "Surest thing you know, Charles. Just as soon as the men are all gone." Toward noon, as the last of the wounded were carried out, the two officers stood next to each other, just as they had shared the command hole through the past five days. "George," Whittlesey said quietly to his friend as they watched the stretcher men walk gingerly down the hill, "we will never again be in finer company than we are right now."

When the wounded had finally gone, with Holderman and McMurtry the last out, Whittlesey looked around him to see two hundred filthy, hollow-eyed men standing quietly. Some were uninjured, while others bore wounds that they insisted were not serious. Not a single man had tried to depart by hitching a ride on a stretcher or pretending to help the wounded, despite the tantalizing odors of hot cocoa wafting up from a little hut that a couple of YMCA men had set up down in the ravine. Not until Whittlesey looked at them and said, "Let's go" did they move. They lined up for cocoa at the hut, or threw themselves to the ground in exhaustion. A few mustered up the energy to cadge hot water from the YMCA men so they could shave. Whittlesey had shaved cold that morning.

The reporters found Whittlesey sitting hunched on a stump, thoughtfully watching his men. Foremost among the newsmen were Thomas Johnson of the *New York Sun*, "a serious-minded young fellow of appalling industry"; Will Irwin of the *Saturday*

Evening Post; and a "skinny fellow" in a tailored uniform, Damon Runyon of the *New York American.* Runyon especially stood out to the soldiers, not just because of his odd Fifth Avenue officer's apparel, but for the fact that it, like theirs, was caked with mud.

Two days earlier, just before dawn on October 6, Private Max "Fly" Gilbert of the 307th Regiment was sitting in an advanced observation post south of the pocket when an officer crawled into his hole with Runyon trailing behind. "This guy wants to spend a little time with you and move up farther," said the officer. "He's a correspondent." The officer left as Gilbert, an orphaned Jewish kid from the Bronx, looked the newcomer over. He was unimpressed. "You're a sucker," he drawled. "Go back where it's comfortable."

But Runyon shook his head. Although Fly didn't know it, the reporter had sought him out on purpose. Before the war, boxer Benny Leonard had fished Gilbert out of an orphanage and brought him home to live with his family. Benny taught Fly everything he knew about fighting, in the ring and in life, and the two became like brothers. Gilbert watched Leonard beat Freddie Welsh to become lightweight champion of the world at the Manhattan Casino in May 1917, and when Gilbert was drafted and sent to Camp Upton later that year, Leonard followed him to teach the boys something about boxing. After Gilbert went to France the two kept up correspondence, Gilbert asking "Brother Ben" to reserve two seats at the Palace Theatre for Christmas Eve, 1918, and then changing it to "Reserve a room for me in a Turkish bath for one week, as I am 'cootied.'"

Runyon, who had watched Leonard fight at the Casino and at Camp Upton, must have sought out Gilbert at the boxer's request.

"I know you from around Benny Leonard's camps," he said. "My name is Runyon of the *New York American*." Choosing a direct approach over pretense, he continued: "I've got a lot of circulation back home. This is a good story."

In a while the reporter won the doughboy's confidence, easing his mood by telling jokes and tall tales, and sharing his hardships. Occasionally Runyon went to Bar-le-Duc to check happenings at the press pool, but he always returned to the same muddy hole occupied by the same muddy private—no big shot but a poor Jewish kid from the Bronx who happened to be friends with a Jewish boxer who was worried about him. In the two days they hung out together the reporter and the private became friends. Thirty years later Gilbert would remember Runyon as a "hero" who risked his life to see that their stories were told. "He didn't have to be there," he recalled. Of course, Runyon also wanted to keep as close to the Lost Battalion as he could get.[4]

Runyon and Irwin had happened to be stopping by division headquarters on their way back from the lines on the morning of October 8 when they heard the long-awaited news of the Lost Battalion's relief. Alexander had just returned from the pocket bearing the German surrender ultimatum, which Whittlesey had given to him. The general proudly waved the paper in the reporters' faces, telling them of Whittlesey's heroism in refusing to surrender, and of his own bravery in pushing his men forward until they finally broke through to the pocket.

Irwin, not so interested in what Alexander had to say about himself, turned the conversation back to the surrender memo. "And what did Whittlesey tell them?" he asked. "What would he tell them?" the general yelled, puffing out his chest. "He told them to go to hell!" The reporters took notes. But a germ of skepticism had crept into Runyon's mind. It was time to get to the front, talk to the men, and find out what really happened. In Irwin's mind going to the front amounted to little more than "hero-hunting"; but for Runyon the quest represented something much bigger.[5]

Runyon and Irwin arrived just in time to join the group of reporters waiting to interview Whittlesey and his men in the ravine. Finding the commander sitting on a stump, they gathered around him and all started asking questions at once. Whittlesey interrupted them. "Don't write about me," he said, "just about these men." To reinforce the point, he pulled aside a passing soldier, a tall, skinny kid, and set him in front of the reporters. He was Private Irving Liner of Brooklyn, the son of Austrian Jewish immigrants who had tried to get a law degree and then settled into life as a clothing salesman. "Just to think," he told the reporters, "a year ago I was studying law, and I had every comfort, too. Now, I have been lousy for two weeks."

The reporters took notes and turned back to Whittlesey. But he stayed evasive. Someone asked him if he had seen any difference in performance between the westerners and the New Yorkers under his command. Wanting to be agreeable, Whittlesey said something about how the westerners were bigger and accustomed to outdoor life. But then he stopped himself. "They were all fine," he emphasized.

Another reporter asked how he had held out for so long. "It was kind of hard to stick it out sometimes," Whittlesey softly replied. Channeling and taking ownership of the sentiments expressed by the now evacuated Lieutenant Revnes, whom of course he did not name, Whittlesey continued: "especially when we heard them trying to get through to us, getting nearer and nearer, then being driven back. It was hard not to have a wash, too. In fact, when they did get through, it was quite a relief." Pausing in embarrassment, he added, "I wasn't trying to make a pun."

Runyon wrote with the others. But he also studied Whittlesey attentively, seeking clues to his personality. His first glance took in "a tall, lean-flanked fellow around 35 years old." Runyon liked the officer's shy personality and "funny little smile." This did not strike him as a "go to hell" kind of leader. As the other reporters scattered to talk to the men, Runyon and a few others stayed to chat with Whittlesey.

Irwin, also skeptical of Alexander's bombast in light of what he now saw, asked Whittlesey what he said when rejecting the German surrender ultimatum. The officer simply replied that he had said nothing. Runyon directly asked him if he had said "go to hell," and got an explicit denial. He had just smiled, Whittlesey said—and Runyon decided that it must have been with his "funny little smile." But something about it was unsettling.

Runyon learned more about Whittlesey from his men. "We held out because he did," one of them said. "We was all right if we could see him once a day." The reporter grew fascinated with their characters. These were the men, as he would write in the first dispatch he sent back to the United States, that he had seen parading "in straggling columns down Fifth Avenue between walls of cheering people." Back then they had been wearing old straw hats, Palm Beach suits, and overalls. Some were from the street gangs that Runyon, himself a former kid gangster, knew well: outfits like the Hudson Dusters and the Gophers. Many came from "the lower East Side, Broad and Harlem, Broadway and the Bronx"; or from "ornate houses on Park and Madison avenues or the upper reaches of the Seventies and Eighties." There were Chinese, Japanese, and Italians, all talking in their own language. He had watched them gather together as they prepared to depart for Camp Upton, hung over from farewell parties, and gravitate into groups of their own kind. He had even seen a few fistfights break out between dockworkers and college boys, and officers' ineffectual attempts to intervene.

Runyon knew them all—and he didn't. He saw the "'Big Town's' polyglot population" emerged from days in the Argonne and transformed into something different: "one-time counter-jumpers, brokers' clerks, gangsters, newsboys, truck drivers, collegians, peddlers, and what not" merged into something new, and stronger. The reporter recognized one of them, a "little chap" from whom he had once bought papers in Times Square. Now, Runyon observed, "he was covered with mud. His eyes were heavy with battle sleep, but he was grinning broadly." Runyon also stopped for a while with a desperately tired captain named George McMurtry, who spoke briefly but kept wiggling his shoulders to alleviate pain in his back from where he said a potato masher grenade had hit him.

But Runyon did not just have eyes for the city boys, though he knew they were the ones his New York City readers would want to read about. He noticed that many of these soldiers had once been western cowboys, ranchers, farmers, and hard-drinking small-town men like his father, and like the ones he had met in his early days tramping the news beat in Colorado. These too were types that he understood.

Runyon was keenly aware that although he too had once been a soldier, these fellows had experienced things he never had or would. In some intimate way, though, he could connect with them in respects that his fellow reporters could not understand. Runyon had moved from the West to the big city and incorporated both of them into his unique personality. In the pocket, westerners and New Yorkers had merged as well—to become comrades unlike any others.

Other reporters, including those who visited the pocket and others like Palmer who never left headquarters or got to know any of the men, chose to zero in on the "go to hell!" myth that Alexander had propagated, despite Whittlesey's denials, to create a mythology of cardboard heroes. Runyon, who had initially thought the death of Eddie Grant would make a better story than that of the Lost Battalion, now decided instead to tell the story of how these men had merged to become living, and suffering, symbols of the United States of America.[6]

The reporters departed that afternoon, giving Whittlesey and his men time to prepare for their next ordeal. Although they had received food and treatment, and seemingly escaped any immediate danger from the enemy, they had not rested. The food had overwhelmed many of them, inducing vomiting and bouts of diarrhea. They still looked and smelled like death, and trembled with fatigue.

The generals, however, decided that the bedraggled doughboys should walk out with their heads held high—and for the world to see. While the Lost Battalion survivors waited in the ravine for the convoy of trucks that they assumed would take them out, orders arrived that they were to clean themselves up for the cameras. A film unit from the Signal Corps, which had been tasked to make a visual documentary record of the AEF in the Great War for propaganda and posterity, was waiting to film the men as they walked—not rode—out of the pocket. Uniforms were to be brushed and cleaned as much as possible; every man who had not already done so was to shave; and bandages were to be hidden or removed. The cameras had no sense of smell.

At three o'clock in the afternoon Whittlesey called his remaining men to order, and walked at their head as they left the ravine. The Signal Corps men had stationed their bulky camera on a tripod next to the only clearing they could find. It was open, but with a small ditch in it that the soldiers would have to cross (and which they could have avoided if they had been permitted to walk out along the wagon road). As the cameraman cranked his contraption's handle the doughboys plodded slowly past. Other 77th Division men were there too, watching but too overpowered with emotion to speak.

Some of the departing doughboys kept their heads up, according to orders. But there were few officers or noncoms to guide them, and most bent them down, walking with leaden steps. Some men stumbled, but by a miracle none of them fell. Afterward the cameramen pulled Whittlesey, Cullen, and a few men aside for another short photo shoot. For a brief moment, Whittlesey turned to the camera and summoned his "funny little smile," but his eyes were blank.[7]

Generals Pershing and Alexander never plumbed the depths of Whittlesey's expression. They were satisfied. He had won their victory.

As Major Whittlesey and his officers and men walked out of the Argonne, Corporal Alvin York walked in.

He had not slept at all the previous night. It had rained on and off as the troops lay in the mud alongside the Aire. Flashes of gunfire lit up the dark sky, accompanied by a cacophony of unidentifiable sounds that jerked men awake or kept them watchful from fear and uncertainty. At three o'clock in the morning on October 8, Captain Danforth alerted his men to prepare to move. As the sky shifted from black to gray, they formed into a column of squads, crossed the Aire on rickety footbridges, and trudged uphill.

The going was easy for York, who had climbed many a hill in his time, but not for doughboys more used to city sidewalks. No obvious paths marked the way. Shell holes, stumps, coils of wire, and other obstructions tripped up the men, who cursed furiously and shouted to find each other in the dark. Because of their slow progress they were unable to reach the crest of Hill 223 before daylight, and German dawn patrols took them under observation. Shells fell fast, followed by the sickening plop and hiss of gas canisters. York remembered his drill and quickly got on his mask. Most of his comrades got theirs on in time too.

The All-Americans reached the top of the hill, took off their masks and wrongly thought themselves safe. Overnight the skilled German infantry had infiltrated the porous American defenses and emplaced what seemed like scores of sniper pits and even a few machine gun nests around the ridge. Guns opened fire from all directions, joining in with intermittent German artillery fire to disrupt the attempts of Danforth and other officers to organize their attack. American artillery remained silent, even when the time for the American advance into the Argonne arrived at ten minutes after six o'clock. Danforth blew his whistle and the infantry advanced anyway.

York's platoon was one of two on the far left of the regimental line, advancing downslope toward the Argonne with fixed bayonets. In theory there were supposed to be 28th Division men off to his left. He could see no one there, but he did see the platoon just in front of his own dissolve under enemy machine gun fire from ahead and to the left and right. Many in his own platoon were hit as well. Every doughboy hit the turf. Danforth disappeared. York's platoon leader, Lieutenant Kirby Stewart of Bradenton, Florida, was practically chopped in half by a burst of machine gun fire. The German machine guns kept churning up the ground. The attack was paralyzed. York knew that if they stayed there, they would die.

Fortunately, acting platoon leader Sergeant Harry M. Parsons, a feisty theatrical manager from Brooklyn, was a man of action. Surmising that the German defenses were anchored on a small hill just inside the woods to his left front, Parsons ordered three squads in his platoon, seventeen men in total, to outflank and capture it. The attempt would be led by Sergeant Bernard Early, an Irish-born bartender from New Haven, Connecticut, and three corporals: York; William Cutting, a half-Irish farm laborer from Massachusetts who had enlisted under an assumed name; and York's good friend Murray Savage, a devout farmer from East Bloomfield, New York.

Early, a hard-drinking brawler, did not get along with York. But he was a good noncom, and at this moment of decision he and his corporals worked well together. The sergeant pointed out a partially covered declivity that led to a gap just south of the enemy-held hill and suggested they make for that. Everyone agreed and off they went. Ironically the continuing German shellfire, now joined by well-meaning but inaccurate American artillery fire, provided some measure of cover and distraction. Miraculously, all seventeen men made it to the tree line undetected, and entered the forest.

It was all trees and thick, pathless underbrush: typical Argonne terrain. York felt in his element. Early and the others unconsciously leaned on the red-headed woodsman, who led them in single file and then in open skirmishing order deep into the woods. For a moment they thought they had gone far enough and should turn north into the German flank, but York insisted they go a little farther and they did. Incredibly, they remained unobserved. But their luck could not hold out forever.

Near a stream the Americans startled two German medical orderlies wearing Red Cross armbands, who fled in an instant. Doughboys—but not York, who might himself have been a medical worker if given his choice—opened fire and missed. Then they all gave chase, knowing that once the Germans gave the alert the game was up. As they ran their direction changed. Without noticing it, they had begun charging the German-held hill directly from the west.

Tearing through the underbrush along a small trail leading toward the hill, just on the heels of the two Germans, the Americans encountered a small stream. They leapt across and exploded into a small hillside clearing in front of the astonished eyes of several dozen Germans scattered around a little wooden hut. It was a German headquarters unit. Expecting that the machine guns on the hill above them would keep holding off the Americans to the east, and not fearing the inaccurate American artillery, they were sitting or standing in shirtsleeves, eating meager German army provisions, chatting, and considering scribbled field reports. Their first reaction on seeing the Americans was to drop anything they were holding and to throw up their hands. York took their leader, Lieutenant Paul Vollmer, into custody while Sergeant Early ordered his men to line up the rest and search them. For one fatal instant the Americans let down their guard.

Up the ridge above the clearing was a German machine gun nest. These men were not at rest but keyed up from fighting and trigger happy. As soon as they saw the Americans behind them they whirled their gun and opened fire, pouring a long stream of bullets into the clearing. The gun took down Americans and Germans alike. Early toppled, and Cutting. Savage, York's closest buddy who had spent long hours with him studying the Bible, went down before his eyes in a mass of blood and rags, his uniform torn nearly off his body. Several other soldiers fell, screaming in German and English, and everyone hit the ground. York's world, so carefully cultivated in faithful routine, exploded instantaneously into a maelstrom of violence.

The moment was terrifyingly intimate, and to York shockingly familiar. This world of woods, hills, and killing was his world, his people's world, for generations. He fell into it like a uniform—not the awkward, tight-fitting uniform of the AEF, but the worn, dirt-stained overalls he had worn in the deep hollows of the Upper Cumberland. There was no time to pray. But he still had his gun.

There were eight Americans unwounded. But York did not notice them, and all they could do was watch what happened next. He himself did not really think about what he was doing. It seemed like there were hundreds of enemy machine guns around him, tearing up the woods. He was fighting for survival, that was all.

Dashing from cover to cover, York worked uphill until he had a downhill view of the German machine gun nest that had started the action. It was surrounded by gun pits containing riflemen, all oblivious to the single American soldier who had gained their flank. Unslinging his beloved rifle, York took aim and fired at the Germans one at a time. Each bullet found its mark in a head or neck that snapped back and erupted in blood. The Germans were at first too fixated on the crowd in the clearing to notice their rapidly diminishing numbers. When they did, and tried to locate their tormentor, it was already too late. He just kept picking them off one at a time. York killed and killed and killed again, until there were near twenty dead Germans, the machine gun barrel drooped down to the ground, and the hillside fell silent.

The silence didn't last long. As York paused and began heading back for the clearing, a group of Germans debouched from a nearby trench and charged him with fixed bayonets. Postwar publicists, seeking to entrench the tow-headed soldier-cum-hero in faux hillbilly lore, described York picking off the Germans like turkeys, back to front, as they obligingly ran toward him in single file. But at the time York didn't much think about it. He just dropped his rifle, pulled out his .45—also well cherished—and killed, killed, and killed. Percy Beardsley, a farmer from Roxbury, Connecticut, fired at the Germans too and helped to break up the attack. The German platoon leader fell in front of York, a bullet in his gut, shrieking in agony. York wasn't near done. But Lieutenant Vollmer couldn't take any more.

Taking his life in his own hands to save those of his men, Vollmer stood up and approached York. He was lucky the American did not turn around and shoot him between the eyes. But though York pointed his pistol at the lieutenant's head, some instinct told him to keep his finger still on the trigger.

"If you don't shoot any more," Vollmer begged in thickly accented English, "I will make them give up."

York didn't drop his gun. His staring eyes held all the hardbitten toughness and cruelty of the Scots-Irish guerrilla fighters of the Tennessee hills—the same men who had come over the mountains to wallop General John Burgoyne, defied the guns of the southern Confederacy, and then made war on each other and on God for generations. York told Vollmer he had better do what he said, and held his gun straighter, his gaze steady, to reinforce the sentiment. If the German had so much as flinched he would have perished on the spot. Death stared in his face.

Vollmer carefully reached into his tunic, pulled out a whistle, and blew. There was tense silence for a moment as the lieutenant shouted in German. Of course, York couldn't understand a word. As shapes emerged from the trees above him to reveal German soldiers, one after another, hands in the air, York kept his pistol pointed at Vollmer's head. Then, as the remaining doughboys rose and lifted their guns, York backed off a little and pointed his pistol at the newcomers, his face still set hard and staring.

One German soldier tried to be a hero. He had concealed a grenade behind his back, and when he got close he threw it at the pistol-wielding American corporal. York didn't even duck. The grenade sailed past his head and exploded behind him. Several Germans and Americans screamed, but York didn't hear them. He was too busy pumping bullets into the grenade-thrower's head.

There was no more resistance after that.

A strange procession assembled to depart the Argonne. Still suspicious, York kept Vollmer and another German officer at the front of the column, his pistol pointed menacingly at their backs. The rest of the Germans followed behind in columns of twos, carrying the wounded and guarded by the other doughboys. Before they left, Vollmer asked York how many men he had. "I have plenty," the Tennessean snapped. When the American hesitated over which route to take back to his own lines, Vollmer suggested they turn north. York promptly chose to take the opposite way, close to the one he had taken into the woods.

As the men moved out, another German platoon appeared and the Americans leveled their rifles. Misjudging the number of doughboys guarding the column, the Germans dropped their guns and surrendered. Later another detachment led by a German lieutenant appeared and deployed for a fight. York shoved his pistol at the base of Vollmer's spine and held it steady. Tell them to surrender, he ordered, or he would kill the lieutenant and all of them too. Knowing he would be the first to go down with his guts blown out in any fight, Vollmer talked his comrades out of the woods and convinced them to join the captives.

All except one, a boy, who refused to drop his gun. York shot him to death. He didn't think about it until later.

As he approached the tree line, York judged that the direct approach was the best, and led his column right out into the open. The rest of the battalion must have wondered why the German-held hill had gone quiet, but didn't do anything about it until the strange column appeared before their eyes. Most of the men were German, and some of the doughboys along the base of Hill 223 prepared to open fire.

But they didn't. Maybe they were alert, or just too dazed and tired. Equally fortunately, enemy fire from the north and south had tapered off thanks to the persistence of 28th and 82nd Division troops in both directions. Harassed only by occasional German artillery shells, the Americans and their prisoners made it across the clearing without incident. York took them up to the first American officer he saw, a lieutenant, saluted, and presented his prisoners. The lieutenant asked how many prisoners he had in tow.

"Honest, lieutenant, I don't know," York replied.

There were 132.

Farther back, the column encountered General Julian R. Lindsey, who commanded York's brigade. "Well, York, I hear you have captured the whole German army," he said. But neither he nor York yet realized the scale of what the Tennessean had accomplished. Other troops had made progress into the woods on either side. Other brave men had helped to capture the prisoners. But mainly it was York, through his instinctive action founded in skills he had learned in a lifetime spent among outsiders, who had wiped out a heavily defended strongpoint and so broken the back of the German defenses in the eastern Argonne.

At ten thirty that morning, shortly after receiving news of the action that had unhinged his line, General Wellmann passed on orders for his troops to begin evacuating the Argonne Forest.[8]

None of the men involved appreciated their roles in bringing about this outcome. General Liggett didn't know that his finger on the map had dragged York into the Argonne. York didn't realize what brought him to this point in his life, or why he behaved as he did despite his renunciation of violence years before. He certainly didn't know anything about the Lost Battalion, and had never heard of Charles Whittlesey or George McMurtry. His only encounter with New York City had been a few days spent cleaning up after the Metropolitan Division at Camp Upton in the fall of 1917. Perhaps then he had wandered into the 308th Regiment's empty camp theater, and wondered who had built it and why they had wasted their time.

Whittlesey had no way of knowing about the Tennessee corporal from another division who had helped to bring the German Argonne defenses crumbling to ashes. Neither did McMurtry. But then, they still understood little of what they had accomplished. Whittlesey didn't realize he had saved his men, but he had. McMurtry did not consciously decide to become Whittlesey's rock, but he did. Nor did Whittlesey, McMurtry, or any of the other men of the Lost Battalion know how their impetuosity and then their resolution had created a crisis that threatened to undermine the entire American war effort, or how their bravery led to Liggett's decision to deploy the 82nd Division, and Corporal York, into the eastern Argonne, resulting in their relief and the first major breakthrough of Pershing's offensive.

Damon Runyon also did not get any of this. Just as York, Whittlesey, and McMurtry had thought only of challenges as they came—of preserving the lives of their men, and of survival—the man from the *New York American* was only interested in finding out about the men, and telling their stories. But now it was his turn: his, and that of his fellow newspaper, book, and even movie men, and of the American political and military authorities. They would decide how America handled the likes of heroes such as these, and how the country would celebrate, or discard, them.

Beneath the surface, though, the glue that bound York, Whittlesey, and McMurtry for the rest of their lives, uplifting and consuming them, and forever changing the United States of America, had already formed.

York awoke sometime that night and wondered what he had done. His memory was spotty, his mind in the process of blotting out things he didn't want to remember. A terrifying feeling told him that in future he must sleep "by the dead and with the dead." And so he rose, corralled the two stretcher-bearers, crossed the clearing, climbed the now silent hill, and walked down into the woods. He was searching for survivors. He was hunting for meaning. He was seeking God. And he was yearning for redemption.

(CHAPTER FOURTEEN)

UNKNOWN SOLDIERS

They had departed New York City in a snowstorm. They returned in the full bloom of springtime, accompanied by a chill wind reminiscent of autumn in the Argonne.

In September 1917, listless crowds had lined Fifth Avenue to watch the Metropolitan draftees saunter through the city on their way to the Polo Grounds and Camp Upton. On May 6, 1919, the 77th Division paraded through the city again in front of a vast cheering throng. New York City embraced the Metropolitan Division as a "mother of warriors opened her arms to her children." Charles Whittlesey and George McMurtry were enfolded in that same embrace. Alvin York would be too, just over two weeks later.

Fifth Avenue had been cleaned for a five-mile stretch north of Washington Square Arch until the streets and sidewalks were nearly spotless. Crowds gathered that morning, concentrated at the arch and at the Metropolitan Museum where the mayor, the secretary of war, and miscellaneous military and civilian dignitaries stood atop a reviewing stand. A firm blue line of New York police held the crowds back from the street. As they waited, a gray cloud bank whipped the sun from view and a cold, steady breeze swept off New York Harbor across Manhattan, forcing the lightly clad spectators to stamp and clap their arms.

Trumpets blared at ten o'clock and expectant watchers broke into loud cheering, craning their necks for a look at their boys. But then a wave of silence rippled through the crowd and men doffed their hats. A horse-drawn carriage rattled slowly up the avenue bearing a man-sized replica of the Statue of Liberty, bedecked in hundreds of daffodils. Ten solemn-faced soldiers marched alongside and behind, each bearing a white banner sparkling with golden stars. There were 2,356 stars—one for each Metropolitan doughboy who had made the ultimate sacrifice. Muffled drumbeats accompanied the procession, and as it passed the reviewing stand the police band broke into a rendition of "Till We Meet Again."

General Alexander's turn came next.

A procession of police bearing red and white guidons followed the carriage. Behind them, cheerleaders rushed to take their places along the line. As General Alexander appeared in view, riding a brown charger borrowed from a policeman who had shown it at the Madison Square Garden horse show, the cheerleaders shouted and cavorted to give the man who had pushed the 77th Division through the Argonne his due. The crowd followed their lead, and their roars followed Alexander all the way up the avenue. Back straight, cap tilted at a jaunty angle, one hand clutching the bridle and the other resting on a sheaf of flowers, his face "glowing with boyish delight," the general basked in adulation.

And Alexander was still pushing. Before the parade, he had boasted that his men would cover the distance from the arch to 110th Street in ninety minutes flat. Every officer and soldier had been ordered to meet the general's expectations and so confirm his promise. They did as they were told, marching behind Alexander with a smart, swift step, bayonets fixed, helmets slung bouncing from their shoulders, caps perched smartly on their heads.

But this was New York City, and the boys—whether from Manhattan, Brooklyn, the Bronx, Rochester, Big Hole, or Billings—belonged to it, not to General Alexander. As he rode north to choreographed cheers, explosive shouts like a thousand Black Toms rocked the crowds behind him as the soldiers passed. As always at events in the big city, spectators all carried newspapers to read while waiting, and to hold overhead in case of rain. At some point a citygoer tore his or her paper into bits and hurled it on the soldiers. Then groups, then the whole crowd did the same, showering the men in homemade confetti. The soldiers beamed, knowing to whom they belonged.

The crowd of one million (according to the *New York Times*), representing every cross section of Greater New York including "bearded patriarchs" and immigrants of every shape and color from the Lower East Side, arrayed along the streets, in windows, on rooftops, on lamp posts, loved all the doughboys. But they were especially eager to see Whittlesey and his men. They had to wait.

The 153rd Brigade marched first, accompanied by machine gun units and celebrities such as "Bangs" the wolfhound who had been captured from the Germans in the Argonne and served his new masters faithfully. A stray dachshund, a Manhattan native despite his Teutonic ancestry, adopted the parade and accompanied it all the way up Fifth Avenue. As the dog waddled smugly along behind the general's horse, Alexander proudly enjoyed raucous cheers for the cheeky dachshund that he thought spectators had reserved especially for him.

Wounded men followed each unit, some pale faced and limping painfully as they struggled to keep up with the general's frenetic pace, others riding in cars, laughing and smiling and waving crutches. But as one unit followed another, impatient spectators began yelling: "Where's the Lost Battalion?" "Where's Whittlesey?" Too happy to be offended, the doughboys jokingly yelled back: "It's lost again!" or "What's the matter with us?"

Whittlesey and McMurtry marched at the head of their battalions of the 308th Regiment near the end of the procession. The regimental band played strangely out of key, for some of the brass instruments had been damaged in the fighting and not repaired. The doughboys marched as required, and McMurtry even smiled—he had been working since April to help plan the parade as a tribute to his men. But Whittlesey's eyes were blank and he refused to speak to reporters.

General Alexander had one more accolade to receive—from his men. At 110th Street he and his entourage wheeled to the right and turned to inspect the troops as they marched past, fortunately for them, on time. "Eyes right!" yelled an officer, and the men turned to pay tribute to Alexander, who received it in silence.

The perfection of the scene was marred only by two airmen who buzzed the general and his aides at a height of just a few hundred feet, causing reporters and soldiers to expend more energy worrying about a potential crash than paying their respects to the general. He didn't mind. "Jubilant as a school boy" at showing proof that he still had push, Alexander told assembled reporters as the parade ended: "I told you we'd do it [passing the reviewing stand] in forty-five minutes. And here we've made it in forty-three minutes. Imagine a division passing a given point in forty-three minutes. It is remarkable."

At a posh dinner that night at the Waldorf-Astoria, General Alexander announced that the Metropolitan Division had been renamed the Liberty Division. Other officers had warned him that the 77th Division would be "chewed up" in the Argonne, he declared. But he had proven them wrong. They had "never stopped" and "were not chewed up." Their success was due to their high morale. "It is the spirit that conquers," he said. His honored guests made sure everyone knew to whom the credit belonged. Napoleon and Hannibal had been unable to conquer the Argonne, one speaker proclaimed. "It was not Alexander the Great, but Alexander the Greater who did it." The general beamed.[1]

Alvin York arrived in the metropolis on May 22. He received a hero's welcome. A tugboat circled the transport *Ohioan* as it entered the harbor, bearing York and other members of his 328th Regiment. About fifty members of the Tennessee Society of New York, wealthy businessmen with Volunteer State origins, crowded the decks of the tugboat shouting, "York! York! We want York!" Meanwhile, a throng of VIPs stepped out of sleek limousines to join a throng of movie and still cameramen, reporters, and flag-waving spectators crowding the government pier at Hoboken where the *Ohioan* would dock. York fled and locked himself in the stateroom.

When the ship docked, the crowd rushed on board looking for York, without waiting for the homesick soldiers to get off. Twenty minutes passed before somebody figured out he was hiding in the stateroom, but he refused to answer their frantic knocks. When an officer arrived and ordered him out, he emerged, "poked his bristly red head out the door, blushed purple and ducked back again." Five minutes more passed before he came out again. The crowd was merciless.

Committee members for the society warmly patted York's back and shook his hand, which a watching city reporter thought looked as big as a young ham. Everyone shouted at once. All he could do was stare back, tears in his eyes, looking terrified and confused. Shoved along "more like a prisoner than a hero," York passed through a mandatory delousing station and then was harried onto the pier. Newsmen snapped his picture and movie cameras rolled for thirty minutes as he tried to deflect questions and give credit to God. The abduction culminated when York was dragged into a limousine and driven off for a tour of the city. The Tennesseans, supported by York's congressman Cordell Hull, and organized into the "York Must See New York Committee," had insisted upon this as a badge of recognition for the red-headed doughboy and themselves.

A caravan of cars drove York across the city and pulled up in front of the Waldorf-Astoria, all of the automobiles unloading simultaneously. York was carried as much as he walked into the hotel lobby, where another crowd awaited. Bellboys fought over the right to carry his bag, but were thwarted by the manager who hefted them himself and cleared a way through the crowd to the elevator. The manager, the bellboys, and as many of the Tennessee committee who could fit crowded with York into the elevator, which carried them to a suite of adjoining rooms usually reserved for the president of the United States. The manager clapped his hands for maids to open the door, and all of them—manager, bellboys, maids, reporters, and multiple elevator carfuls of Tennesseans—roiled into the suite around the bewildered hero.

The spectators chuckled as York looked for a place to hang his cap—they assumed he was looking for a nail—and laid it on a divan in the richly appointed room that included a grand piano. A committeeman grabbed York's elbow and dragged him over to a table where his group had placed a silver-framed photo of the soldier's mother. Dr. James J. King, chairman of the society and a doctor from Columbia, Tennessee, south of Nashville (the same folks that York's people had fought in the Civil War), asked York if he wanted a bath, holding open the doors to the luxurious bathroom. "Somebody said something about dinner," the soldier responded, "and I guess I'll just have a roll up and a roll down."

Fascinated, the growing crowd watched as York rolled up his sleeves and rolled down his collar and washed up. Another committee member brushed his coat. When he emerged from the bathroom someone asked York to take off a shoe, which he did, and a committeeman knelt down to trace the outline of his foot. Inspecting his woolen socks, they decided he deserved better and brought in a pair of silk ones with matching elegant shoes. After that, crowds gawked while he got a shave and a haircut. Then they watched him eat dinner.

Afterward the phone rang at the desk telephone in a committee member's drawing room. After hours of trying, a call to Tennessee had been put through. It was York's mother. He was given fifteen minutes alone to talk, and emerged with a broad grin. The talk had given him strength. After all his reticence at dinner, York finally opened up.

Turning to assembled reporters, York smiled confidentially and said, "Look here. I'll show you what the German battalion commander tried to kill me with." With that he pulled out a shiny Mauser automatic pistol that he had taken from the body of the officer he shot in front of Lieutenant Vollmer. York had refused to sell it despite numerous offers. "Got the lieutenant right through the stomach," he said with obvious satisfaction. "He dropped, screaming. Then I shot the others. All of them screamed when they were hit. Like pigs. They were only about twenty yards away. I couldn't miss." A reporter asked him if the twenty-five Germans he had killed weighed on his conscience. York responded without hesitation. "My conscience is clear. The blame is on the Germans for starting this war."

Despite his bravado, York was sweating, and the reporters couldn't help noticing it. One cub reporter, trying to be witty, remarked that York probably wouldn't have gone through all that fuss in the Argonne if he had known what he would have to face in New York City. York's face darkened and he fixed the reporter with narrow, menacing eyes. "Friend," he drawled, "I never thought about anything more than what I was doing there. And I did what I did because I just had to do it. That's all."

"Don't you part with it, son," said a committeeman, indicating the pistol. "Money don't mean a thing to you. You're gonna have so much that you can light your pipe with it if that strikes your fancy." He told York they were giving him a fifty-thousand-dollar farm and two thousand dollars in cash. Tomorrow, York would get a reception in the hotel ballroom and then a dinner with a thousand guests and General Duncan in attendance. York was delighted, his shyness gone. Seeing the twin beds in his room, he laughed and said, "You can't fool me! I'll sleep all over both of 'em!" He went to sleep, alone at last, well after midnight.

The media assumed that York would sleep late the next morning, but were unprepared for his early habits. Up at five thirty, he had a huge breakfast of ham and eggs, hot biscuits, hominy, strawberry shortcake, and pancakes with plenty of coffee and then disappeared walking west along 34th Street. When he wandered back into the lobby at noon, he told worried members of the Tennessee committee that he had visited the dentist, but they had no time for explanations and whisked him off to the Stock Exchange.

Watching the frenetic activity on the exchange floor from the visitors' gallery, York said, "Kinda reminds me of the battle of the Meuse-Argonne. When do we eat?" But he had been spotted. When the traders put up a cheer for the visiting hero, he bowed quickly and tried to depart, but a batch of brokers cut him off, hoisted him on their shoulders, and carried him around the floor. They propped him on a platform and made him talk. He said only: "I did the best I could and that was all I could do." Then they grabbed him again. Trading had been called off, but the brokers had found a new commodity and so they offered York for sale. Bidding was frenzied and he was sold for a high price, then sold again and again until they finally let him go.

"I tell you I'm pretty weary," York groaned as the limousine carried him away from the Stock Exchange past the Woolworth Building and back to his hotel. "New York is certainly a great city," he complained, "but it do tire a fellow out some." He would get no rest. Dinner that night hosted the promised thousand guests, including Duncan and war artist Joseph Cummings Chase, who had just painted the sergeant's portrait. After a speech by Duncan, York was thrust to the podium and the assembly shouted bloodthirstily for the story of how he had killed all those Germans. But York was no longer in the mood. "I'd love to entertain you-all with a speech tonight," he said, "but I just can't do it." They tried again and again, supported by Duncan, but he continued to refuse.

That evening, Cordell Hull took him on board a train to Washington, DC. On May 24, he visited the House of Representatives, and heard a speech by Hull crediting York with "the greatest individual feat of bravery in the war." The delegates cheered and

York saluted. Then he went to the War Department to meet the secretary of war, and to the White House to meet with President Wilson's secretary Joseph Tumulty. Wilson was in Paris, and since York had already encountered him there while on furlough in the city earlier that year, the soldier declared finally that he had "seen it all."

Except the New York City subway. During dinner at the Waldorf, York had said he wanted to see the subway. There was no time, but the city authorities promised to catch him on his way back from Washington. On May 25, York was taken to Long Island where he had another gala dinner at the Garden City Hotel, and was hailed as the future governor of Tennessee. After a night in a suite used by former president Taft, York was taken on a tour of Manhattan. Shoved in the back of a limousine "between two of New York's most dashing younger society women," he got to see Central Park and Grant's tomb. And he finally got his subway ride, again with crowds of committeemen and reporters in tow. While on the train, York just grunted, but when a reporter asked him at Penn Station what he thought of the subway, York said, "You've got to hand it to New York."

That evening, after a "stag dinner" with the Tennessee Society, York took a box seat for a revue at the Winter Garden. The audience cheered and begged him to take the stage, but he bowed and refused. They asked him to make a speech from his box, but he said, "No, I jest won't," and clamped his jaws shut. After the performance, however, he was taken backstage and crushed by a swarm of barely clad chorus girls. After that, dazed but happy, he escaped for a time. York had to get his discharge from the army at Camp Merritt. And a lady waited for him back home.[2]

For most men of the 77th and 82nd Divisions, the celebrations ended with the parades in New York City or their hometowns. The expectation was that they would return to their families, or maybe get married and find jobs. No one found it easy. Marriages failed and families split apart because of veterans' struggles to cope with civilian life, or civilians' problems in adjusting to the return of their changed loved ones. An economic downturn—temporary, but they didn't know it then—drastically reduced employment opportunities. No official mechanism existed for aiding soldiers struggling with physical and mental debilities.

But they did not have to cope entirely on their own. Instinctively, veterans turned to the people they trusted most: each other. Almost every division, including the 77th and 82nd, formed a voluntary aid association. So did many smaller units, and so eventually would the Lost Battalion. Conscientious field officers who still felt responsible for their men often led and staffed them. But it was the ex-noncoms and common doughboys who made the organizations work. Through these associations, men received advice, instructions, connectivity, informal group therapy, and occasionally a little monetary aid. The support was especially welcome for men returning to life in the big cities. In smaller towns and in the country, community support was vital.

And the American community in some ways became wider. Racial divisions remained profound—after 1919 the Ku Klux Klan would become more powerful than ever before—but that resulted in part from the AEF's failure to properly integrate African Americans or credit their contribution to victory. But although divisions between city and country, native born and immigrant, did not go away, significant barriers fell. Before the war, first- and second-generation immigrant communities lived almost entirely walled off from mainstream society, even in big cities. New York

City was suspected of being un-American, and profound divisions separated city and country. After the war, though, new attitudes developed. Now they were all Americans.

The Lost Battalion presented a microcosm of this phenomenon. By their bravery, resolution under adversity, and group spirit they had shown how Jews, Christians, unbelievers, country boys, city boys, Anglo-Saxons, southern and eastern Europeans, Asians, Native Americans, rich and poor could work together under one flag and become one. Nobody needed to tell them what had happened—they knew and believed it. But the American media, by zeroing in on what had happened in the Charlevaux Ravine and telling the story to the world, ensured that the public would recognize and appreciate the example.

Damon Runyon had initiated the process when he met the Lost Battalion survivors as they emerged from the pocket. Almost alone among his fellow reporters, he skipped the official line in order to learn what happened from the soldiers themselves. His fascination with the doughboys—not just the archetype athlete-warrior, but the everyday guy who loved boozing, gambling, womanizing, smoking, cussing, telling bawdy jokes, and beating up on the Germans—ensured that everybody got in on the game, not just the cookie-cutter heroes. His reports from the pocket had been the first to emphasize the humanity, the common American quality of the men in the pocket, and his continuing reports from the front would set the tone for many years to come.

Yet there was a sinister strain emerging in other media coverage that would manipulate the commonest (but also most complex) of men, Alvin C. York, as a tool to divide.

The postwar publicity machine operated at a fever pitch by the spring of 1919. Damon Runyon, now lionized as a "famous war correspondent," refused to take part in it. Even in reporting war, he remained his own man. Others could say what they wanted—it was the common doughboys who interested him.

Runyon stuck with the 77th Division through October 1918 as it occupied the Argonne. Pershing had what some witnesses described as a nervous breakdown in mid-October and turned over command of First Army to General Liggett, who led it through to the end of the war. Runyon didn't catch the command transfer or the reasons for it—he was too busy mixing with the troops, recording their conversations, and seeking out city and athletic celebrities. During his rambles he learned details about the death of Eddie Grant and reported them, pointing out that the ex-ball-player had died trying to relieve the Lost Battalion. Although he met and admired Liggett, as well as a "mild looking, retiring man" named Colonel George C. Marshall whom he correctly identified as one of the logistical architects of victory, Runyon followed the troops all the way to November 11. The night before the armistice, he and Thomas Johnson tried desperately to get back to the 77th Division so they could gather some local color for their readers, but couldn't make it in time and ended up with another outfit near the town of Sedan. Unfazed, Runyon settled down with the men and asked them how they felt about the peace.[3]

When the war ended, many reporters rushed off to Paris to seek official reactions or follow political developments. Not Runyon. He stayed with the troops, meeting returning prisoners of war and recording their reactions to German captivity. Then he followed the army, switching from one formation to another, as it marched out of France and into Luxembourg and Germany to form the army of occupation. Once again, his primary interest was not headquarters but the doughboys. He published a series of "Doughboy Dialogues" based on conversations he had heard in the lines in the Argonne and other parts of France, and in Germany.

While in Germany, Runyon still followed athletes, watching boxing matches and ball games. He became particular friends with Red Sox catcher and infantryman Hank Gowdy, and with famed ace and former race car driver Eddie Rickenbacker. These were his kind of men. Still, he mixed mostly with everyday soldiers, not paying much attention to the trends and "hot stories" followed by his fellow journalists, and thus missing out on the growing brouhaha about Alvin C. York. In January 1919, Runyon had a brief but frightening bout with influenza. This and his continuing frustrations with military censorship convinced him that it was time to go home.[4]

The massive transport ship *Leviathan*, a former German liner of the Hamburg America Line, docked at Hoboken on March 6. It carried Runyon and nine thousand soldiers of the 27th "Empire" Division, New York State National Guard, which had fought under British command in Flanders. The troops received an enthusiastic reception, followed in April by a parade in Manhattan. While on board, Runyon typically hadn't bothered with interviewing the officers, including the division's celebrity commander, Manhattan attorney John F. O'Ryan. Instead he hung around the infantry, writing down their conversations and jokes for publication after his arrival.

Almost as soon as he set foot back in the city, Runyon set to interviewing and writing the life story of boxer Jack Dempsey, due to fight Jess Willard for the world heavyweight title on July 4, 1919. Dempsey fascinated Runyon as a new type of boxer, kind in person but "ferocious . . . almost primitive in the ring"; a man who "sheds punches as fast as a machine gun sheds bullets." He was so preoccupied with this that he missed the arrival of the first large contingent of 77th Division soldiers in New York on the liner *Aquitania* on April 24. In another respect, though, he would not miss the significance of the day.[5]

The division's arrival had been anticipated for months. New Yorkers were determined that the draftees should be welcomed just as warmly as the National Guardsmen, and that they should also get a parade. For several weeks the War Department held back, insisting that one expensive parade was enough for New York City. Thanks to support from General O'Ryan and Acting Secretary of the Navy Franklin Delano Roosevelt, and following a demonstration of 77th Division wives in Washington, DC, the War Department backed down. By the time the *Aquitania* docked the department had promised a parade.

As the *Aquitania* and other vessels bearing 77th Division troops sailed into New York Harbor in April and May, troops crowded the decks to adoringly cheer the same Statue of Liberty that had seen them off over a year earlier. The first contingent of doughboys then debarked in the rain, proudly wearing their new shoulder patches bearing the same Statue of Liberty. Huge crowds welcomed them. Then, appropriately, they rushed off to the city ballparks. It was opening day, and Damon Runyon had no intention of missing it.

"It all came back yesterday afternoon like the fulfillment of a precious dream," he wrote for the following morning's edition of the *New York American*, "the good old game of baseball! Not the half-dead-and-half-alive baseball of the dark wartime period; not the pallid wraith of the pastime that stalked ghostily across the dreary days of Summer for the past few years, but the old game itself, full lunged, and red, red blooded." As he heard the crowds roar, it seemed to Runyon like "the sweetest music in all the world—the great booming of human pipes pouring out the enthusiasm of the soul." They even celebrated when Babe Ruth hit a home run for the Red Sox.

Runyon hoped to find forgetfulness in sports. Charles Whittlesey and his officers never enjoyed the same catharsis. They were not among the returning heroes on April 23. They had come back to the city long ago, completely unheralded.[6]

The 77th Division had fought in the Meuse-Argonne region throughout the remainder of October 1918. Whittlesey wanted nothing more than to stay with his men. "Out here in the woods . . . where the hidden things of life begin to show, one learns new things," he wrote a friend on October 12. Friendship in particular acquired new meaning. Before the month was out, however, and while his soldiers kept fighting, Whittlesey was ordered home, ostensibly to help raise a new regiment but more likely to be available for anticipated publicity.[7]

Whittlesey arrived in New York just after the armistice on November 14. To his shock, people treated him like a hero. For this he had his former adjutant Arthur McKeogh, stateside since October 8, to thank. McKeogh had seen nothing of the fighting in the pocket, but as a former newspaperman he did not hesitate to talk to the press about Whittlesey, McMurtry, and other men he had known with the 308th. Reporters had already tracked down and interviewed Whittlesey's former landlady, who insisted that he would never swear and thus could not have said "go to hell." Ignoring her, Runyon, and Irwin, newspapers decided to call him "Go to Hell Whittlesey" at every opportunity.[8]

Whittlesey tried and failed to avoid the notoriety. In command performances across the city, beginning at the Williams Club, he insisted that he and his men had "simply stuck" and denied that he had said "go to hell" or been any kind of hero. Reporters brushed aside his denials, apparently with increasing annoyance, and repeated the same stories.

One of Whittlesey's first acts was to write a lengthy letter to the mother of Lieutenant Gordon Schenck, most of which she refused to release to the press. He then attended a funeral service for Schenck on Thanksgiving in Clinton Congregational Church in Brooklyn, and consoled the deceased's family. On December 5, President Wilson announced that Whittlesey and McMurtry (still in France) would be awarded the Medal of Honor. On the same day, Whittlesey received his discharge from the army.[9]

But the media quickly fell out of love with Whittlesey. Like York, he consistently refused to regale reporters with action-packed tales of his exploits, insisting that he had just done his duty. But unlike the "hillbilly" from Tennessee, it was impossible to poke fun at this solemn, tortured intellectual. At public appearances he stood awkwardly, and turned away from curious reporters. When he spoke at all it was to stick to the facts, deny legend, pay tribute to the men, and, worse, call for an end of hate and promote the humane treatment of Germany. He stood as stiffly as ever when he received the Medal of Honor from General Clarence Edwards on Boston Commons on Christmas Eve. Afterward Whittlesey returned to his family.

On January 19, 1919, *Seattle Times* reporter J. C. Wade tracked Whittlesey down to Pittsfield and succeeded in securing an interview with him and his mother. Wade found her sitting in an armchair, gazing lovingly at her son perched alongside. After a few minutes Mrs. Whittlesey excused herself, and her boy stood, kissed her, and patted her lovingly on the shoulder before returning to his seat. Wade, noticing the deep scar alongside Whittlesey's nose, started to ask him about his role in the pocket, only to be cut off midsentence. Holding up his hand with a frozen smile, Whittlesey dismissed the wound as a scratch; and before the reporter could begin again he crossed his legs, stared sternly, and said, "I would much rather talk about the boys who came to our rescue than about the details of our experience in the ravine."

Whittlesey then spoke of Eddie Grant. Perhaps he had read Runyon's articles about the fallen ballplayer. Whittlesey had been friends with Grant at Harvard, and reminisced about sitting with him on the law school steps and walking on the commons. The two men had gone to Plattsburg together and then to Camp Upton. "I can just see and hear that boy," Whittlesey said with a distant look in his eyes, "when he heard that my battalion was trapped in the woods saying, 'Well, if there is any chance to get my old friend "Whit" out of that hole, I want to be the man to do it.'

"When the shell burst and killed that boy America lost one of the finest types of manhood I have ever known," Whittlesey continued with his eyes misting up. "His memory will always remain dear to me." Wade, fully putting his foot in it now, mumbled something about the men of the Lost Battalion "calmly awaiting death." Leaping up, eyes flashing behind his spectacles, with hands on his hips, Whittlesey tore into the reporter. "I want to tell you that the boys of our battalion did not calmly await death," he growled. "They were certainly quiet, through force of circumstances, but they were not calm. When a bullet goes through your helmet, just grazing your scalp, and the next instant a fragment of a bursting shell skims your back and you stay in that little funk hole waiting for the next—well, I don't see how anyone could be very calm." As he spoke, Whittlesey must have heard screams in his ears.

Sitting, lighting a cigarette, and shifting nervously in his chair, Whittlesey did his best to field a battery of inane questions. Wade asked if there had been any humorous moments. "Well, hardly," Whittlesey drawled. Then Wade spoke of sacrifice. "Sacrifices!" Whittlesey snapped angrily through a curling cloud of cigarette smoke. "Why, this war has been just one continual succession of sacrifices." But then he remembered a sturdy, handsome, "well-knit" boy from the West who volunteered to serve as a runner with a smile and sparkling eyes. Whittlesey prayed for the boy's life as he left, and heard the shot that killed him. He recalled men dying begging for water. One lieutenant allowed a man to go and try to get water for his friend, only to see him fall to a sniper's bullet on his way to the spring.

Whittlesey told what it felt like to starve. He spoke of having to deny mortally wounded men their dying wishes. And when Wade asked him what it felt like when General Alexander grasped his hand after the relief and promoted him to lieutenant colonel on the spot, Whittlesey snarled contemptuously: "Oh, well, naturally I was so thrilled at the general's words that I simply trembled." And that, Wade decided, was enough of that. Over the following weeks reporters had similar experiences with Whittlesey and just gave up trying.[10]

Whittlesey probably hoped he could fade into obscurity. But where he refused to talk, reporters found plenty of his men who were more forthcoming. And increasingly, the press tended to be critical. Shortly after returning to France, likely as a matter of military routine rather than out of any sense of vindictiveness, Whittlesey formally preferred charges against Lieutenant Revnes for advocating surrender. This led just after Christmas to a formal hearing and investigation in France, exposing simmering tensions.

McMurtry and Holderman, who had both urged Whittlesey to file charges, supported him to the hilt. Others, however—not knowing the orders imposed by Alexander, Johnson, Stacey, and others—accused Whittlesey of having been too impetuous in advance and too stubborn to retreat. Revnes was convicted, but then it was overturned, and by February 1919 he had been acquitted. Whittlesey, however, had become an ambiguous kind of hero. Some soldiers leaked their critiques of his leadership to the press. Three days after he and his division paraded in New York, the *Tribune* published an interview with two fliers who blamed Whittlesey's ignorance of proper signaling for their inability to accurately drop supplies to the pocket.[11]

McMurtry was able to avoid the notoriety that Whittlesey and York feared. Nobody questioned his heroism or pestered him with questions about his service. He received his Medal of Honor from General Pershing at a ceremony with several other recipients in Paris on March 2, 1919. A few days later he returned to the division's encampment and helped to form the 77th Division Association, which was tasked with helping to get Metropolitan doughboys jobs after they returned home. McMurtry served as treasurer. He devoted most of his free time to it after returning from France with the rank of major on April 28, although the photo taken of him on shipboard just before he debarked reveals the anguish on his face. He marched alongside Whittlesey in New York on May 6.[12]

York couldn't hide from the spotlight like McMurtry, but he had more time to prepare for it than Whittlesey. After October 8, 1918, York had remained with his unit as it fought through the Meuse-Argonne. He was promoted to sergeant on November 1, a welcome development since it entailed higher pay, and stayed with his unit, except for brief furloughs in Paris, through the long wait for demobilization. York and his buddies got to meet President Woodrow and First Lady Edith Wilson on Christmas 1918, but he was given no particular fanfare and looked forward to resuming life as a humble mountain farmer.

It was not to be. Just before the war ended, Captain Danforth initiated an investigation into York's conduct that resulted in an award of the Distinguished Service Cross on November 30. Dissatisfied, Danforth suggested that York be considered for the Medal of Honor. General Duncan concurred, but had to initiate an intensive investigation. Unlike many of its sort, this one would be conducted publicly.

In January 1919 the war artist Joseph Cummings Chase painted York's portrait along with those of several dozen other Distinguished Service Cross recipients. Finding York's story fascinating, he recommended it to George Pattullo of the *Saturday Evening Post*. Pattullo was a Canadian-born author who had penned popular Wild West stories before becoming a war correspondent. A fervent United States nationalist, he got along well with the American military authorities. As a reporter covering the occupation in Germany, Pattullo described Germans as fat and wealthy despite the British naval blockade. He also accused the British and French of trying to cover up the fact that providence had chosen the United States as a tool for winning the war. Chase and Pattullo talked with Duncan, who decided that Pattullo was "able, conservative and reliable." He invited the artist, the reporter, and York to accompany him to the Argonne battlefield to determine what had happened there, and why.[13]

The men tramped over the battlefield in early February 1919. The air blew cold, and snow covered the ground. York pointed out, to the best of his memory, which likely was only partially accurate considering the circumstances of the fight, how he had gotten around Hill 223 and where the subsequent action had taken place. Every now and then he stopped to pose for photographers. While they walked around, Pattullo spoke with York. In the process the reporter decided that only a miracle could explain what had happened on October 8, 1918; that York was America's greatest hero; and that Pattullo was the man to tell his story.

After extensive interviews with other soldiers involved in the fighting that day, York's Medal of Honor was approved and he received it from Duncan in France on April 18, 1919. Almost simultaneously Pattullo's story about York, "The Second Elder Gives Battle," was published in the *Saturday Evening Post*. The story gave York sole credit for the victory, and attributed it to the Tennessean's clean living and strong morals. It also presented him as the quintessential American: "Have you ever seen a gunman of the old Southwest? A real gunman, not the loud, quarrelsome, spurious, saloon hero? Well, that's York." Pattullo gave no credit to York's comrades, perhaps not coincidentally given that those who survived were mostly recent immigrants and city dwellers. The article was a huge hit. It made Pattullo a celebrity, and York too, as he would find out when he landed in New York a month later.[14]

Print media no longer held a monopoly on publicity. Movies had become a big thing in the United States during the war. Lowell Thomas, a twenty-five-year-old Princeton lecturer in rhetoric and part-time journalist who possessed the instincts of a showman, went to war in May 1917 with a commission from the Wilson administration to promote the war effort through film. After wandering about France and finding nothing especially glorious there, he went to Italy and then to Jerusalem in search of the kind of romance the American public would appreciate. He discovered T. E. Lawrence. Thomas convinced the Englishman to advise and star in a film about the liberation of Jerusalem. Two movies resulted: *With Allenby in Palestine* and *With Lawrence in Arabia*.

In the spring of 1919, with the war ended but opportunities for personal promotion and profit nearly unlimited, Thomas took his films to New York City. He rented the Century Theatre in Central Park West with his own money, and used it as a forum to introduce his movies to the public. At each performance, Thomas appeared onstage when the curtain rose, declaring sonorously: "Come with me to lands of history, mystery and romance." He unveiled a massive photograph of Lawrence in Arab clothing and headdress, dubbing him the new Richard the Lionheart. The films swelled with adventure and romance, and produced the anticipated hit. After sell-out performances in Madison Square Garden, however, Thomas took his show on the road to Great Britain. The New York stage went dark, but others had already noticed his example.[15]

Lawrence was an Englishman, but Americans had plenty of heroes of their own. Damon Runyon's boss, William Randolph Hearst, wanted in on it, so in the spring of 1919 he commissioned Edward A. McManus, a former *McClure's Magazine* editor under contract to make movie serials for Hearst, to make a movie about the Lost Battalion. McManus joined forces with director Burton King, who in turn contacted General Alexander to help him out with the filming. Alexander, who took a "keen interest" that there should be "no error in the slightest detail," leapt at the chance to advise on set and appear on camera, and insisted that some of his officers and men should come along—perhaps so that he could bask in their reflected glory.

Whittlesey's reputation had by then become somewhat tarnished with the media, but Alexander felt that he could not make the movie without the ex-colonel's involvement. Maybe he even felt he could help polish the poor man a little, and give him the celebrity he deserved. How Alexander managed to persuade Whittlesey, who had no particular affection for his former general, is now impossible to say. Just before the victory parade, on "Argonne Day," May 1, Alexander had dragooned Whittlesey and some of his men into making a public demonstration on Park Avenue of the bayonet drill by which his men had "cleared the Argonne." Perhaps Whittlesey felt that by working on the movie with Alexander he could ensure that his men received the credit they were due. He made a terrible mistake.

McManus and King already planned to use their own team of silent actors, largely unknowns, to depict a corny love tale and a drama between two Chinese gang rivals drafted to serve at the front. This took up well over half of the finished picture. But Alexander wanted his own men in the story too, and asked Whittlesey to select and appear with them on camera. McMurtry, Cullen, Krotoshinsky, and a few others—but not Holderman, who had yet to receive a Medal of Honor despite Whittlesey's fervent advocacy—did so (Cher Ami got a stand-in). McKeogh appeared as Whittlesey's adjutant even though he hadn't participated in the battle.

King went all out. The filming took place, so producers claimed, somewhere near the actual battlefield. He set off bombs to create craters, and blew up trees and boulders. Shrapnel shells and signal flares exploded in the air. Barbed wire was draped with scraps of uniforms. "Soldiers" fired real bullets from machine guns and rifles through the foliage, and writhed in agony from feigned wounds. It was all very realistic by the standards of the time. Whittlesey, McMurtry, and the rest had not only to watch, but to participate in the on-site recreation of the most terrifying moments of their lives.

The sufferings of the veterans involved were taken by King and Alexander as proof that they were doing something right. One journalist wrote: "The realism of the production as it was played by the soldiers themselves overwhelmed them in its intensity.... The continuous firing and din unnerved not a few of the players, and the bits of realism that were injected by the soldiers themselves appalled them." The idea was to alternately amuse and horrify. Audiences would be delighted, and they bought the tickets.

Alexander, credited in film titles as "once a doughboy," appeared in multiple scenes as a relaxed, even jolly commander with a common touch. Of course, the filmmakers presented the relief of the Lost Battalion as his victory, with no mention of Liggett's flank attack. Cullen appeared signaling American airplanes, and McMurtry walked across the pocket, expressionless but undaunted under fire. Krotoshinsky, ramrod stiff, brought word of the Lost Battalion's predicament to their comrades. Whittlesey never appeared on camera alone, but in two brief scenes, inscrutable behind his glasses, in a command hole with McMurtry. It hardly mattered. McManus, King, and Alexander were only using the officers and men as window dressing intended to give the film an air of "authenticity."

Alexander loved the outcome. Back in the United States in July, he first presided over a screening of the film to some blue bloods and a few survivors at the Ritz-Carlton on July 2. Then he invited Secretary of War Newton D. Baker and several officers from the War College to a special screening. Afterward he boasted that the film, whose military tactics he claimed to have choreographed, could be used to train West Point cadets (a clear dig at the professional soldiers he had long despised).

The film opened in theaters across the country in August. A movie reviewer who slipped in late to see a special screening at New York City's George M. Cohan Theatre in September 1919 encountered a teary-eyed theater manager who whispered, "Oh, you missed the best part of it—you missed the romance." After that, whether because of poor attendance or other factors, the movie disappeared from view for two years.[16]

To many entertainers, York seemed a better prospect than the elusive Whittlesey. During the Tennessean's tour in New York, producer Jesse Lasky of the Famous Players-Lasky Corporation witnessed the commotion and decided that he wanted to buy the rights to his story for a motion picture. He talked with Flo Ziegfeld about it, who considered putting York in the Follies with Will Rogers. But although Lasky sent one of his flunkies to pull York aside and try to purchase the rights, the hero refused.

These offers received no publicity at the time, and later accounts suggesting that salesmen and movie moguls offered York hundreds of thousands of dollars for product endorsements and movie rights were probably as false as the story that New York gave him a ticker-tape parade. Many of these tales originated with an Australian war veteran and confidence man named Tom Skeyhill, who observed York's arrival in New York and thought hard about how he could use the hero's name for profit. Skeyhill, and Lasky, would be back.[17]

Alvin York took the usual route home. His train pulled in at Crossville, Tennessee, on May 29, 1919. A small, cheering crowd waited at the station with reporters nearby. He hesitated to get off the train, but friends finally dragged him over to a waiting convoy of six Ford Model Ts that had come to meet him from Jamestown. They whisked him off quickly, for he was in a hurry to depart. That evening they arrived in Jamestown, where he had a tearful reunion with his mother in front of more reporters.

Normally only a crazy man would try to make it from Jamestown to Pall Mall by car. But York was special and the drivers determined to try. Just in case the Model Ts couldn't handle it, a squad of men rode ahead by mule. As the cars bounced and jounced York along the steep, deeply rutted dirt roads, folks rushed out of their cabins to call mountain greetings: "Hello, Al!" and "How are you, Al?" to which he usually responded: "Oh, fair to middlin'." Henry Ford's cars lived up to their billing, and brought York to Pall Mall and the short walk home to his family.

Another small crowd loitered outside his farm door. Pastor Pile stood there too, to welcome him back into the church. Reporters plied York with the usual questions. He was polite but short with most of them. The fifty-thousand-dollar farm he supposedly now owned was still just a dream. York still only counted on what he could see and touch. "What Ah like best of all," he said, "is just to get back. It's where Ah've been all my life an Ah reckon it's the best place for me." A week later he married Gracie in Pall Mall.[18]

For two years, York tried to focus on tilling his mountain farm. He didn't want to relive his war experiences in any way. But he couldn't seem to settle down and relax. After marrying, he and Gracie celebrated in Nashville and honeymooned in Utah. Tributes and celebrations followed them everywhere, much to Gracie's discomfort and Pastor Pile's disgust. When York finally came back to Pall Mall, he became preoccupied with the idea of opening up his isolated region to the rest of an America, and a world, that he couldn't forget no matter how hard he tried.

York invested some of his tribute money into having a paved road built to the Wolf River Valley. He went on to establish the York Foundation to further rural education, make his people better farmers, and help them learn to read and write. But the foundation required money, and the fifty-thousand-dollar farm he had been "given," as it turned out, amounted to some four hundred acres of land worth half that amount, without any buildings. Worse, it was less than half paid for. York now had to find the money to pay it off even as he struggled to raise funds for the York Foundation. He was not much of a businessman, and could think of only one way to earn the money he needed: go on the road, and trade on his celebrity.

York did agree to give some product endorsements for money, providing they were products he had actually used. But he still refused any deal to appear or give his story to the movies, or to appear on stage. He went public about it, telling audiences at Rotary Club gatherings and other venues that he refused to "commercialize the honor I have gained under the flag" even though he could supposedly earn a thousand dollars a day by doing so.

From a publicity standpoint the appeal worked. Newspapers spread the word: York and his wife, now with a small baby, faced poverty unless the American people reached out to help. Tributes poured in. To keep them coming, York had to stay on the road, giving speeches about his war experiences and his faith. In the summer of 1921 he horrified evangelical audiences by telling them that vaudeville had just made another offer to him, reassuring them for the moment that he still was "not interested in making money out of patriotism." They gave in equal parts gratitude and hope that he would never have to sell his soul.

York was no shyster. He needed the money to provide for his family on a farm that supposedly had been given to him as a gift. The York Foundation also promised to help the bitterly impoverished people of northeast Tennessee. But these efforts also helped York himself, by giving him a place to channel his inward turmoil and continuing grief. Somehow, some way, he desperately desired to turn evil into good. On December 3, 1921, he finally got good news: donations had reached a level that allowed him to pay off the mortgage on his farm.[19]

George McMurtry had no money worries. He returned to his wife, Mabel, and their flat at 812 Fifth Avenue opposite the Central Park Zoo, and went back to his brokerage business. The couple rented a summer cottage at White Sulphur Springs, West Virginia, where George played golf and put on big dinner and dance parties at Kate's Mountain Club. His life was not devoid of drama—his brother Alden, a police officer, was badly injured while gunning down two burglars; and his two-year-old son, George Jr., died at the summer cottage in September 1920. For consolation, McMurtry took Mabel on a grand tour of western Europe, but their joint passport photo reveals a deeply unhappy couple whose marriage was crumbling. No media bothered him, however, and so he had time to work behind the scenes helping out troubled Lost Battalion survivors. Charles Whittlesey was one of those who needed the help.[20]

The war did not leave Whittlesey any more than it left York, McMurtry, or even Runyon. Whereas they found ways to channel their emotions, Whittlesey found none. The aftereffects he carried were not just mental. During the summer of 1918 he had inhaled a strong whiff of poison gas that he failed to report. By the time the war ended, Whittlesey had developed a cough that tormented him with all the maddening persistence of tinnitus. His brother Elisha, who had served as an ambulance driver during the war, suffered from the same complaint, and he would die when his tormented lungs finally gave out in 1922.

Work was a challenge too. Whittlesey ended his legal partnership with John Pruyn and practiced banking law for a Wall Street firm. But his attention wandered easily. Although his reticence had driven away the media for the most part, Whittlesey was still targeted for public speaking and fund-raising events for veterans' aid societies, including the American Legion and Red Cross, in Boston and New York. Again and again he appeared in public, awkward and retiring, sometimes with McMurtry and other former officers by his side, talking about his war experiences and world affairs—and wishing himself anywhere else.

There were light moments. He received piles of fan mail, and a bronze bust that a fan had fashioned and put on exhibit in Chicago. King Nicholas I of Montenegro awarded Whittlesey the Order of Prince Danilo I, also by mail. In February 1921 the reluctant hero went to Hollywood and met with comedian "Fatty" Arbuckle. Whittlesey admitted that appearing in front of the camera scared him to death, but he nevertheless embraced the cinema. "You can starve a man; you can wound him with bullets," he joked, "but you can't dim his love for the movies." Increasingly, though, moments of relaxation and release came fewer and further between. By the autumn of 1921 he had stopped going to the Williams Club, which had once been one of his favorite resorts. But he still campaigned as an advocate for disabled veterans.

The Lost Battalion sought out Whittlesey. He worked hard to get proper recognition for Captain Holderman until the Californian received the Medal of Honor in 1921. Veterans struggling to reestablish themselves in civilian life, some of them the same men who had criticized Whittlesey behind his back in 1919, wrote him letters, called his office, and knocked on his door. Some were traumatized. Others were ne'er-do-wells. Many were both. All of them begged for jobs, money, or just conversation.

Unable to lift the crushing weight of personal responsibility, Whittlesey gave freely to all the veterans, wives, widows, and family members who crowded his doorstep. He provided money and support, and legal aid. He even helped the cousin of one of his Polish soldiers who tried to enter the country as a stowaway and rewarded Whittlesey's support by fleeing police at Ellis Island. In July 1921, Whittlesey left his sickbed to attend the funeral of one of his runners who had fallen into alcoholism and died on the city streets, lying unclaimed in the morgue for days.

And the dead haunted his dreams.[21]

The United States was a deeply competitive society in the 1920s. People measured everything in order, from best to worst, including their heroes. Who was the greatest American hero of the war? Who decided? The military authorities, or popular acclamation? And who cared?

Damon Runyon was not interested in sorting out the heroes. The Western Front had provided catharsis, helping him to process his Spanish-American War experiences and the soldier he had never quite become. He believed that he had left all of that behind him. The now was what mattered, and the real action seethed on the streets. From 1919 onward, he focused on writing about sports and city life for the *New York American*. As a celebrity, he earned a celebrity's salary: the then phenomenal sum of twenty thousand dollars yearly for his daily column alone, or about double the average wages for comfortable living in New York City.

But the war lived on underneath the surface. Although Runyon still had a wife and children, he saw little of them. He wrote in abundance to the point of obsession, glorying in the title of the most prolific writer in America. He smoked maniacally, womanized expansively, and spent much of his time prowling the streets. During the war he had spent all of his time wandering in or behind the lines, recording conversations. Now he did the same in Manhattan.

Reminders of the war stalked every street corner. Many of the men he listened to, athletes or not, were veterans who spoke about the war and their struggles to readjust. Their personalities and everyday lives had changed because of what they had experienced. In the years to come, Runyon became a primary witness of the changes the veterans wrought on everyday life in the big city—albeit without always consciously understanding what he saw. But although Runyon continued his friendship with Eddie Rickenbacker, whom he tried to convince to run for president, and served as an honorary pallbearer at Bat Masterson's funeral on October 28, 1921, he made no attempt to analyze the war or dredge up the past.[22]

The need to memorialize the war, and to identify and appreciate its heroes, nevertheless preoccupied many Americans. In the first glow of triumph they had applauded men like York, Whittlesey, and McMurtry, and cheered at parades. They had removed their hats at memorials to the dead and clapped for the wounded, but then forgotten them as they passed by. By 1921, though, the urge had arisen to select heroes from the dead and the living so that Americans could fix their memories.

From here on to the limitless future, an Unknown Soldier would represent the dead servicemen of all American wars, following an example set by the British the year before. Someone else, though, must represent the living—a man to be designated the finest American hero, somebody who could stand for every man, but without appearing flawed or vulnerable. For this, York and Whittlesey had become in some ways tarnished, and so no longer fit the bill, and McMurtry never had.

Preparations for the identification of the Unknown Soldier were highly ritualized and elaborate, reflecting the impassioned feelings of the American people in the aftermath of their first modern global war. On October 24, 1921, after a random selection process, Sergeant Edward F. Younger, son of German immigrants and a Chicago postal worker, chose America's Unknown Soldier. He did so by laying a wreath of roses on one of four coffins containing unidentified remains of doughboys killed in action on different parts of the Western Front, including the Meuse-Argonne. A short time later the coffin was loaded on a ship to be carried home for burial in Arlington National Cemetery.

The ceremony would be vast and ornate, perhaps unlike any public event in American history since President Abraham Lincoln's funeral in 1865. Hundreds of thousands if not millions of spectators were expected, including newly elected president Warren G. Harding, former president Wilson, hundreds of civilian and military officials, thousands of veterans, thousands of war mothers and wives, and hundreds of Medal of Honor recipients from many wars. Decorated heroes would be given pride of place in the ceremony—behind politicians and generals, of course. Eight would serve as pallbearers. Dozens more would be honorary pallbearers, not actually carrying the coffin but following it and joining a select group at the graveside. York, Whittlesey, and McMurtry were all invited to be a part of the honorary group.

Only one man, though, would represent the United States infantry and all living servicemen, thus taking pride of place among the veterans at the ceremony. Unlike the randomly chosen Unknown Soldier, Pershing would select this individual, whom the media (but not Runyon, who was on a sports assignment in Georgia) would dub America's greatest living military hero. As the final days of October passed, newspapers indulged in speculation. Many assumed the soldier would be York, or Whittlesey, or maybe even Pershing himself. They were wrong. On November 1, Pershing announced his choice: Sergeant Samuel Woodfill of the 5th Division, United States Army.

Woodfill was a hero, and also a safe choice. Born on an Indiana farm near the Kentucky border, he was like York a woodsman and a marksman. He had joined the army at age eighteen and stayed there, serving in Alaska (where he became a skilled big-game hunter) and along the Mexican border. In World War I Woodfill rose to the rank of captain and fought in the Meuse-Argonne. Five days after the relief of the Lost Battalion and four days after York's exploit in the Argonne, he single-handedly demolished several enemy machine gun nests holding up his regiment's advance, and killed bunches of Germans with his rifle, his pistol, his bayonet, and a trench pick.

Woodfill received a Medal of Honor for these feats, even though the army returned him to the prewar rank of sergeant when hostilities ended. In 1921, unlike the deeply troubled Whittlesey and the financially challenged York, Woodfill stayed in the army after reenlisting. And he kept his life together. Calm, erect, square jawed, and well spoken, he had not received much publicity to this point but had no trouble handling it when it came.

Newspapers immediately decided that Woodfill represented the "first" American, the "hero of heroes," "greater" than York (second) or Whittlesey (third). They pointed out that no one had given him the credit he deserved, implying that York and Whittlesey had received too much attention by contrast, and said that he had borne the unfair slight (their words, not his) in silence. Woodfill was modest: "My only regret," he said, "is that I could not have done more." But he was also articulate. Although gruff and unemotional about his exploits, he willingly talked about them with reporters. Perhaps most important, Woodfill carried no obvious whiff of inner torment or of scandal. The newspapers loved him. In the run-up to the Unknown Soldier ceremony, media only mentioned York and Whittlesey in asides.

Woodfill arrived in Washington, DC, on November 4, 1921. He was cheered by the House of Representatives, and presented to the president. Five days later, after further tributes, Woodfill stood with Pershing at the dockside in the Washington Navy Yard to greet the ship *Olympia*, bearing the body of the Unknown Soldier. As he waited, Woodfill stood obligingly, stomach in and chest out, gaze inscrutable, while Secretary of War John W. Weeks fingered the medals decorating his tunic in front of whirring cameras. After the ship docked, Woodfill led the other seven pallbearers representing each branch of the service onto the deck, lifted the coffin, and carried it down to a waiting caisson. They walked alongside it through mist and rain, past silent crowds, to the Capitol where it lay in state for two days.

Vast crowds surged into Washington, DC, on the morning of November 11. Traffic jams prevented some outraged dignitaries from joining the ceremonies. At eight thirty in the morning Woodfill and the other pallbearers lifted the coffin from the Capitol's dome room and carried it to the caisson. The assembled procession then moved slowly down Pennsylvania Avenue to the accompaniment of muffled drums and a funeral dirge. Walking alongside and immediately behind were the pallbearers, the president, Pershing, Chief Justice Taft, the House of Representatives, the Senate, and former president Wilson in his carriage. Harding and Pershing kept gesturing with their hands to urge the crowd to silence. In the cold and light mist, spectators stood attentive and bare headed. From the Capitol steps, a ripple of grief passed through the crowd as mothers and fathers, brothers and sisters, wives and girlfriends, and children broke down sobbing and fled, fell to their knees, or were led away.

The procession halted briefly in front of the White House so that the president could take his place in the reviewing stand. As it did so a group of generals and politicians crowded around Woodfill to congratulate him. But he saw nothing to celebrate. Fulfilling his role throughout with professionalism and profound respect for his comrades, Woodfill accepted his role but not once presented himself as a hero. Embarrassed and possibly offended, he acknowledged the generals' and politicians' plaudits only by standing stiffly to salute.

The procession, the marine band at its head playing Chopin's Funeral March, reached Arlington Cemetery at eleven thirty that morning. It continued past silent crowds to the right colonnade. From there pallbearers carried the casket before chiefs of the army and navy to the flower-decked amphitheater, filled with some five thousand honored guests including servicemen and -women in uniform. As the marine choir sang, the pallbearers placed the coffin on a bier in front of a platform on which stood a small assembly of honored guests: among them Vice President Calvin Coolidge and his wife, Grace; honorary pallbearers including York, Whittlesey, and McMurtry; and a Native American chief who would deliver the final blessing.

After more hymns, the marine band broke into the "Star-Spangled Banner." Three aircraft circled the amphitheater in tribute. After a bugle call, the crowd observed two minutes of silence. President Harding, arrived from the White House in a car, then rose to give a speech fit for the occasion. As he did so, the clouds broke and the amphitheater erupted in sunlight.

Harding spoke well, and was broadcast on the radio. While testifying to the bravery of those who had and had not fallen, and espousing the cause for which they fought, he condemned war and hatred unequivocally. "This American soldier went forth to battle with no hatred for any people in the world," he said, "but hating war and hating the purpose of every war for conquest.... In advancing toward his objective was somewhere a thought of a world awakened; and we are here to testify undying gratitude and reverence for that thought of a wider freedom." The president concluded: "It is fitting to say that his sacrifice, and that of the millions dead, shall not be in vain. There must be, there shall be, the commanding voice of a conscious civilization against armed warfare."

After a few more hymns, the pallbearers bore the coffin to the hill followed by a procession of admirals, generals, princes, and potentates. With the Capitol in view, the Unknown Soldier entered his final resting place. A Christian graveside service followed. A selected procession of mothers and other honored guests laid wreaths and tributes beside the mausoleum. Finally, a western Native American chief in a magnificent bonnet conducted a Native American rite of burial. He concluded by laying his bonnet on the coffin. The ceremony ended with taps, and rifles firing a military salute.

York, Whittlesey, and McMurtry sat silently, and anonymously, on the stage throughout the ceremonies, with Holderman not far away. Inevitably they must have greeted each other, but no one reported their meeting or whether they reflected on what had brought them to this place. The cameras ignored them. No reporters asked them what they thought. York had been mentioned in newspapers only to point out that Woodfill had been chosen ahead of him. Whittlesey's name rarely appeared in print anymore. Neither man complained, but they could not have escaped the perception that they had served their purpose with a public that no longer needed them.

During the ceremony, with York sitting silent and awkward nearby, Whittlesey looked at the casket of the Unknown Soldier. He felt accused. Instinctively, he turned to McMurtry. In their hardest times together in the pocket, these men had shared everything that could be said and never be said. They knew each other to the cores of their souls as nobody would ever know either of them again. "George," Whittlesey confided, "I should not have come here. I cannot help but wonder if that may not be one of my men from the Pocket. I shall have nightmares tonight and hear the wounded screaming once again."

A friend would later say of Whittlesey: "The funeral in Arlington apparently was the climax to all the sadness he went through."[23]

On November 19, Whittlesey attended a Red Cross charity event at which he shared the stage with French marshal Ferdinand Foch, generalissimo of all Allied forces in 1918. Several wounded men, many badly mangled by shrapnel, sat or stood next to them. Attendees thought Whittlesey "moody and morose."

On Thanksgiving Day, the twenty-fourth, Whittlesey visited his friend and former law partner, John Pruyn, and his wife, and played with their baby; but his cheerfulness was excessive and forced. On the following day, after cleaning up his law office desk and sealing a number of papers in envelopes, Whittlesey seemed strangely relaxed. That evening he went out with a friend to see *The Lost Battalion*, newly revived in the theaters. For a few moments Whittlesey's glasses reflected images of himself, play-acting a drama turned farce and in some measure selling his soul.

On November 26, 1921, a Saturday, Whittlesey saw off his dying brother Elisha, on a train back to join the rest of their family in Pittsfield. Late that morning he climbed on board the United Fruit liner *Taloa*. The ship was bound for Havana, where Whittlesey had never been and where he had no business. He spent the day alone in his cabin, or gazing out to sea. That evening he joined the captain and others for dinner, and adjourned to the smoking room where he chatted with passengers about the recent Army-Navy game. At eleven fifteen he told them good night and walked out on deck, disappearing into the fog. No one ever saw him again.

A steward found several sealed envelopes in Whittlesey's cabin the next morning. One of them, addressed to Pruyn, read: "Just a note to say good bye. I'm a misfit by nature and by training, and there's an end of it."[24]

One of the letters was addressed to George McMurtry, who read and then burned it. He didn't tell anyone what his friend had written, but he never forgot.

(CHAPTER FIFTEEN)

HOMECOMINGS

In 1921 a freelance writer named Samuel K. Cowan left his native Nashville for Pall Mall. He settled down there temporarily to collect local color for a book about York. Though a Tennessean, Cowan was a lowlander with little understanding of highland ways. York nevertheless agreed to talk with him a few times and even revealed some pages from his diary. Cowan wasn't much interested in York, though, but rather in what he supposedly represented: the racially superior American pioneer, uncorrupted by the immigrant wave of the past several decades.

The postwar era was the Ku Klux Klan's heyday, especially throughout the South and Midwest. The Klan had little influence in the highlands, however; in this region of poor subsistence farmers slavery had been rare before the Civil War, and the African American population was quite small. For York and his kin, race was a nonissue; though proud of their ancestors, they didn't waste time comparing them, or themselves, to anyone else.

The same was not true in places like Nashville, however, and Cowan struck a chord with readers to whom the Lost Battalion's racial mélange offered little appeal. They preferred to see York, and

Woodfill, as representatives of a white race so pure that it eclipsed even contemporary Europeans. Cowan presented highland folkways and religion with all the authenticity of a Disney theme-park ride, but he called York among "the purest Anglo-Saxons to be found today and not even England can produce so clear a strain." And so the Raleigh, North Carolina, *News and Observer* could trumpet that "the boast of the purity of our mountain stock is no idle one... those of us who have unpolluted English blood in our veins, as most of us have [in North Carolina], are right glad."[1]

York didn't exploit Cowan's race-baiting, but he welcomed publicity insofar as it aided his campaigns on behalf of the York Institute. He hoped to create schools for local boys, teaching them the skills they would need to improve themselves and the Upper Cumberland, and maybe escape the violence and alcohol abuse that plagued their lives. After years of giving speeches and product endorsements, and securing some welcome large donations of land and supplies, he was able to break ground for the eventual Alvin C. York Industrial Institute near Jamestown in May 1926. But it came at a cost.

York's outspoken support for teaching evolution, including at his school, made enemies after he gave an interview on the subject to the *New York World*. He also became embroiled in legal tussles with local authorities in Fentress County, including board members of his own institute. Most upsetting to York was the impact of all the traveling and speaking on his personal finances and his relationship with his family. Just as with other veterans, though, his restlessness was well-nigh uncontrollable.[2]

Several years after Cowan skedaddled back to Nashville, a new biographer turned up in Pall Mall: Australian veteran Tom Skeyhill, who had been badly wounded at Gallipoli and in France and had been touring the States on and off since 1918. Skeyhill had all the bona fides of a combat veteran. He also had undergone his own personal trials, claiming to have "miraculously" had his sight restored after being blinded by a shell burst.

Professing himself a deeply religious man, especially since his healing, Skeyhill urged audiences to support the "true church," especially since "American churches are more true, more clean, than the churches of any other country in the world." The Australian adored the American South, calling it a new "promised land" and thus impressing his audiences in that region. Skeyhill was a showman—some said a con man—who designated himself a "soldier-poet" and traded on his "thrilling escapes" at the front to earn money on the lecture circuit. He had a dubious relationship with the truth, but there was no doubting his popularity. From 1919 to 1927 Skeyhill traveled all over North America and Europe, giving thousands of lectures to venues sometimes packed with tens of thousands of people.[3]

Explaining his interest in York, Skeyhill claimed that he had witnessed the Tennessean's arrival in New York in 1919 (he also described a welcoming ticker-tape parade that did not in fact take place). Skeyhill said that he was driving through Tennessee eight years later when the notion struck him to drop by and see York—a detour of several hundred miles from the highway to Nashville over difficult roads in days when the region was still extremely isolated. As ill luck would have it, York was absent and Skeyhill recoiled at the poverty of Fentress County. He left disappointed, but returned some months later after striking up a correspondence with York.

Skeyhill knew just how to reach the shy Tennessean. He told stories of his time in the trenches, wounding, and miraculous recovery; and prayed reverently in Pastor Pile's church. He also confessed how lucrative his career had become on the speaking circuit, and spoke of new opportunities. York was entranced. He opened up about his war experiences; hit and miss speaking engagements mostly through local Rotary clubs; financial troubles; and dreams of transforming Fentress County.

When Skeyhill broached the idea of writing his biography York, who had received only trifling royalties from Cowan's earlier book, showed the Australian the terse diary he had kept at the front. Skeyhill told him it was just the thing he needed to craft a popular book that would earn the money York desperately needed to pay his personal debts and support his growing but troubled foundation. Showman Lowell Thomas was in the process of doing the same thing for Woodfill. York gave in—and immediately earned fifteen thousand dollars in advance and serialization rights from the Famous Speakers Bureau in New York City. Skeyhill earned just as much up front, and there would be plenty more for both men in speaking fees.[4]

Skeyhill later claimed to have spent most of the winter of 1927–1928 with York in the mountains, studying the diary, gathering stories, and getting to know the people. The truth is that the Australian's lecture engagements kept him almost entirely on the road in New England and the upper Midwest during that period. Skeyhill probably wrote *Sergeant York: His Own Life Story and Diary* at his desk during the summer of 1928 using scraps of York's diary, newspaper reports, and such official records as he could gather. There were no portable tape recorders in the 1920s, so of course Skeyhill didn't record York's words. Nor did he collect a full point-to-point narrative from the sergeant's mouth. Instead, the Australian concocted a faux hillbilly dialect and used it to describe experiences and conversations that he largely invented in his own head.

Though not as crass as Cowan, Skeyhill still dwelt on York's Scots-Irish background and pioneer heritage (with which Skeyhill, as an Australian, could surely sympathize). In one especially artificial section of his fictionalized biography, Skeyhill had York give an extended history lecture describing his people as "the fightenest men" who were "the old Anglo-Saxon type and among the purest in America" (only lightly diluted by Germans and French) and "kinder seasoned and hardened in the roughness of this-here new continent of ours." They "left the other side rather than bow down to kings and dictators," and then beat up on a series of enemies from Indians to Europeans to "Wellington's veterans, the ones who helped to bust Napoleon."

Still, Skeyhill knew how to write. Through his pen, York became the quaint, lovable, Christian mountain man that people expected and wanted to see. The Tennessean also came to represent an idealized vision of America. In his squad, York melded with an amalgam of city boys, who like the men of the Lost Battalion originated from all over the world. But Skeyhill emphasized that York, the pure American, won the battle on his own by fighting in a purely American way; for example, by picking off attacking German soldiers from rear to front as if they were turkeys, a scenario that Skeyhill likely concocted himself. The end result was a masterpiece of yarn spinning, calculated to appeal to the public. It paid off rich dividends, far beyond York's wildest dreams.[5]

In the 1920s New York City became the centerpiece of a new America and a far different place than it had been before the war. The Manhattan skyline continued to shift and grow with the beginning of a new skyscraper boom. The people had changed too, thanks to the war. In the summer of 1922, city officials decided to put on a patriotic concert in Central Park. Naturally they turned to Harry Barnhart. As conductor of the New York Community Chorus, he had stirred up and annoyed the crowds with his gusty singing at the Polo Grounds in 1917.

Since then, however, the normally ebullient Barnhart had become consumed with guilt. So many of those young men he had sent off to war had died, and he felt responsible. He would conduct the Central Park concert, he told city authorities, but he refused to play the "Star-Spangled Banner" because it was "gloomy and stimulates hatred." Officials canceled Barnhart and replaced him with a military band.[6]

Below the skyscrapers, veterans returned to their families and jobs and moved on as well as they could. Just as their experiences in Europe had transformed them, so they changed everyone around them, from friends to coworkers to families and communities. Immigrant soldiers spoke with pride of their wartime services and acted as if they belonged. They did. Nobody in future would question whether they, or New York City, was really American.

The Great Depression of the 1930s hit New York City like a ton of bricks. It also devastated the heartland and the West. Veterans instinctively banded together in the crisis. Men from all over the country, including members of the 77th and 82nd Divisions and the Lost Battalion, marched to Washington, DC, in the summer of 1932 as members of the Bonus Army, only to be routed by troops under General Douglas MacArthur. But this didn't fracture their unity. Members of the Lost Battalion met informally throughout the Depression to confide in each other just as they had done to their late commander. In September 1938 they formed the Lost Battalion Survivors Association under the leadership of George McMurtry, who dedicated himself to it for the rest of his life.

The same year saw the publication of *The Lost Battalion* by Thomas Johnson and Fletcher Pratt. Johnson had been among the journalists covering Whittlesey's command in the Argonne, and after the war he remained in touch with some of the survivors. Pratt was a military historian whose job was to keep Johnson honest. The job was not too difficult. Although Johnson clearly dramatized parts of his tale, and cast almost every soldier in a positive light, he was a good journalist and to some extent an eyewitness. *The Lost Battalion* was not a con job like Skeyhill's book; but it also did not earn nearly as much money.[7]

The onset of World War II in 1939 and America's entry into the conflict in 1941 devastated some veterans. They had felt the same revulsion toward Europe and its problems that most Americans had in the 1920s, and cherished hopes that their personal sacrifices would rule out another world war. But war returned, and fathers sent their sons off to war. Troubled veterans responded by falling into depression and alcoholism. Others recaptured the pride and patriotism they had felt on returning home in 1919. They had earned it. Now it was their sons' turn.

Throughout it all, the Lost Battalion continued to endure, and served as an example for future generations. On April 21, 1948, McMurtry attended the dedication of the Whittlesey Room in New York's Williams Club. McMurtry unveiled a portrait of Whittlesey by Edward Bartlett, one of the late commander's former lieutenants. Williams president James Phinney Baxter hoped that "from this portrait which we hang today, and from the lips of men still living, younger men will catch the spirit of our honored dead.... When at long last a better world beats finally its swords to plowshares, we shall remember, with the architects of peace, the men who died that their country might live." McMurtry summed it up himself at each meeting of the survivors' association, which continued until 1968. "As long as you and I live," he said with a toast to Whittlesey, "we will never be in finer company."[8]

McMurtry continued to preside as other men passed away. General Johnson died in 1923. General Alexander, who returned to his prosperous law career but never managed to recapture the flicker of fame he had enjoyed in 1919, died in New York City in 1941. Nelson Holderman concluded his formal military career in 1919 but dedicated the remainder of his life to serving veterans, managing the Veterans Home of California. He died in 1953. William J. Cullen, loyal to the survivors' association to the last, passed away in 1971. Maurice Revnes moved to Beverly Hills and worked for MGM as a producer. He died in Florida in 1985. His obituaries said nothing of his service with the Lost Battalion.

George McMurtry continued his life as a stockbroker and prospered financially. Personally he did not. Married three times, he had a daughter named Louise and maintained his Park Avenue apartment, also frequenting the Harvard, Knickerbocker, and other city clubs. But he earned a reputation as a difficult, hot-tempered figure with family and acquaintances (he had few friends) in New York, West Virginia, and his retirement home in Bar Harbor, Maine. Although McMurtry ran and funded the Lost Battalion Survivors Association, maintaining the respect of his former comrades, he never regained the father-confessor status that he had in 1918. McMurtry made no book or movie deals, and never tried to tell his story. He dealt with his memories, and his demons, alone. He died in 1958 at age eighty-two, a New Yorker tried and true to the end.[9]

Damon Runyon maintained his love affairs with New York City, sports, women, and violence. War never truly left him. His writing on the Lost Battalion, and on the doughboys generally, had helped to humanize them to the reading public and to demonstrate that in their individual differences and vibrancy they were all Americans. During the jazz age, as he continued his sports writing and especially as he haunted the Great White Way, Runyon's writing incorporated veterans, and violence, and helped to define a new America.

Noir fiction and cinema owed a huge debt to Runyon, and through him to World War I. Like fellow journalist Walter Winchell and authors like F. Scott Fitzgerald, James M. Cain, Dashiell Hammett, and Raymond Chandler, whose primary characters were often war-scarred veterans, Runyon wrote the war into his own short fiction. He presented gangsters more realistically than any other writer had done. And he reveled in killing and other forms of violence.

Runyon's characters spoke about guns in language they had learned in places like the Argonne. His vocabulary for the sound of gunfire ranged in practically infinite variety from "big whoom" to "big blooey-blooey." These were words he had picked up during the war, but also that guys on the city streets had learned, and repeated, and kept improvising with each other. Increasingly fascinated with boxing, Runyon described it usually as hand-to-hand combat between warrior-soldiers.[10]

Although Runyon probably never met Alvin York, the red-headed Tennessean did not entirely escape his notice, thanks to the 1941 movie *Sergeant York* with Gary Cooper. Runyon recognized York as a deserving hero, and praised how the movie's religious sentiments (which the reporter did not share) would attract new patrons to box offices. The New York journalist could not help lamenting, however, that Hollywood had neglected to pay tribute to men like fellow war hero (and Unknown Soldier honorary pallbearer) Sam Drebin, "the Fighting Jew." "In times like these," Runyon asserted as new war shadows gathered around the banner of Nazi Germany, "we cannot have too many documents on men like York and Drebin, native and alien born, who have contributed to the undying glory of the Stars and Stripes."[11]

Runyon talked about going to the front again during World War II, but never did. Instead he remained in his beloved city, the place he loved as passionately as he despised it. There was plenty of fighting going on there in the streets anyway. As New York grew and changed, and forgot about World War I, Runyon became as alienated and lonely as any of the veterans who had experienced the war with him. As biographer Edwin Hoyt wrote, Runyon "was lonely and desperately unhappy but only a handful of those close to him suspected he was capable of a real emotion. No one understood the depth of his alienation from society, although for those who followed his newspaper column it was written down for anyone to see."[12]

World War II approached its end, and Runyon slowly succumbed to throat cancer brought on by his long chain-smoking habit. His final thoughts turned back to the first great war, the one he had seen and reported and lived. Eddie Rickenbacker remained one of the journalist's closest friends. The barnstorming ace represented everything Runyon wished that he, and the war, had been, but was not. For a long time, the reporter had hoped that Rickenbacker would campaign for political office and so help define a new America. The aviator never fulfilled this wish, but he was in a position to carry out a dying request that symbolically united Runyon, the war, and the city he had helped to define as the beating heart of America.

On December 18, 1946, a few days after Damon Runyon died in New York City, a DC-3 aircraft took off from LaGuardia Field. The plane belonged to Eastern Airlines, owned by Rickenbacker. But the World War I ace did not pilot the aircraft. Instead, he sat in the back along with Runyon's second wife and son, holding an urn containing Runyon's ashes. The plane banked through thin clouds flecked with particles of snow, and flew over Woodlawn Cemetery where the journalist's first wife, from whom he had separated in 1928, was buried. The DC-3 soared over the Statue of Liberty, scarred by the Black Tom explosion but still standing proudly as it had when beckoning immigrants to Ellis Island, saying farewell to the departing 77th Division doughboys in 1917, and welcoming them home in 1919 wearing patches bearing her image.

From Lady Liberty the plane banked again and flew over southern and central Manhattan. Through the plane windows Rickenbacker witnessed a city emerging transformed from another victorious war, replete with skyscrapers built in the jazz age that Runyon had chronicled so well. He could see cars and people moving, living, struggling in a million individual stories just as Runyon had chronicled them. Though the Polo Grounds and the new Yankee Stadium, built in 1923, stood off in the distance—there were no games going on anyway—the plane passed over Madison Square Garden and followed the Great White Way to Times Square.

As his aircraft soared over Times Square, Rickenbacker tipped the urn, and Runyon's ashes fluttered down, merging with tiny particles of mist and snow and swirling undetected among cars and people on Manhattan's immortal streets.

Runyon had asked in his will for Rickenbacker to scatter the ashes "over the island of Manhattan, the place that I have truly loved and that was so good to me."[13]

Across America, millions of servicemen and -women returned from World War II. They came home to cities and the countryside, each carrying his or her experiences. They changed the United States as they had been changed. And the country continued to grow.

As New York and other cities rose and expanded, so rural America seemed to fade in the national consciousness. But though it no longer remained so separate from urban America as it once had been, thanks in part to the experiences of men thrown together during the two world wars, the country's heartland stayed strong. Millions of Americans continued to call it home, returning to farms small and large, and tilling the land.

The mountains of East Tennessee no longer stood so separate and isolated from the rest of the country. Alvin York helped open the mountain gateways by paying to build the first paved road to Fentress County. With the advent of the Tennessee Valley Authority in the 1930s, the region really opened up. Many residents left, traveling across the country, voluntarily abandoning the separateness and supposed purity of their forebears. In a way they too became immigrants, and were merged into the communities around them, as American as any Chinese from California, Polish Jew from Manhattan, or cowboy from Arizona.

Alvin York left his beloved mountains again at the beginning of World War II. His views on war had changed profoundly. Twenty years earlier he had struggled to understand the war's meaning, but now, even before Pearl Harbor, he spoke out as an opponent of isolationism. As early as 1937 he was publicly advocating military action to stop imperial Japan and Nazi Germany. But York became most vulnerable when he got involved in a cause. In the winter of 1939–1940, Jesse Lasky approached York again with a movie deal. He initially found the old soldier reluctant, but then appealed: "Sergeant, you risked your life for your country in the World War, and you'd do it again if your country needed you, wouldn't you? That need exists right now and I know that you're going to give your life to your country—through the powerful medium of the screen."

The ploy worked. York and Lasky signed the contract in May 1940, and the money was good: twenty-five thousand dollars and the same again upon the movie's release; a salary of five hundred dollars per week for York's work on the movie as "technical consultant"; and a percentage of gross receipts if the movie earned over three million dollars. He needed every penny. York stipulated that Skeyhill's book and a subsequent children's book called *Last of the Long Hunters*, to which the Tennessean owned the rights, would be used as a basis for the picture. Skeyhill did not participate, for he had died in an airplane crash in 1932 while on the lecture circuit. York firmly deleted a line in the contract that said he would make himself available as an actor.

The movie *Sergeant York* starring Gary Cooper was released in July 1941. York attended the opening at New York's Astor Theatre in front of adoring crowds and representatives of a number of patriotic organizations. Then it was off to Washington, DC, where he got the same treatment again and President Franklin D. Roosevelt welcomed him back to the White House. York had enjoyed working on the film. He liked how it followed Skeyhill's script, which foregrounded his faith and humility, and (this time in false Hollywood hillbilly language) treated his people with respect. He also liked Cooper's portrayal of himself, and had good reason to appreciate the receipts, which topped ten million dollars.

For a while York again became a public figure. When the United States entered World War II he spoke at patriotic events and did his part to support the war effort. But although he would live until

1964, his health suffered from chronic arthritis and respiratory problems perhaps (although he never claimed this) brought on by wartime exposure to poison gas. By the 1940s York no longer looked the same trim, rangy figure he once had, but the eyes were still there, revealing his ongoing inner struggle soothed by faith.

After the war ended, however, the national stage no longer held appeal. York continued to funnel money to his charitable initiatives (to his own detriment, for he suffered from money problems for the rest of his life), but he stepped down from managerial responsibilities with the York Foundation. Increasingly he found nothing in the outside world worth grasping, or anyone outside his family whom he could touch in any vital way. His public appearances dwindled away to nothing, and he liked it that way.

In the end, York turned away from life's battlefield and climbed back up the mountains into the woods of his beloved East Tennessee. During his remaining years he would spend most of his time on his farm, working the fields, spending time with his family, and, in the way of generations immemorial, sitting on his porch and telling stories. In time, the restlessness faded away in a way it had never done for Whittlesey, McMurtry, or Runyon. Giving had consumed Whittlesey, and to some degree McMurtry, until there was nothing left. But for York, giving consumed his suffering and pointed the way toward peace and hope. Well might he have recited Psalm 121 as he followed the winding path to his mountain home:

I will lift up mine eyes unto the hills, from whence cometh my help.[14]

ACKNOWLEDGMENTS

On this project, I am particularly indebted to historians who have blazed trails ahead of me. Robert J. Laplander's dedication to uncovering and preserving the story of the Lost Battalion is evident in his definitive work, *Finding the Lost Battalion*, which served as an invaluable guide throughout the preparation of my own book. He and Alan D. Gaff, author of the superb *Blood in the Argonne*, provided me with friendly advice and several useful references. I am grateful to Alan especially for referring me to a number of obscure newspaper articles that I would otherwise have missed, materially aiding my research, and for correcting some of my initial misconceptions about Damon Runyon. Kevin C. Fitzpatrick, author of the valuable guide *World War I New York*, also provided helpful suggestions and advice.

Personal details of individual Lost Battalion members come in part from perusal of genealogical records digitized on Ancestry.com.

Alvin York, somewhat surprisingly, remains a controversial figure among historians. The best biography is *Alvin York* by Douglas V. Mastriano, which I consulted frequently in the course of my research. Michael Birdwell, the foremost expert on York's personal papers, kindly shared with me his deep understanding of the Tennessean as a man. I am also grateful to Michael J. Kelly for allowing me to consult a manuscript copy of his new book, *A Hero on the Western Front*, based upon close study of the battlefield, and to the great historian Ed Bearss for sharing his own observations with me.

Mark Fastoso and Luis Blandon of Echo Productions provided me with exceptionally valuable conceptual insight into the crafting of this work in the course of numerous conversations about the preparation of a proposed documentary film on the subject. In the course of their work they also provided me with a number of useful sources, both written and visual, to assist my research. Luis identified many of the photos.

A personal note of thanks goes out to my friend and eminent historian William T. Walker, author of the important book *Betrayal at Little Gibraltar* about another vital aspect of the Meuse-Argonne. Bill's encouragement, insight, and support have been indispensable over the past two years. This book could not have been written without him.

Bob Pigeon of Da Capo Press has been a wonderful editor, reading the manuscript carefully and providing useful insights and corrections. Thanks also to my agent David Patterson of Stuart Krichevsky Literary Agency.

As always, all mistakes and misinterpretations are my own.

NOTES

PROLOGUE: FOUR MEN

1. Thomas J. Skeyhill, *Sergeant York: His Own Life Story and War Diary* (Garden City, NY: Doubleday, Doran, 1928), 177–79.

CHAPTER ONE. PLAYING THE GAME

1. Jules Witcover, *Sabotoge at Black Tom: Imperial Germany's Secret War in America, 1914–1917* (Chapel Hill, NC: Algonquin Books, 1989), 11–20; *Brooklyn Daily Eagle*, July 30–31, 1916; *New York Herald*, July 31, 1916.
2. Witcover, *Sabotoge at Black Tom*, 21–22, 162.
3. *New York Herald*, July 31, 1916.
4. Edwin P. Hoyt, *A Gentleman of Broadway* (Boston: Little, Brown, 1964), 86–88.
5. Ross J. Wilson, *New York and the First World War: Shaping an American City* (Franham, Surrey: Ashgate, 2014), 138–41.
6. Kevin C. Fitzpatrick, *World War I New York: A Guide to the City's Enduring Ties to the Great War* (Guilford, CT: Globe Pequot, 2017), 2–3; *The Brooklyn Daily Eagle*, April 6, 1917; *New York Times*, April 8, 1917.
7. *New York Times*, April 8, 1917.
8. *New York Times*, April 12, 1917.
9. *New York Times*, April 20–21, 1917.
10. Wilson, *New York and the First World War*, 156–58; Edward G. Lengel, *To Conquer Hell: The Meuse-Argonne, 1918* (New York: Henry Holt, 2008), 35–36.

11. *New York Times*, May 4, July 13, 1916; *Ithaca Journal*, May 17, 1916; *Evening World*, June 6–7, 1916.

12. Robert J. Laplander, *Finding the Lost Battalion: Beyond the Rumors, Myths and Legends of America's Famous WW1 Epic*, 3rd ed. (privately published, Lulu Press, 2017), 40–47; Alan D. Gaff, *Blood in the Argonne: The "Lost Battalion" of World War I* (Norman: University of Oklahoma Press, 2005), 119–21; *Harvard Alumni Bulletin* 21, no. 14 (January 2, 1919), 260; Williams College Archives, online biography, http://archives.williams.edu/manuscriptguides/whittlesey/bio.php.

13. *Brooklyn Daily Eagle*, July 19, 24, August 6, 1916; *New York Sun*, July 21, 1916; *New York Times*, July 16, 19, 24, 1916; Laplander, *Finding the Lost Battalion*, 47.

14. *New York Times*, August 10, September 5, 7, 1915; *New York Sun*, August 17, September 7, 1915; Donald M. Kington, "The Plattsburg Movement and Its Legacy," *Relevance: The Quarterly Journal of the Great War Society* 6, no. 4 (Autumn 1997).

15. Anne E. Mosher, *Capital's Utopia: Vandergrift, Pennsylvania, 1855–1916* (Baltimore: Johns Hopkins University Press, 2004), 43–45; Laplander, *Finding the Lost Battalion*, 159.

16. Kevin Baker, "Emory Upton and the Shaping of the U.S. Army," *Military History* 29, no. 1 (May 2012), 38.

17. *New York Sun*, July 17, 1917; New York, *Evening World*, July 17, 1917; *Brooklyn Daily Eagle*, August 22, 1917.

18. Gaff, *Blood in the Argonne*, 10–11; Roger Batchelder, *Camp Upton* (Boston: Small, Maynard, 1918), 5.

19. *Brooklyn Daily Eagle*, August 18, 27, 1917; *New York Tribune*, August 25, 1917; *Kane Republican*, August 27, 1917; *Reading Times*, August 30, 1917.

20. *New York Times*, September 5, 1917.

21. *Brooklyn Daily Eagle*, September 4, 1917.

CHAPTER TWO. WAR'S STORY

1. *Salt Lake Tribune*, September 9, 1917.

2. *Tennessean*, October 10, 1917.

NOTES TO CHAPTER TWO

3. *Tennessean*, October 11, 1917; *Salt Lake Tribune*, October 12, 1917.
4. *Tennessean*, October 16, 1917.
5. *Pittsburgh Daily Post*, November 15, 1917.
6. Damon Runyon and Charles Farwell Edson, "Hold 'Em, Yale!" marching song for the sammies (Los Angeles: Frank J. Hart Southern California Music Company, 1917), 3.
7. Jimmy Breslin, *Damon Runyon* (New York: Ticknor & Fields, 1991), 29–36; Hoyt, *A Gentleman of Broadway*, 9.
8. Hoyt, *A Gentleman of Broadway*, 12–16; Breslin, *Damon Runyon*, 43.
9. Hoyt, *A Gentleman of Broadway*, 12–21.
10. Breslin, *Damon Runyon*, 24, 51–55; Hoyt, *A Gentleman of Broadway*, 21, 24, 26. On January 14, 1917, a former colleague of Damon Runyon, named "W. O. Mc.," wrote a column in the *Salt Lake Tribune*'s "Tad's Tid-Bits" reading: "Say stupid: What do you mean all the sports writers . . . are stay-at-home birds? Private Alfred Damon Runyon, late of the Thirteenth Minnesota volunteers, and myself, late of the First California volunteers, did our best to get into a war in 1898. Anyhow, we traveled 7000 miles to the Philippines and got shot at as much as the law allowed. It was kind of skimpy shooting and a frost as a war—that Spanish-American thing and the Filipino insurrection that followed. Sure we dug trenches and slept in them when they were wet and we ducked with great dexterity when shot at. So for the love of Mike, give us credit for trying. It wasn't our fault that they were cheese wars. We did our level and you know that Damon and I are not athletes. Two laps around a billiard table would flounder us."
11. *Lippincott's Monthly Magazine* 80 (July–December 1907), 794.
12. Breslin, *Damon Runyon*, 57, 63; Hoyt, *A Gentleman of Broadway*, 26, 42, 49, 61–63, 72, 77–78.
13. Breslin, *Damon Runyon*, 22, 85–100; Hoyt, 86, 90, 94–95, 107; Daniel R. Schwarz, *Broadway Boogie Woogie: Damon Runyon and the Making of New York City Culture* (New York: Palgrave Macmillan, 2003), 6–9; Runyon passport application, August 1918, Ancestry.com.
14. Breslin, *Damon Runyon*, 126–36.
15. Breslin, *Damon Runyon*, 163–171; Hoyt, *A Gentleman of Broadway*, 125–29.

16. Quoted in Hoyt, *A Gentleman of Broadway*, 137.
17. *New York American*, July 1, August 14, 1917.
18. *New York American*, September 5, 1917.

CHAPTER THREE. THE COUNTRY AWAKENS

1. Troy D. Smith, "Champ Ferguson: An American Civil War Rebel Guerilla," *Civil War Times* 40, no. 6 (December, 2001), 40–47; Thurman Sensing, *Champ Ferguson: Confederate Guerilla*, reprint edition (Nashville, TN: Vanderbilt University Press, 1994), 68–188.
2. Skeyhill, *Sergeant York*, 11.
3. William Lynwood Montell, *Killings: Folk Justice in the Upper South* (Lexington: University of Kentucky Press, 1986), 23–64; Skeyhill, *Sergeant York*, 7–12.
4. William York's Tennessee death record, Ancestry.com.
5. John Perry, *Sgt. York: His Life, Legend & Legacy* (Nashville, TN: Broadman & Holman, 1997), 19–20.
6. Douglas V. Mastriano, *Alvin York: A New Biography of the Hero of the Argonne* (Lexington: University Press of Kentucky, 2014), 27–28. Mastriano has delved deeply into the complexity of York's thinking on this subject.
7. Mastriano, *Alvin York*, 36.
8. *New York Times*, May 23, 1919; Skeyhill, *Sergeant York*, 79–80.
9. Skeyhill, *Sergeant York*, 84–87; Mastriano, *Alvin York*, 25–28; Perry, *Sgt. York*, 17–32; David D. Lee, *Sergeant York: An American Hero* (Lexington: University Press of Kentucky, 1985), 98.
10. Cornelius Willemse, *Behind the Green Lights* (New York: Alfred A. Knopf, 1931), 354.
11. *Brooklyn Daily Eagle*, March 31, 1917.

CHAPTER FOUR. THE ADVENTURE BEGINS

1. Gaff, *Blood in the Argonne*, 16.

2. W. Kerr Rainsford, *From Upton to the Meuse with the Three Hundred and Seventh Infantry* (New York: D. Appleton, 1920), 3–4; Gaff, *Blood in the Argonne*, 18.

3. Gaff, *Blood in the Argonne*, 13–24.

4. Rainsford, *From Upton to the Meuse*, 2–4.

5. Louis Wardlaw Miles, *History of the 308th Infantry, 1917–1919* (New York: G.P. Putnam's Sons, 1927), 115; Gaff, *Blood in the Argonne*, 32–33, 36.

6. Miles, *History of the 308th Infantry*, 140–41.

7. Alexander T. Hussey and Raymond M. Flynn, *The History of Company E, 308th Infantry (1917–1919)*, (New York: Knickerbocker Press, 1919), 5–6.

8. *Philadelphia Enquirer*, November 19, 1917; Gaff, *Blood in the Argonne*, 24–25.

9. Gaff, *Blood in the Argonne*, 38–39.

10. *Brooklyn Daily Eagle*, February 23, 1918.

11. *New York American*, September 11–13, 1917.

12. Thomas M. Johnson and Fletcher Pratt, *The Lost Battalion*, reprint edition (Lincoln: University of Nebraska Press, 2000), 22; Julius Ochs Adler, ed., *History of the Seventy Seventh Division August 25, 1917–November 11, 1918* (New York: 77th Division Association, 1919), 166–67; *Brooklyn Daily Eagle*, February 4, 1918.

13. *New York Herald*, February 4, 1918; *New York Tribune*, February 4, 1918.

14. *Brooklyn Daily Eagle*, February 4, 1918; *New York Times*, April 29, 1919.

15. *Brooklyn Daily Eagle*, February 22, 1918; *New York Times*, February 23, 1918; Rochester, New York, *Democrat and Chronicle*, February 23, 1918.

16. Rochester, New York, *Democrat and Chronicle*, February 23, 1918.

17. Rainsford, *From Upton to the Meuse*, 6–7.

18. *Brooklyn Daily Eagle*, March 12, 1918.

19. Rainsford, *From Upton to the Meuse*, 15–20; Laplander, *Finding the Lost Battalion*, 57–60; Gaff, *Blood in the Argonne*, 42–50; Hussey and Flynn, *The History of Company E*, 8–10; Louis Felix Ranlett, *Let's Go! The Story of A.S. No. 2448602* (Boston: Houghton Mifflin, 1927), 11–12.

20. *Official History of the 82nd Division American Expeditionary Forces, "All American" Division* (Indianapolis: Bobbs-Merrill, 1919), 1–4; *Brooklyn Daily Eagle*, March 22, 1918.

21. Skeyhill, *Sergeant York*, 98–103.

22. Skeyhill, *Sergeant York*, 109; Mastriano, *Alvin York*, 43–45.

23. Ranlett, *Let's Go!*, 19–20; Jonathan H. Ebel, *Faith in the Fight: Religion and the American Soldier in the Great War* (Princeton University Press, 2010), 70.

24. Gaff, *Blood in the Argonne*, 54–60; Ranlett, *Let's Go!*, 26–32; *Official History of the 82nd Division*, 4–11; Skeyhill, *Sergeant York*, 110–114.

CHAPTER FIVE. FIRST BLOOD

1. Mastriano, *Alvin York*, 48–56; Skeyhill, *Sergeant York*, 114–28.

2. Francis P. Duffy, *Father Duffy's Story: A Tale of Humor and Heroism, of Life and Death with the Fighting Sixty-Ninth* (New York: George H. Doran, 1919), 114–15; Laplander, *Finding the Lost Battalion*, 61–64; Gaff, *Blood in the Argonne*, 60–72.

3. Gaff, *Blood in the Argonne*, 74–75, Laplander, *Finding the Lost Battalion*, 64–65; Ranlett, *Let's Go!*, 94–99; Miles, *History of the 308th Infantry*, 54–60.

4. Hussey and Flynn, *The History of Company E*, 23–25.

5. Miles, *History of the 308th Infantry*, 97–98; Hussey and Flynn, *The History of Company E*, 29–34.

6. Edward G. Lengel, *Thunder and Flames: Americans in the Crucible of Combat, 1917–1918* (Lawrence: University Press of Kansas, 2015), 353–54; Gaff, *Blood in the Argonne*, 82–89.

7. Laplander, *Finding the Lost Battalion*, 73.

8. Ibid., 67–69.

9. Gaff, *Blood in the Argonne*, 91–92; Laplander, *Finding the Lost Battalion*, 69–71; Robert H. Ferrell, *Five Days in October: The Lost Battalion of World War I* (Columbia: University of Missouri Press, 2005), 6–7; Johnson and Pratt, *The Lost Battalion*, 29–30.

10. Gaff, *Blood in the Argonne*, 94–97.

11. Miles, *History of the 308th Infantry*, 116–18.

12. Nathan A. Haverstock, *Fifty Years at the Front: The Life of War Correspondent Frederick Palmer* (Washington, DC: Brassey's, 1996), 3–12, 26,

198–206; Mitchel P. Roth, ed., *Historical Dictionary of War Journalism* (Westport, CT: Greenwood Press, 1997), 230–31.

13. Frederick Palmer, *America in France* (New York: Dodd, Mead, 1918), 406–7.

14. Skeyhill, *Sergeant York*, 135–37; American Battle Monuments Commission, *82nd Division Summary of Operations in the World War* (Washington, DC: United States Government Printing Office, 1944), 10–14; Mastriano, *Alvin York*, 62–65.

15. Quoted in David F. Trask, *The AEF and Coalition Warmaking* (Lawrence: University Press of Kansas, 1993), 105.

16. Robert Alexander, *Memories of the World War, 1917–1918* (New York: MacMillan, 1931), 158–70.

17. American Battle Monuments Commission, *82nd Division Summary of Operations in the World War*, 21; Gaff, *Blood in the Argonne*, 107–9; Laplander, *Finding the Lost Battalion*, 88–90.

18. Miles, *History of the 308th Infantry*, 119–22; Edward Newell Lewis, "In the Argonne's Mist and Mystery," *American Legion Weekly* 1, no. 13 (September 26, 1919), 7; Hussey and Flynn, *The History of Company E*, 45–46.

CHAPTER SIX. THROUGH THE FOREST GATE

1. Rainsford, *From Upton to the Meuse*, 164–68; American Battle Monuments Commission, *77th Division Summary of Operations in the World War* (Washington, D.C.: United States Government Printing Office, 1944), 31–32; Hussey and Flynn, *The History of Company E*, 45–46; Lewis, "In the Argonne's Mist and Mystery," 7–9.

2. Lewis, "In the Argonne's Mist and Mystery," 7–9, 29; Arthur McKeogh, "The Lost Battalion," *Collier's*, November 16, 1918, 5–6; Gaff, *Blood in the Argonne*, 116–21; Laplander, *Finding the Lost Battalion*, 105–10.

3. Laplander, *Finding the Lost Battalion*, 115–25; Lewis, "In the Argonne's Mist and Mystery," 29, 32; McKeogh, "The Lost Battalion," 6; Hussey and Flynn, *The History of Company E*, 46–47.

4. Miles, *History of the 308th Infantry*, 127–29; Laplander, *Finding the Lost Battalion*, 128–43; Lewis, "In the Argonne's Mist and Mystery," 32.

5. Laplander, *Finding the Lost Battalion*, 134–36, 146–47.

6. Lewis, "In the Argonne's Mist and Mystery," 33; Hussey and Flynn, *The History of Company E*, 47.

7. Miles, 131, 325–26; *Brooklyn Daily Eagle*, September 10, 1918.

8. Lengel, *To Conquer Hell*, 158–59; Laplander, *Finding the Lost Battalion*, 152–58, 161–75; Hussey and Flynn, *The History of Company E*, 48; Miles, *History of the 308th Infantry*, 129–32.

9. Lengel, *To Conquer Hell*, 180–83, 189–90; Miles, *History of the 308th Infantry*, 132–39; McKeogh, "The Lost Battalion," 6; Gaff, *Blood in the Argonne*, 123–38; Laplander, *Finding the Lost Battalion*, 178–206, 211–31.

10. Lengel, *To Conquer Hell*, 221–23; Laplander, 234–61; Gaff, *Blood in the Argonne*, 132–36; John W. Nell, *The Lost Battalion: A Private's Story* (San Antonio, TX: Historical Publishing Network, 2001), 85–86; Johnson and Pratt, *The Lost Battalion*, 22; Ferrell, *Five Days in October*, 13.

CHAPTER SEVEN. INTO THE POCKET

1. Gaff, *Blood in the Argonne*, 140–41; Ferrell, *Five Days in October*, 14–15; Johnson and Pratt, *The Lost Battalion*, 21–24; Laplander, *Finding the Lost Battalion*, 286–90.

2. Lengel, *To Conquer Hell*, 223–25; Laplander, *Finding the Lost Battalion*, 299–301.

3. Laplander, *Finding the Lost Battalion*, 307–8.

4. Ferrell, *Five Days in October*, 16–17; Gaff, *Blood in the Argonne*, 141–44; Johnson and Pratt, *The Lost Battalion*, 30–31.

5. Johnson and Pratt, *The Lost Battalion*, 27–29, 32, 36.

6. Johnson and Pratt, *The Lost Battalion*, 38; Laplander, *Finding the Lost Battalion*, 327.

7. Ferrell, *Five Days in October*, 18; Gaff, *Blood in the Argonne*, 144–46; Johnson and Pratt, *The Lost Battalion*, 33–38.

8. Lengel, *To Conquer Hell*, 225–28; Laplander, *Finding the Lost Battalion*, 325–26.

9. Ferrell, *Five Days in October*, 19–21; Gaff, *Blood in the Argonne*, 147–48; Johnson and Pratt, *The Lost Battalion*, 41–44, 54–55; Laplander, *Finding the Lost Battalion*, 328–44.

CHAPTER EIGHT. SURROUNDED

1. Holderman's military records in Ancestry.com; Laplander, *Finding the Lost Battalion*, 248–49; Johnson and Pratt, *The Lost Battalion*, 50; Gaff, *Blood in the Argonne*, 151.

2. Johnson and Pratt, *The Lost Battalion*, 48–50; Laplander, *Finding the Lost Battalion*, 327–50; Ferrell, *Five Days in October*, 22–23; Gaff, *Blood in the Argonne*, 151.

3. Johnson and Pratt, *The Lost Battalion*, 62–63; Gaff, *Blood in the Argonne*, 153.

4. Lengel, *To Conquer Hell*, 227–29; Ferrell, *Five Days in October*, 23; Gaff, *Blood in the Argonne*, 148–50; Johnson and Pratt, *The Lost Battalion*, 66–69, 78–79; Hussey and Flynn, *The History of Company E*, 51–53; Laplander, *Finding the Lost Battalion*, 366–68.

5. Jasper Copping, "Honoured: The WW1 Pigeons Who Earned Their Wings," *Daily Telegraph*, January 12, 2014; Gaff, *Blood in the Argonne*, 156–57.

6. Laplander, *Blood in the Argonne*, 353.

7. Johnson and Pratt, *The Lost Battalion*, 72–77; Ferrell, *Five Days in October*, 25; Laplander, *Finding the Lost Battalion*, 364, 373; Gaff, *Blood in the Argonne*, 154–55.

8. Ferrell, *Five Days in October*, 23–24; Gaff, *Blood in the Argonne*, 155–56; Laplander, *Finding the Lost Battalion*, 384–85.

9. Johnson and Pratt, *The Lost Battalion*, 90–96, Laplander, *Finding the Lost Battalion*, 386.

10. Miles, *History of the 308th Infantry*, 154.

11. Johnson and Pratt, *The Lost Battalion*, 80–89; Ferrell, *Five Days in October*, 58–60; Laplander, *Finding the Lost Battalion*, 389–94.

12. Lengel, *To Conquer Hell*, 228–30; Ferrell, 26–27; Gaff, 157–60; Laplander, 394–98.

CHAPTER NINE. FRIENDLY FIRE

1. Ferrell, *Five Days in October,* 29; Johnson and Pratt, *The Lost Battalion,* 120–21; Gaff, *Blood in the Argonne,* 169; Laplander, *Finding the Lost Battalion,* 414.

2. Johnson and Pratt, *The Lost Battalion,* 114–15, 121; Ferrell, *Five Days in October,* 30–31.

3. Johnson and Pratt, *The Lost Battalion,* 147; Gaff, *Blood in the Argonne,* 173.

4. Ferrell, *Five Days in October,* 32–33; Gaff, *Blood in the Argonne,* 173–74; Laplander, *Finding the Lost Battalion,* 419–20.

5. Lengel, *To Conquer Hell,* 230–33; Laplander, *Finding the Lost Battalion,* 435–36.

6. Ferrell, *Five Days in October,* 35–36; Gaff, *Blood in the Argonne,* 176–81; Johnson and Pratt, *The Lost Battalion,* 134–41, 144; Nell, *The Lost Battalion,* 94; Laplander, *Finding the Lost Battalion,* 437–39.

7. *Brooklyn Daily Eagle,* June 10, November 25, 1918; Johnson and Pratt, *The Lost Battalion,* 144.

8. Gaff, *Blood in the Argonne,* 174–87; Ferrell, *Five Days in October,* 34; Laplander, *Finding the Lost Battalion,* 444–48.

9. Lengel, *Thunder and Flames,* 44–62.

10. Lengel, *To Conquer Hell,* 245; Johnson and Pratt, *The Lost Battalion,* 150–53; Laplander, *Finding the Lost Battalion,* 453–56.

11. Lengel, *To Conquer Hell,* 245–46.

12. Skeyhill, *Sergeant York,* 140–44; Mastriano, *Alvin York,* 73–77; *82nd Division Summary of Operations,* 18.

13. *Lincoln Star,* 20 July 1918; *Evening Herald,* 22 July 1918.

14. Breslin, *Damon Runyon,* 174; Hoyt, *A Gentleman of Broadway,* 141–42; "The Clarendon: Hearst's Opulent Quintuplex," *New York Times,* May 1, 1994; Runyon passport application, Ancestry.com.

15. Mitchell Yockelson, *Forty-Seven Days: How Pershing's Warriors Came of Age to Defeat the German Army in World War I* (New York: Dutton, 2016), 188–89; Richard Slotkin, *Lost Battalions: The Great War and the Crisis of American Nationality* (New York: Holt, 2006), 372–73; Johnson and Pratt, *The Lost Battalion,* 265; Ferguson passport

application, Ancestry.com; and Laplander, *Finding the Lost Battalion*, 502.

CHAPTER TEN. THE TEST

1. Gaff, *Blood in the Argonne*, 189–90, 195–98; Johnson and Pratt, *The Lost Battalion*, 157–59.
2. Gaff, *Blood in the Argonne*, 200–3; Lengel, *To Conquer Hell*, 252–53.
3. Gaff, *Blood in the Argonne*, 198–200.
4. Ferrell, *Five Days in October*, 142; Gaff, *Blood in the Argonne*, 193; Lengel, *To Conquer Hell*, 252–53; Miles, *History of the 308th Infantry*, 163.
5. Laplander, *Finding the Lost Battalion*, 479–80.
6. Ferrell, *Five Days in October*, 39; Johnson and Pratt, *The Lost Battalion*, 172–73.
7. Ferrell, *Five Days in October*, 43–51; Gaff, *Blood in the Argonne*, 211–23; Johnson and Pratt, *The Lost Battalion*, 155–57; Laplander, *Finding the Lost Battalion*, 461.
8. Gaff, *Blood in the Argonne*, 214–15.
9. Ferrell, *Five Days in October*, 51.
10. Mastriano, *Alvin York*, 78.
11. Laplander, *Finding the Lost Battalion*, 491–93; Gaff, *Blood in the Argonne*, 207.
12. Ferrell, *Five Days in October*, 54; Laplander, *Finding the Lost Battalion*, 500.

CHAPTER ELEVEN. THE QUALITY OF COURAGE

1. *New York Evening World*, May 23, 1919; *82nd Division Summary of Operations*, 18–19; Mastriano, *Alvin York*, 78–79.
2. David Laskin, "The Great War and Jewish Memory," *Hadassah Magazine*, June/July 2014, http://www.hadassahmagazine.org/2014/06/13/great-war-jewish-memory/; Lee J. Levinger, *A Jewish Chaplain in France* (New York: MacMillan, 1921), 84–85.

3. Johnson and Pratt, *The Lost Battalion*, 176.

4. *Seattle Sunday Times*, January 19, 1919.

5. Johnson and Pratt, *The Lost Battalion*, 214–15; Laplander, *Finding the Lost Battalion*, 507; *New York Times*, November 30, 1921.

6. Johnson and Pratt, *The Lost Battalion*, 206–8; Laplander, *Finding the Lost Battalion*, 530–34.

7. Lengel, *To Conquer Hell*, 252–53, 450; Gaff, *Blood in the Argonne*, 204–5; Johnson and Pratt, *The Lost Battalion*, 210–12; Ferrell, *Five Days in October*, 38–39; Laplander, *Finding the Lost Battalion*, 536–38.

CHAPTER TWELVE. THE CRISIS

1. Gaff, *Blood in the Argonne*, 133–35.

2. Johnson and Pratt, *The Lost Battalion*, 219–23, 232, 243–44; Gaff, *Blood in the Argonne*, 227–31; Laplander, *Finding the Lost Battalion*, 556.

3. Lengel, *To Conquer Hell*, 269–71; Gaff, *Blood in the Argonne*, 238–43; Ferrell, *Five Days in October*, 63–64; Johnson and Pratt, *The Lost Battalion*, 225–28, 239–40, 244–46. Robert Laplander has suggested a different progression of movements and discussion after Hollingshead arrived, but the essential elements remain the same; Laplander, *Finding the Lost Battalion*, 578–84.

4. Ferrell, *Five Days in October*, 62–66; Johnson and Pratt, *The Lost Battalion*, 233–34, 247–49; Gaff, 244–46; Laplander, *Finding the Lost Battalion*, 588–91.

5. Edward G. Buxton Jr., *Official History of 82nd Division American Expeditionary Forces, 1917–1919* (Indianapolis: Bobbs-Merrill, 1920), 53–56; Skeyhill, *Sergeant York*, 143–45; *82nd Division Summary of Operations*, 22–23; American Battle Monuments Commission, *28th Division Summary of Operations in the World War* (Washington, DC: United States Government Printing Office, 1944), 66–68.

6. Laplander, *Finding the Lost Battalion*, 585–86, 593–94; Gaff, *Blood in the Argonne*, 248.

7. Laplander, *Finding the Lost Battalion*, 596.

8. Laplander, *Finding the Lost Battalion*, 598–602; Ferrell, *Five Days in October*, 66–67; Gaff, *Blood in the Argonne*, 247–53; Johnson and Pratt, *The Lost Battalion*, 252–55.

CHAPTER THIRTEEN. HEROES

1. *Brooklyn Daily Eagle*, November 24, 1918; Robert Manson, "Through Six Days of Heroism with the Lost Battalion," *Literary Digest* 60, 44, 47.
2. Laplander, *Finding the Lost Battalion*, 617–19.
3. Laplander, *Finding the Lost Battalion*, 618–20; Johnson and Pratt, *The Lost Battalion*, 263–64; Ferrell, *Five Days in October*, 78–83; Gaff, *Blood in the Argonne*, 253–54.
4. *Vidette-Messenger*, August 29, 1947; *New York Evening World*, December 24, 1918.
5. Laplander, *Finding the Lost Battalion*, 629–30.
6. Gaff, *Blood in the Argonne*, 244, 259–60; Hoyt, *A Gentleman of Broadway*, 141–43; Louisville, Kentucky, *Courier Journal*, September 30, 1938; Haverstock, *Fifty Years at the Front*, 211–12.
7. The film still exists in the Signal Corps collection at the National Archives. Gaff, *Blood in the Argonne*, 256, 261; Laplander, *Finding the Lost Battalion*, 628.
8. Lengel, *To Conquer Hell*, 278–82; Skeyhill, *Sergeant York*, 150–84; Mastriano, *Alvin York*, 93–116; Buxton, *Official History of 82nd Division*, 58–62.

CHAPTER FOURTEEN. UNKNOWN SOLDIERS

1. *New York Times*, May 7, 1919; *New York Tribune*, May 7, 1919.
2. *New York Evening World*, May 23, 27, 1919; *New York Times*, May 24, 26, 27, 1919; *New York Tribune*, June 1, 1919; "Conscience Plus Red Hair Are Bad for Germans," *Literary Digest*, June 14, 1919, LXI, 42–48.
3. *Pittsburgh Daily Post*, November 13, 1918; Louisville, Kentucky, *Courier Journal*, September 30, 1938.

4. Hoyt, *A Gentleman of Broadway*, 142–48.

5. *Pittsburgh Press*, April 16–20, 1919.

6. *New York American*, April 24, 1919; *New York Herald*, April 8, 25, 1919.

7. *Berkshire Eagle*, September 22, 2017.

8. *Elmira Star-Gazette*, October 13, 1919; *New York Evening World*, November 14, 1919.

9. *Brooklyn Daily Eagle*, November 25, December 5, 1918.

10. *Seattle Sunday Times*, January 19, 1919. Thanks to Alan Gaff for pointing out this revealing but forgotten article to me.

11. *New York Tribune*, May 9, 1919; Laplander, *Finding the Lost Battalion*, 652–56.

12. *New York Times*, March 2, 1919; *Elmira Star-Gazette*, March 24, 1919.

13. US Congress, Committee on Military Affairs, House of Representatives, statement by Cordell Hull, October 20, 1919; *Anniston Star*, May 12, 1919.

14. George Pattullo, "The Second Elder Gives Battle," *Saturday Evening Post* 191, no. 43, April 26, 1919, 3; Mastriano, *Alvin York*, 133–40; Michael E. Birdwell, "Alvin C. York: The Myth, the Man, and the Legacy," *Tennessee Historical Quarterly* 71, 4 (Winter 2012), 323.

15. Juliet Nicolson, *The Great Silence 1918–1920: Living in the Shadow of the Great War* (London: John Murray, 2009), 144–45.

16. *Charleston Daily Mail*, June 12, 1919; *Washington Post*, June 29, 1919; *New York Times*, April 27, July 3, 1919; *Tennessean*, July 20, 1919; *New York Tribune*, September 9, 1919.

17. Mastriano, *Alvin York*, 149–53.

18. *New York Times*, June 1, 1919.

19. *Philadelphia Inquirer*, April 15, 1920; Olean, New York, *Times Herald*, August 26, 1921; *Washington Times*, December 2, 1921; J. W. Williamson, *Hillbillyland: What the Movies Did to the Mountains and What the Mountains Did to the Movies* (Chapel Hill: University of North Carolina Press, 1995), 211; Mastriano, *Alvin York*, 162–66.

20. *New York Tribune*, February 16, 1920; *New York Herald*, May 6, July 21, September 25, 1920; *New York Times*, September 4, 1920.

21. *New York Times*, September 8, 1920, July 16, October 17, 1921; *Sun and Erie County Independent*, February 10, 1921; *Springfield Republican*,

February 11, November 13, 1919; Laplander, *Finding the Lost Battalion*, 657–61; Gaff, *Blood in the Argonne*, 280–83.

22. Schwarz, *Broadway Boogie Woogie*, 25; Breslin, *Damon Runyon*, 180.

23. *Minneapolis Star Tribune*, November 1, 1921; *Washington Herald*, November 1, 1921; *New York Tribune*, November 1, 2, 6, 1921; *New York Evening World*, November 7, 29, 1921; *Washington Post*, November 10, 13, 1921; Laplander, *Finding the Lost Battalion*, 662.

24. *New York Evening World*, November 29, 1921; Lengel, *To Conquer Hell*, 433–34; Laplander, *Finding the Lost Battalion*, 662–68.

CHAPTER FIFTEEN. HOMECOMINGS

1. Samuel K. Cowan, *Sergeant York and His People* (New York: Funk & Wagnalls, 1922), 77; *Raleigh News and Observer*, May 14, 1922.

2. Mastriano, 166–69; Davenport, Iowa, *Quad-City Times*, January 22, 1926.

3. *Raleigh News Observer*, January 23, 1919; *Greenville News*, February 3, 1919; *Roanoke News*, February 6, 1919; *Akron Evening News*, April 3, 1920.

4. Perry, *Sgt. York*, 160–61, 186–90.

5. Lee, *Sergeant York*, 94–99; Skeyhill, *Sergeant York*, 15–18; *Tennessean*, April 21, 1928.

6. Jefferson Morley, "Star-Spangled Confederates: How Southern Sympathizers Decided Our National Anthem," *Daily Beast*, July 4, 2013, http://www.thedailybeast.com/star-spangled-confederates-how-southern-sympathizers-decided-our-national-anthem.

7. Laplander, *Finding the Lost Battalion*, 676–78.

8. *Pittsfield Berkshire Eagle*, April 16, 1948; *North Adams Transcript*, April 21, 1948; Lost Battalion reunion newsletters at http://wmi.longwood.k12.ny.us/cms/One.aspx?portalId=2549374&pageId=7129225.

9. *New York Times*, November 24, 1958; Laplander, *Finding the Lost Battalion*, 176.

10. Breslin, *Damon Runyon*, 17; Schwarz, *Broadway Boogie Woogie*, 38–39, 81, 147, 243.

11. *Tennessean*, July 3, 1941.

12. Schwarz, *Broadway Boogie Woogie*, 11; Hoyt, *A Gentleman of Broadway*, 4.

13. *New York Times*, December 19, 1946; *Brooklyn Daily Eagle*, December 19, 1946.

14. Mastriano, *Alvin York*, 173–89; Perry, *Sgt. York*, 277–300; King James Bible, Psalm 121:1–2.

BIBLIOGRAPHY

Adler, Julius Ochs, ed. *History of the Seventy Seventh Division August 25, 1917–November 11, 1918.* New York: 77th Division Association, 1919.

Alexander, Robert. *Memories of the World War, 1917–1918.* New York: MacMillan, 1931.

American Battle Monuments Commission. *82nd Division Summary of Operations in the World War.* Washington, DC: United States Government Printing Office, 1944.

———. *77th Division Summary of Operations in the World War.* Washington, DC: United States Government Printing Office, 1944.

———. *28th Division Summary of Operations in the World War.* Washington, DC: United States Government Printing Office, 1944.

Baker, Kevin. "Emory Upton and the Shaping of the U.S. Army." *Military History*, 29, 1 (May 2012), 38–43.

Batchelder, Roger. *Camp Upton.* Boston: Small, Maynard, 1918.

Birdwell, Michael E. "Alvin Cullum York: The Myth, the Man, and the Legacy." *Tennessee Historical Quarterly* 71, 4 (Winter 2012): 318–339.

Breslin, Jimmy. *Damon Runyon.* New York: Ticknor & Fields, 1991.

Buxton, G. Edward Jr. *Official History of 82nd Division American Expeditionary Forces, 1917–1919.* Indianapolis: Bobbs-Merrill, 1920.

Cooke, James J. *The All-Americans at War: The 82nd Division in the Great War, 1917–1918.* Greenwood, CT: Praeger, 1999.

Copping, Jasper. "Honoured: The WW1 Pigeons Who Earned Their Wings." *Daily Telegraph*, January 12, 2014.

Cowan, Samuel K. *Sergeant York and His People.* New York: Funk & Wagnalls, 1922.

Duffy, Francis P. *Father Duffy's Story: A Tale of Humor and Heroism, of Life and Death with the Fighting Sixty-Ninth.* New York: George H. Doran, 1919.

Ebel, Jonathan H. *Faith in the Fight: Religion and the American Soldier in the Great War*. Princeton, NJ: Princeton University Press, 2010.

Faulkner, Richard S. *Pershing's Crusaders: The American Soldier in World War I*. Lawrence: University Press of Kansas, 2017.

———. *The School of Hard Knocks: Combat Leadership in the American Expeditionary Forces*. College Station, TX: Texas A&M University Press, 2012.

Ferrell, Robert H. *America's Deadliest Battle: Meuse-Argonne, 1918*. Lawrence: University Press of Kansas, 2007.

———. *Five Days in October: The Lost Battalion of World War I*. Columbia: University of Missouri Press, 2005.

Fitzpatrick, Kevin C. *World War I New York: A Guide to the City's Enduring Ties to the Great War*. Guilford, CT: Globe Pequot, 2017.

Gaff, Alan D. *Blood in the Argonne: The "Lost Battalion" of World War I*. Norman: University of Oklahoma Press, 2005.

Hallas, James H., ed. *Doughboy War: The American Expeditionary Force in World War I*. Mechanicsburg, PA: Stackpole Books, 2000.

Haverstock, Nathan A. *Fifty Years at the Front: The Life of War Correspondent Frederick Palmer*. Washington, DC: Brassey's, 1996.

Hoyt, Edwin P. *A Gentleman of Broadway*. Boston: Little, Brown, 1964.

Hussey, Alexander T., and Raymond M. Flynn. *The History of Company E, 308th Infantry (1917–1919)*. New York: Knickerbocker Press, 1919.

Johnson, Thomas M., and Fletcher Pratt. *The Lost Battalion*. Lincoln: University of Nebraska Press, 2000. Originally published in 1938.

Kelly, Michael J. *A Hero on the Western Front: Discovering Alvin C. York's Great War Battlefield*. London: Frontline Books, 2018.

Kington, Donald M. "The Plattsburg Movement and Its Legacy." *Relevance: Quarterly Journal of the Great War Society* 6, no. 4 (Autumn 1997).

Klausner, Julius, Jr. *Company B 307th Infantry: Its History Honor Roll Company Roster*. Privately printed, 1920.

Laplander, Robert J. *Finding the Lost Battalion: Beyond the Rumors, Myths and Legends of America's Famous WW1 Epic*, 3rd ed. Privately printed, Lulu Press, 2017.

Lee, David D. *Sergeant York: An American Hero*. Lexington: University Press of Kentucky, 1985.

Lengel, Edward G. *Thunder and Flames: Americans in the Crucible of Combat, 1917–1918*. Lawrence: University Press of Kansas, 2015.

———. *To Conquer Hell: The Meuse-Argonne, 1918*. New York: Henry Holt, 2008.

Levinger, Lee J. *A Jewish Chaplain in France*. New York: MacMillan, 1921.

Lewis, Edward Newell. "In the Argonne's Mist and Mystery." *American Legion Weekly*, 1, 13, September 26, 1919, 7–9, 29, 32–34.

Lewis, W. David. *Eddie Rickenbacker: An American Hero in the Twentieth Century*. Baltimore: Johns Hopkins University Press, 2008.

Liggett, Hunter. *A.E.F.: Ten Years Ago in France*. New York: Dodd, Mead, 1928.

———. *Commanding an American Army: Recollections of the World War*. Boston: Houghton Mifflin, 1925.

Manson, Robert. "Through Six Days of Heroism with the Lost Battalion." *Literary Digest* 60 (January–March, 1919), March 29, 1919, 44, 47.

Mastriano, Douglas V. *Alvin York: A New Biography of the Hero of the Argonne*. Lexington: University Press of Kentucky, 2014.

McKeogh, Arthur. "The Lost Battalion." *Collier's*, November 16, 1918, 5–6, 18, 22, 24, 26.

———. *The Victorious 77th Division (New York's Own) in the Argonne Fight*. New York: John J. Eggers, 1919.

Miles, Louis Wardlaw. *History of the 308th Infantry, 1917–1919*. New York: G.P. Putnam's Sons, 1927.

Montell, William Lynwood. *Killings: Folk Justice in the Upper South*. Lexington: University of Kentucky Press, 1986.

Mosher, Anne E. *Capital's Utopia: Vandergrift, Pennsylvania, 1855–1916*. Baltimore: Johns Hopkins University Press, 2004.

Nell, John W. *The Lost Battalion: A Private's Story*. San Antonio, TX: Historical Publishing Network, 2001.

Nicolson, Juliet. *The Great Silence 1918–1920: Living in the Shadow of the Great War*. London: John Murray, 2009.

Palmer, Frederick A. *America in France*. New York: Dodd, Mead, 1918.

———. *Our Greatest Battle: The Meuse-Argonne*. New York: Dodd, Mead, 1919.

Perry, John. *Sgt. York: His Life, Legend & Legacy*. Nashville, TN, Broadman & Holman, 1997.

Rainsford, W. Kerr. *From Upton to the Meuse with the Three Hundred and Seventh Infantry*. New York: D. Appleton, 1920.

Ranlett, Louis Felix. *Let's Go! The Story of A.S. No. 2448602*. Boston: Houghton Mifflin, 1927.

Roosevelt, Theodore, Jr. *Rank and File: True Stories of the Great War*. New York: Charles Scribner's Sons, 1928.
Roth, Mitchel P., ed. *Historical Dictionary of War Journalism*. Westport, CT: Greenwood Press, 1997.
Runyon, Damon. "Hold 'Em, Yale!" marching song for the sammies. Los Angeles: Charles Farwell Edson, 1917.
Schwarz, Daniel R. *Broadway Boogie Woogie: Damon Runyon and the Making of New York City Culture*. New York: Palgrave Macmillan, 2003.
Sensing, Thurman. *Champ Ferguson: Confederate Guerilla*. Reprint edition. Nashville, TN: Vanderbilt University Press, 1994.
Skeyhill, Thomas J., ed. *Sergeant York: His Own Life Story and War Diary*. Garden City, NY: Doubleday, Doran, 1928.
Slotkin, Richard. *Lost Battalions: The Great War and the Crisis of American Nationality*. New York: Henry Holt, 2005.
Smith, Troy D. "Champ Ferguson: An American Civil War Rebel Guerila," *Civil War Times* 40, no. 6 (December, 2001).
Through the War with Company D, 307th Infantry, 77th Division. New York. Privately printed, 1919.
Trask, David F. *The AEF and Coalition Warmaking*. Lawrence: University Press of Kansas, 1993.
Willemse, Cornelius. *Behind the Green Lights*. New York: Alfred A. Knopf, 1931.
Williamson, J. W. *Hillbillyland: What the Movies Did to the Mountains and What the Mountains Did to the Movies*. Chapel Hill: University of North Carolina Press, 1995.
Wilson, Ross J. *New York City and the First World War: Shaping an American City*. Farnham, Surrey: Ashgate, 2014.
Witcover, Jules. *Sabotage at Black Tom: Imperial Germany's Secret War in America, 1914–1917*. Chapel Hill, NC: Algonquin Books, 1989.
Yockelson, Mitchell. *Forty-Seven Days: How Pershing's Warriors Came of Age to Defeat the German Army in World War I*. New York: Dutton, 2016.

INDEX

A Company (77th Division, 308th Regiment, 1st Battalion), 135, 145
Adler, Julius Ochs, 21
AEF (American Expeditionary Forces)
  Cantigny as first victory of, 96, 182–183
  Chaumont, France, headquarters of, 192, 214
  and Meuse-Argonne strategy, 110–111
  "push forward" doctrine of, 207
  unpreparedness of, 73, 88–89, 96
  and "the will to win as sufficient to victory," 139
  See also Pershing, John J.
African American soldiers, 19, 20, 71, 79, 112, 277
Aire River valley, 111, 112, 118 (map), 128, 186, 236–237, 256–257
Aisne River valley, 109, 111, 118 (map)
Alexander, Robert
  background of, 104–105
  as bully, 112, 169, 206–207
  death of, 314
  and German surrender memo, 251, 253, 255
  and *Lost Battalion* film, 289–290, 291–292
  and Lost Battalion relief, 185–186, 204–205, 206–207, 214, 245, 246–248, 251, 256, 285
  as media-conscious, 193
  and Meuse-Argonne strategy, 111, 112, 113
  and 77th Division homecoming, 268–271
  and 77th Division initial advance in Meuse-Argonne offensive, 120–121, 123, 125, 126, 128
  and 77th Division order to continue in Meuse-Argonne offensive, 131, 132–133, 138–139, 141–142, 143–144, 148–149, 169
"All-American" Division. *See* 82nd "All-American" Division
All Quiet on the Western Front (Remarque), 182
Alsace-Lorraine, 97–100, 110

INDEX

Alvin C. York Industrial Institute, 308
American Expeditionary Forces. *See* AEF (American Expeditionary Forces); Pershing, John J.
Anderson, Herman G., 197, 198, 222, 223
Aquitania (ship), 281
Arbuckle, "Fatty," 296
"Argonne Day," 290
Argonne Forest, German 1918 spring and summer offenses in, 180–181, 182, 183, 185. *See also* Meuse-Argonne offensive
Argonne Ravine, 131–132, 142, 144, 149–150, 206
Arlington National Cemetery, 299, 302–304
Averill, Nathan K., 85, 102, 103

B Company (77th Division, 308th Regiment, 1st Battalion), 122, 145
Babe Ruth, 12, 78, 282
Baker, Newton D., 19, 184, 185, 291
"Bangs," 269
Bar-le-Duc, 208–209, 214, 251
Barnhart, Harry, 33, 34, 35, 311–312
Baxter, James Phinney, 313
Beaty, "Tinker Dave," 55, 57, 60
Bebee, Kid, 40
Bell, James F., 31, 33, 35–36, 73–74, 77, 80, 83
Belleau Wood offensive, 96, 129, 182–183

Bendheim, Lionel, 179, 229
Black Tom explosion, 7–10, 14, 16, 46, 87, 269, 317
Bleckley, Erwin, 215
Boston Braves, 33, 35–36
Boston Red Sox, 12, 50, 280, 282
Boyce's Tigers, 35, 69, 72, 170
Breckenridge, Lucien, 103
British Allied troops, 95, 109, 132, 155, 181, 182, 280, 287
British training camps, 96–97
Brooklyn Daily Eagle, 29, 36
Brooklyn Dodgers, 12, 36, 50
Brown, Clifford R., 228–229, 247
Budd, Kenneth P., 102, 112–113, 117, 121, 122, 123, 124–125, 127
Bulger, Bozeman, 93
Bundy, Omar, 189
Burgoyne, John, 261
Businessmen's Camp. *See* Plattsburg camp
Buxton, G. Edward, 63–64

C Company (77th Division, 308th Regiment, 1st Battalion), 145, 179, 229
Cain, James M., 315
Camp Gordon, 62, 65, 85, 88–89, 90, 96
Camp Lewis, 84
Camp Upton
 Bell as 77th Division commander at, 35–36, 73–74, 77, 80, 83
 building of, 28–30
 82nd Division at, 87–90
 Johnson as 77th Division commander at, 80, 83, 85, 86

(344)

New York trainees at, 30, 31–32,
    71–72
Runyon as reporter at, 78–79,
    191, 250
77th Division at, 30–31, 35–36,
    69, 70–79, 80, 83, 84–87, 113,
    191, 264, 267, 284
  as a "singing camp," 31, 35, 73,
    83
Cantigny, France, 1st Division
    capture of, 96, 182–183
CCCU (Church of Christ in
    Christian Union), 60, 61
Cepaglia, Phil "Zip," 248
Chandler, Raymond, 315
Chaplin, Charlie, 3–4, 70
Charlevaux Ravine ("the pocket")
  "friendly fire" into, 172–173
  German position east of, 118
    (map), 204, 227–228, 245
  and Lost Battalion position, 118
    (map), 172–173, 193, 202, 203,
    204
  and Lost Battalion relief efforts,
    204, 227–228, 240–241, 245
  77th Division advance into,
    142–144, 149–151, 155
  See also Lost Battalion; Meuse-
    Argonne offensive
Chase, Joseph Cummings, 275, 287
Chaumont, France, AEF
    headquarters at, 192, 214
Cher Ami, 156, 175–176, 201, 204,
    290. *See also* pigeons, carrier
Chicago White Sox, 37–39
Civil War, 29, 32, 36, 55, 66–67, 98,
    273, 307
Clemenceau, Georges, 185

combat fatigue, 129, 130–131, 195
Coolidge, Calvin, 303
Coolidge, Grace, 303
Cooper, Gary, 315, 319
Cowan, Samuel K., 307–308,
    310–311
Cretic (ship), 86
Cross, Eben, 22
Cullen, William J.
  death of, 314
  with the Lost Battalion, 161, 168,
    180, 233, 256, 199
  and *Lost Battalion* film, 290, 291
Cutting, William, 258, 260

Danforth, E. C. B., 63, 257, 258, 287
Davis, Richard Harding, 45, 48, 49,
    67, 107
Dead Man's Hill, 111, 121, 123,
    131–132
Dempsey, Jack, 280–281
draft, national, 19–20, 25, 31–36, 37,
    65–66, 76–77, 312
Drebin, Sam, 315–316
Duffy, Francis, 98–99, 216
Duncan, George B., 97, 102–103,
    188, 274, 275, 287, 288

E Company (77th Division, 308th
    Regiment, 2nd Battalion)
  and departure for Europe, 86,
    92
  at the Hippodrome, 81–82
  McMurtry as captain of, 74–75,
    98–102, 112–113, 114, 153
  in Meuse-Argonne offensive,
    112, 114, 117, 120, 123, 125, 127,
    132, 145–146, 151–154, 157

INDEX

E Company (*continued*)
    and New York military parade, 82–83
    in Vesle River region, 99–102
    Wilhelm as interim commander of, 152–153, 157
Eager, Sherman W., 139
Early, Bernard, 258–260
Edrop, Percy, 39–40
Edwards, Clarence, 283
Egan, Ellen, 47–48
82nd "All-American" Division (328th Regiment)
    in the Argonne, 187–188, 191, 207, 236, 237, 246, 263, 264–265
    arrival on front lines of, 97
    at Camp Gordon, 88–89
    at Camp Upton, 87–90
    Duncan as commander of, 103
    ethnic diversity in, 216
    in European training camps, 96–97
    as misfit draftees, 87–89
    return home of, 277
    in Saint-Mihiel offensive, 109
    See also York, Alvin C.
Ellis Island, 7, 8, 9, 13, 17, 75, 297, 317

Fatherland (newspaper), 16
Fentress County, Tennessee, 52, 56, 57, 61, 62, 69, 308, 309–310, 318
Ferguson, Champ, 55, 56, 57, 58, 60
Ferguson, Fred S., 192

Ferguson, Patrick, 55
Fighting 69th Regiment, New York National Guard, 98, 191
films, WWI-era, 288–289. *See also The Lost Battalion*
First Army, US, 109–111, 128, 131, 133, 170, 184–185, 207, 279
1st Battalion (77th Division, 308th Regiment), 82–83, 86, 99, 103, 122, 135–136, 145, 179, 229, 237. *See also* Whittlesey, Charles
1st Division, US, 96, 182, 185, 186–187, 207–208, 210–211
Fitzgerald, F. Scott, 315
Foch, Ferdinand, 110, 305
40th "Sunshine" Division, 113, 136, 148, 149, 241
42nd Division (New York National Guard), 98, 106, 191
Foss, Sidney, 197, 198, 222
4th Division, U.S., 100, 111
French troops, 112, 128, 132, 138, 141, 142, 143, 144, 145, 145 (map), 170, 188, 248
Friedman, Benjamin, 217
Frogg, William, 56

G Company (77th Division, 308th Regiment, 2nd Battalion), 145–146
Gaedeke, Ben, 150, 176
gas warfare, 99, 101–102, 103, 105–106, 119, 129–130, 155, 257, 296, 319–320
Gilbert, Max "Fly," 250–251
Goettler, Harold, 215
Gowdy, Hank, 280

(346)

INDEX

Grant, Eddie, 78, 93, 191–92, 206, 209, 214, 255, 279, 284
Greeley, Horace, 44–45

H Company (77th Division, 308th Regiment, 2nd Battalion), 145, 151–152, 231. *See also* Cullen, William J.
Haig, Douglas, 95
Hammett, Dashiell, 315
Hannay, John, 144
Harding, Warren G., 299, 302, 303
Harlem Hellfighters, 71
Hearst, William Randolph, 12, 15, 16, 44, 46, 48, 49, 50, 190–191, 289
Herschkowitz, Jack, 216, 218
Heuer, Joseph, 149
Hill 180, Meuse-Argonne, 118 (map), 236
Hill 223, Meuse-Argonne, 118 (map), 236–237, 238, 257, 263, 287–288
Hill 244, Meuse-Argonne, 118 (map), 236
Hoboken, New Jersey, 17, 271, 280
Holderman, Nelson
  background of, 147–148
  and final German attack on the Lost Battalion, 219–220, 221
  as K Company commander, 148, 149–151, 152, 154, 156–157, 162, 197, 209
  with the Lost Battalion, 197, 198–199, 219–220, 221, 227, 247–249, 286
  and Medal of Honor, 290
  in Meuse-Argonne offensive, 147–148, 149–151, 152, 154, 156–157, 162
  postwar life and death of, 314
  at Unknown Soldier ceremony, 304
  wounding of, 247, 249
Hollingshead, Lowell, 226–227, 229–232, 234, 334n3
Hoyt, Edwin, 316
Hull, Cordell, 272, 275–276
Huston, T. L., 39

I Corps, 112, 118 (map), 185, 207. *See also* Liggett, Hunter
Iraci, Alfio, 153
Irwin, Will, 249–250, 251–252, 253
Italian Allied forces, 106

Jacobs, Harold, 192
Johnson, Evan
  as career officer, 104–105
  death of, 314
  and Lost Battalion relief, 245, 246
  as 154th Brigade commander, 105–106, 121, 125, 126, 131, 132–133, 138–139, 144, 148–149, 156, 186, 205–206, 245, 286
  and "push forward" command to 154th Brigade, 138–139, 148–149, 156, 186
  as 77th Division temporary commander, 80, 83, 85, 86, 97
Johnson, Thomas, 249–250, 279, 312–313
Justicia (ship), 86

INDEX

K Company (77th Division, 307th Regiment, 3rd Battalion), 148, 149–151, 152, 154, 156–157, 162, 171, 197, 209. *See also* Holderman, Nelson
Kidde, Regnar, 81–82
King, Burton, 289, 290, 291
King, James J., 273
Kipling, Rudyard, 41, 43, 50
Krotoshinsky, Abraham, 227–228, 238–240, 247, 290, 291
Ku Klux Klan, 54, 66, 277, 307

Lapland (ship), 86, 90–91
Larney, James F., 174–175, 177
Lasky, Jesse, 292, 318–319
Lawrence, T. E., 289
Lederie, Louis, Jr., 82
Leonard, Benny, 78–79, 250–251
Leviathan (ship), 280
Lewis, Edward N., 116
Liggett, Hunter
   and final attack in the Argonne, 214, 236, 245–246, 264–265
   as First Army commander, 279
   as I Corps commander, 112, 185, 186–187, 206–207, 214, 236
   and Lost Battalion relief, 204, 206–208, 214, 236, 245, 264–265, 291
   and Meuse-Argonne offensive, 112, 120, 132, 133
Lindsey, Julian R., 263
Liner, Irving, 252
Lost Battalion
   AEF leadership and, 169, 185–186, 203–208, 214, 251, 245, 246–248, 253, 256, 285
   and AEF relief efforts, 170, 197, 202–205, 207–208, 214–215, 219, 240–242, 245, 279
   breakout attempts among, 225–229, 238–240
   Damon Runyon and, 4–5, 249–251, 251–252, 253–255, 314–315
   events leading to isolation of, 135–146, 185
   final attack on Germans by, 234–236
   "friendly fire" assaults on, 172–178, 200–201, 204, 215
   German final attack on, 219–221
   German surrender memo to, 251–252, 231–234, 235
   as heroes, 255–256
   location of, 145 (map)
   and *Lost Battalion* film, 289–292, 305
   machine gunners' plight in, 161–162, 197–198
   and May 1919 New York homecoming parade, 270
   and the press, 4–5, 192–193, 208, 214, 246, 249–250, 251–255, 278–279, 283–285
   relief of, 242–243, 245–248, 251, 279
   and Revnes' advocating of surrender, 222–223, 285–286
   suffering of, 163, 172, 176, 195–197, 198–200, 222, 230, 233, 285
   See also Holderman, Nelson; McMurtry, George; Meuse-Argonne offensive; Whittlesey, Charles

The Lost Battalion (film), 289–292, 305, 312–313
Lost Battalion Survivors Association, 277, 295, 312, 313, 314

Madison Square Garden, 11, 147, 268, 289, 317
Manson, Robert, 246
Marne River, 100, 104, 105, 109, 121
Marshall, George C., 31, 279
Masterson, Bat, 47, 298
McGraw, John, 33–34, 37, 38–39
McKeogh, Arthur, 116, 121, 124, 126, 282, 290
McManus, Edward A., 289, 290–291
McMurtry, George
  background of, 26–27
  at Camp Upton, 69, 74–75, 78–79, 81–82, 85
  and combat fatigue, 130–131
  E Company under, 74–75, 83, 98–102, 112–114, 117, 120, 123, 125, 127, 152, 153–154
  and "friendly fire" attack on Lost Battalion, 200–201
  and German final attack on Lost Battalion, 219–220, 221, 222, 233–235
  and German surrender memo, 231–232
  with the Lost Battalion, 151, 160, 161–163, 174, 177, 180, 198, 200–201, 209–210, 217–220, 221, 222–224, 225, 231–232, 233–235
  and *Lost Battalion* film, 290–291
  and Lost Battalion relief, 242–243, 246, 247, 249, 254
  Lost Battalion Survivors Association led by, 295, 312, 313–314
  Lost Battalion troop connections with, 217–218
  and May 1919 New York homecoming parade, 270, 286
  as Medal of Honor recipient, 283, 286
  and Meuse-Argonne advance into the pocket, 135, 136–137, 139–140, 141, 142, 143, 144, 146
  and Meuse-Argonne initial advance, 112, 114, 117, 120, 121, 123, 125, 127, 132, 133–134
  at Plattsburg, 25, 27, 28–29, 32
  postwar life and death of, 295, 314
  as 2nd battalion temporary commander, 102, 103, 105
  and Unknown Soldier ceremony, 300, 303, 304
  on Vesle River front lines, 100–102, 105
  as war hero, 298–299
  Whittlesey relationship with, 163, 210, 223, 264, 265, 313
  wounding of, 162, 168, 217–218, 246, 247, 249, 254
Mead, Kidder, 192
"Metropolitan" Division. *See* 77th "Metropolitan" Division
Meuse-Argonne offensive
  AEF strategy in, 110–114
  aerial forces in, 201–203

(349)

Meuse-Argonne offensive (*continued*)
   Allied forces and, 112, 128, 132, 138, 141–142, 143, 144, 145, 145 (map), 170, 188, 248
   and Dead Man's Hill, 111, 121, 123, 131–132
   and German evacuation from Argonne Forrest, 260–264
   German Front line in, 145 (map)
   German General Wellman and, 210–211
   German storm troopers and, 95, 211, 220, 235
   Hill 223 and, 118 (map), 236–237, 238, 257, 263, 287–288
   initial advance in, 112, 114, 115–117, 118 (map), 119–121, 122–125, 126–127, 130–132, 133–134
   and 77th Division continued advance into the pocket, 135–146, 145 (map), 149–151, 155
   See also Alexander, Robert; Liggett, Hunter; Lost Battalion; Pershing, John J.; 77th Division
Meuse River, 110, 128
Michalsuk, Steve, 79
Military Training Camps Association (MTCA), 25
Mitchel, John Purroy, 15–16, 17, 21, 31, 32
Mitchell, William "Billy," 202
Monahan, John T. E., 122
Moran, Frank, 11
Mullin, Jerry, 75

Nast, Condé, 22

"National Draft Day," 31–36, 51–52, 72–73, 78, 82, 312
neutrality, American, 14–16
New World, 16
New York American, 4, 46, 51, 189, 249–250, 281–282, 298. *See also* Runyon, Damon
New York City
   baseball in, 12, 33–36, 37–39, 46, 49–50, 53, 71 (*See also teams individually by name*)
   Black Tom explosion near, 7–10, 14, 16, 46, 87, 269, 317
   Mitchel as mayor of, 15–16, 17, 21, 31, 32
   "National Draft Day" in, 31–36, 51–52, 72–73, 78, 82, 312
   newspaper industry in, 12, 44–45, 107 (*See also newspapers individually by name*)
   nineteenth-century immigration to, 13–14
   in postwar years, 277–278, 311–312
   and 77th Division ethnic diversity, 71–72, 75, 84, 87–88, 106, 216–217, 254
   77th Division identity with, 19–20, 30, 35, 36, 39–40, 80, 98–99
   and 77th Division in February 1918 military parades, 82–84
   and 77th Division in May 1919 homecoming parade, 267–270
   and US entry into WWI, 14–19, 31

before WWI, 7–14
WWI-era ethnic sectional identity and paranoia in, 15–16, 17–18, 19–20, 277–278
New York Giants, 12, 33–36, 37, 38–39, 46, 49, 53, 78, 191–192, 206
New York Globe, 107
New York Harbor, 7, 14, 90, 191, 268, 281
New York Herald, 45, 73, 107–108, 192
New York Sun, 21, 29, 249
New York Times, 11, 21, 44–45, 107, 269
New York Tribune, 44–45, 82, 116, 286
New York World, 44–45, 107, 192, 308
New York Yankees, 12, 39

Ohioan (ship), 271
Olympia (ship), 301
153rd Brigade (77th Division), 71, 148–149, 246, 269
154th Brigade (77th Division), 71, 97, 138–139, 148–149, 245, 246
O'Ryan, John F., 280, 281
Owens, Tom, 78

Pall Mall, Tennessee, 5, 54–55, 60, 61, 89, 293–294, 307
Palmer, Frederick, 107–108, 191–192, 214, 255
Parsons, Harry M., 258
patriotism, 18, 27, 28, 62, 66–67, 190, 294, 313
Patton, George S., 50, 184

Pattullo, George, 287–288
Peabody, Marshall G., 198
Pershing, John J.
  as AEF commander, 19–20, 27, 29, 69, 102–103, 108, 173, 184, 188, 191, 208, 214, 236
  First Army under, 109, 184–185, 279
  Frederick Palmer as AEF press chief to, 108, 191, 214
  and Lost Battalion relief, 185–186, 204, 208, 214, 256, 264–265
  mental breakdown of, 185, 279, 208
  and Meuse-Argonne offensive, 110–111, 112, 120, 128, 131, 132, 133, 134, 184–186, 264–265
  on the Mexican border, 48, 49, 104, 148
  and Presidio tragedy, 184
  and "success" in warfare, 129
  and Unknown Soldier ceremony, 302
  war correspondents and, 192–193
  and Woodfill military hero selection, 300, 301
Peterson, Emil H., 226, 229
pigeons, carrier, 125, 132, 155–156
Pile, Rosier C., 60, 61, 62, 293, 309
Plattsburg camp, 20–22, 24–25, 27–29, 32, 51, 152, 159–160, 169, 196
"the pocket." *See* Charlevaux Ravine
Polo Grounds, New York, 12, 33–36, 37, 38, 39, 46, 69, 72, 170, 267, 312, 317

(351)

INDEX

Pool, Thomas G., 149–150, 157, 209–210, 216
Pou, Robert E., 241–243
Pratt, Fletcher, 312–313
Prescott, Austin F., 103, 121
press, Lost Battalion and, 4–5, 192–193, 208, 214, 246, 249–250, 251–255, 278–279, 283–285. *See also* war correspondents
Prinz, Heinrich, 229–230
Probst, Louis, 153
Pruyn, John, 24, 296, 305–306
Pulitzer, Joseph, 12, 44, 45
Pyle, Ernie, 216

racial segregation in US armed forces, 20, 71, 79
Rainwater, Carl, 142
Raleigh (NC) *News and Observer*, 308
Ranlett, Louis, 90, 91
Remarque, Erich Maria, 182
Revnes, Maurice
 background of, 159–160
 with the Lost Battalion, 159–160, 168, 197, 198, 200, 209, 222–223, 252, 285–286
 at Plattsburg, 159–160, 196
 postwar life and death of, 314
 surrender advocated by, 222–223, 285–286
Rice, Cushman, 39
Richards, Omer, 155–156, 160, 171–172, 175–176, 201
Rickenbacker, Eddie, 280, 298, 316–317

Robins. *See* Brooklyn Dodgers
Roosevelt, Franklin D., 281, 319
Roosevelt, Quentin, 21
Roosevelt, Theodore, Jr., 21
Roosevelt, Theodore "Teddy," 26, 32–33, 45, 67, 76–77, 107, 130
Root, Elihu, Jr., 22
Runyon, Damon
 Argonne arrival of, 147, 190–192, 193
 background of, 41–44
 and desire to go to the Front, 93, 189–190
 "Doughboy Dialogues" of, 279–280
 and Lost Battalion, 183, 208–209, 214, 249–255, 265, 278
 and National Draft Day parade, 36, 51–52, 78
 New York City life of, 44–48
 Pancho Villa and, 49
 as poet, 40, 43–44, 78, 189–190
 postwar life and death of, 279–281, 297–298, 314–317
 as reporter at Camp Upton, 68, 78–79
 in Spanish-American War, 42, 43, 297, 325n10
 as sports fan and sportswriter, 37–38, 39, 40, 42, 43, 44, 50, 53, 93, 280–282, 298, 300, 315
 as war correspondent, 4–5, 183, 191–192, 208–209, 214, 250–251, 279–280
Runyon, Ellen Egan, 47–48, 191
Russell, Melvin Herbert, 59–60
Ruth, Babe, 12, 78, 282

Saint-Mihiel offensive, 109–110, 111
Salt Lake Tribune, 325n10
Saturday Evening Post, 249–250, 287–288
Savage, Murray, 2, 258, 260
Scandinavian (ship), 90, 91
Schenck, Gordon L., 179, 209, 217, 221, 228, 229, 283
Schoenfeld, Herman, 82–83
Scribner's Weekly, 45
2nd Battalion (77th Division, 308th Regiment)
    Budd as commander of, 112–113, 117, 121, 122, 123, 124–125, 127
    en route to the Front, 86, 91
    H Company of, 145, 151–152, 231
    McMurtry as temporary commander of, 102, 103, 127, 136, 232
    in Meuse-Argonne offensive, 117, 122, 123, 124–125, 127, 136, 145, 151–152, 231, 232
2nd Division, US, 100, 189
Selective Service Act, 19–20. *See also* draft, national
Sergeant York (film), 315–316, 318–319
Sergeant York: His Own Life Story and Diary, 310. *See also* Skeyhill, Tom; York, Alvin C.
77th "Metropolitan" Division
    Bell as commander of, 31, 33, 35, 73–74, 77, 80, 83
    at Camp Upton, 30–31, 35–36, 69, 70–79, 84–85, 113 80, 83, 191, 264, 267, 284
    casualties in, 113, 129–130, 140, 148, 150, 160, 268
    Duncan as commander of, 97
    ethnic diversity in makeup of, 71–72, 77, 84, 216–217
    and February 1918 New York military parade, 82–85
    on front lines in Alsace-Lorraine, 97–100
    on front lines in Vesle River region, 100–105
    Jewish soldiers in, 210, 216–217, 250
    Johnson as temporary commander of, 80, 97
    and journey to Europe, 85–93
    as "Liberty" Division, 271
    and May 1919 homecoming, 267–271
    as "Metropolitan" Division, 80
    in Meuse-Argonne strategy, 111, 112–114
    at Plattsburg, 20–22, 24–25, 27–29, 32, 51, 152, 159–160, 169, 196
    in training in Europe, 96–97
    and war mobilization efforts, 75–76
    See also Alexander, Robert; Lost Battalion; Meuse-Argonne offensive
77th Division Association, 286
shell shock, 130, 195
Sirota, Irving, 210, 216
Skeyhill, Tom, 292, 308–309, 310–311, 313, 319
Smart, Daniel S., 213–214, 216

Smith, Fred E., 125, 127
Soissons, France, 95, 100
Somme River region, 96
Spanish-American War, 26, 43, 49, 66–67, 97, 104, 209, 297, 325n10
Speich, George F., 171
Stacey, Cromwell
   in the Argonne, 121, 125–126, 127, 131, 132, 133, 134, 135, 138, 139, 140, 141, 286
   and Lost Battalion, 153, 156, 186, 205
   replacement of, 205–206
Statue of Liberty, 7, 8, 9, 14, 87, 90, 268, 281, 317
Stengel, Casey, 12
Stewart, Kirby, 258
Stimson, Henry L., 76
Sunshine Division. *See* 40th "Sunshine" Division

Taft, William Howard, 276, 302
3rd Battalion (77th Division, 307th Regiment), 148, 149–151, 152, 154, 156–157, 162, 171, 197, 209
3rd Division, US, 96, 100
Thomas, Lowell, 288–289, 310
Thorpe, Jim, 33–34
369th Regiment (93rd Division), 71
305th Regiment (77th Division), 71, 76
306th Regiment (77th Division), 71, 145
307th Regiment (77th Division)
   and departure for Europe, 85–87
   and February 1918 New York military parade, 83
   and Lost Battalion relief, 214, 242, 245, 247
   in Meuse-Argonne offensive advance, 122, 138, 141, 143, 148–149, 193
308th Regiment (77th Division)
   and departure for Europe, 85–87, 91
   as February 1918 entertainers at the Hippodrome, 80–81, 85
   and February 1918 New York military parades, 82–83
   on the front lines, 99, 100, 102–103, 105
   and Lost Battalion relief, 214, 245
   and May 1919 New York homecoming, 270
   and Meuse-Argonne offensive advance into the pocket, 138, 141–142, 144, 148–149
   and Meuse-Argonne offensive strategy, 113
   See also McMurtry, George; Meuse-Argonne offensive; 77th Division; Stacey, Cromwell; Whittlesey, Charles
325th Regiment (77th Division), 92
328th Regiment (82nd Division), 90, 188, 236–237, 271
Times Square, New York, 7, 11, 45, 47, 98, 254, 317
trench warfare, 28, 129
Tuite, Martin F., 217
Tumulty, Joseph, 276

INDEX

28th "Bloody Bucket" Division, Pennsylvania National Guard
  in Lost Battalion relief, 245
  in Meuse-Argonne offensive, 128, 185, 186, 188, 207, 236–237, 257, 263
  in Meuse-Argonne offensive strategy, 111, 112
27th "Empire" Division, New York National Guard, 280

Unknown Soldier ceremony, 299–300, 301, 302–304
Upton, Emory, 29. *See also* Camp Upton

Vanderbilt III, Cornelius, 39
Van Loan, Charlie, 44
Verdun, Battle of, 10, 109, 110, 112, 188
Vesle River region front, 100–101
Vigonto, Victor, 87–88
Villa, Pancho, 48–49, 50
Vollmer, Paul, 259, 261–263, 273
voluntary aid associations, veteran, 277
Voorsanger, Elkan C., 216–217

Wade, J. C., 283–285
war correspondents, 4–5, 45, 46, 67, 107–108, 287. *See also* Davis, Richard Harding; Palmer, Frederick; Runyon, Damon
War Department, US, 19–20, 25, 75, 88, 128–129, 276, 281
"war neuroses," 130
Weeks, John W., 301

Wellmann, Richard, 180–181, 182, 183, 210–211, 236, 264
Welsh, Freddie, 78, 250
Whittlesey, Charles
  background of, 22–24
  at Camp Upton, 69, 73, 74, 78–79, 82, 83, 85, 284
  and combat fatigue, 130–131
  criticisms of, 198, 286
  en route to Europe, 86, 90–92
  and "friendly fire" on Lost Battalion, 173, 174–175, 177–178, 188, 200
  as "Galloping Charlie," 116, 218
  and German attacks on Lost Battalion, 178–180, 200, 220–221, 234–235
  and German surrender memo, 231–234, 251–252, 253, 255
  idealism and sensitivity of, 24, 106
  and Lost Battalion breakouts, 225, 227, 228, 230
  Lost Battalion burden of responsibility on, 163, 168–169, 199–200, 201, 218, 297
  as Lost Battalion commander, 4, 5, 147, 148–150, 151–152, 153–154, 155–157, 159, 160, 162–163, 165
  and Lost Battalion communications efforts, 171–172, 175–176, 203
  and *Lost Battalion* film, 290–291, 305
  and Lost Battalion relief, 170, 185–186, 201, 202–204, 205, 207–208, 215, 241, 242–243, 245, 249

(355)

Whittlesey, Charles (*continued*)
  and May 1919 New York homecoming parade, 267, 269, 270, 286
  McMurtry relationship with, 163, 210, 223, 264, 265, 313
  as Medal of Honor recipient, 283
  media and, 282–285, 290, 292, 304
  and Meuse-Argonne initial advance, 115–117, 119–121, 122–125, 126–127, 130–132, 133–134, 135–146, 145 (map)
  and National Draft Day, 32
  and November 1918 return to New York, 282–286
  at Plattsburg, 22, 24–25, 27, 28–29, 32, 51, 73, 124, 152, 284
  postwar life and death of, 295–296, 305–306
  and Revnes' surrender conviction and acquittal, 222–223, 285–286
  and sleep deprivation in Lost Battalion, 171, 195, 200, 218
  as tormented by war, 295–296, 297, 301, 304–306
  and Unknown Soldier ceremony, 300, 301, 303, 304
  as veterans advocate, 296–297
  as war hero, 296, 298–299, 313
  See also Lost Battalion; Meuse-Argonne offensive; 77th Division
Whittlesey, Elisha, 296, 305
Wilhelm, Karl, 152, 153, 157
Willard, Jess, 11, 280
Willemse, Cornelius, 66
Williams, Gracie Loretta, 59, 60
Wilson, Edith, 287
Wilson, Woodrow
  and Allied war efforts, 19, 182, 184, 185, 288
  and McMurtry and Whittlesey Medals of Honor, 283
  media restrictions and, 78
  Pancho Villa and, 48
  at Unknown Soldier ceremony, 299–300, 302
  and US entry into WWI, 14–16, 17, 18, 31–32, 50–51, 73
Winchell, Walter, 315
Wood, Leonard, 20, 22
Woodfill, Samuel, 300–302, 304, 307–308, 310
World War I
  celebration of heroes of, 298–301
  communications obstacles in, 154–155
  in film and literature, 288–289, 315
  and Germany surrender, 251
  and mobilization efforts, 17–19, 75–76
  national draft and, 19–20, 25, 31–36, 37, 51, 65–66, 72–73, 76–78, 82, 312
  US entry into, 14–16, 17, 18, 25, 31–32, 50–51, 73
  US occupation army in Germany after, 279–280
  Woodrow Wilson and, 14–16, 17, 18, 19, 31–32, 50–51, 73, 182, 184, 185, 288

World War II, 101, 179, 216, 313, 316, 317–318, 319

Yankee Stadium, 12, 317
Yaphank, 29, 77. *See also* Camp Upton
York, Alvin C.
    assault on Germans by, 1–4, 5, 260–264, 265, 273–274, 275, 287–288
    background of, 57–59
    at Camp Gordon, 62–63, 88–89, 90
    at Camp Upton, 90
    Cowan book on, 307–308, 310
    and departure for Europe, 89–90, 91, 92–93
    Distinguished Service Cross awarded to, 287
    and draft and questions of war, 52, 59–65
    with 82nd Division in the Argonne, 147, 187–189, 208, 213–214, 236–238, 257–260, 286–287
    from Fentress County, Tennessee, 52, 56, 57, 61, 62, 69, 308, 309–310, 318
    and May 1919 homecoming, 271–276
    as Medal of Honor recipient, 287, 288
    media and, 4, 273–274, 278, 283, 287–288
    in Pattullo "The Second Elder Gives Battle," 287–288
    postwar life and death of, 292–295, 301, 308, 318–320
    and promotion to sergeant, 286–287
    religious faith of, 189, 213, 265, 320
    at Saint-Mihiel, 109
    and *Sergeant York* film, 315, 318–319
    Skeyhill as biographer of, 292, 308–311, 313, 319
    and Unknown Soldier ceremony, 300, 301, 303, 304
    as war hero, 261, 271–276, 288, 292, 294, 298–299, 301, 315
York Foundation, 294–295, 320
Younger, Edward F., 299

Zimmerman, Heinie, 39
Zimmermann telegram, 15

ABOUT THE AUTHOR

White House Historical Association

EDWARD G. LENGEL is a military historian, battlefield tour guide, and travel enthusiast who has published award-winning books on World War I and the Revolutionary War, including *To Conquer Hell: The Meuse-Argonne, 1918*; and *Thunder and Flames: Americans in the Crucible of Combat, 1917–1918*. He has contributed articles for *Military History, Military History Quarterly, American Heritage*, and *American History* and appears frequently on television and radio, including the History Channel, NPR, and other networks.